"With IT'S YOUR MOVE, Cyndi Maxey and Jill Bremer have crafted a tutorial for life through which anybody could benefit. Both reflective and practical, it serves as the best friend you always wanted that forced you to look in the mirror when you most needed to see the truth. Punctuated with delightful stories of lives in progress and the real-world challenges they have faced, IT'S YOUR MOVE provides both passion and insight along with a play-by-play strategy for how to get what you need once you know what you want. Find a pad of paper, a sharp pencil and a comfortable chair and dig in!"

—Bob Nelson, Ph.D., author of *1001 Ways to Reward Employees and 1001 Ways to Take Initiative at Work*

"IT'S YOUR MOVE will inspire you to take action in life and work. It's filled with practical how-to's to get you moving (yes, mingling, too) and achieving your goals. Whether you want to move up at work, challenge yourself in life, or simply shake the doldrums, this book will help you do it. Play the 52 tip-filled cards suggested by Cyndi and Jill, and then share your success!"

—Susan RoAne, Mingling Maven and nation's leading networking expert and author of *How to Work a Room*®, *What Do I Say Next?*, and *RoAne's Rules: How to Make the Right Impression*

"Jill and Cyndi have literally given it all to us. Want to win? Read their rules and play with their wisdom and strategy to gain strength and balance. An absolute must for anyone who wonders, 'Is this all there is?'"

—Marilyn Miglin, President and CEO, Marilyn Miglin, L.P.

In an increasingly competitive world, it is quality
of thinking that gives an edge—an idea that opens new
doors, a technique that solves a problem, or an insight
that simply helps make sense of it all.

We work with leading authors in the various arenas
of business and finance to bring cutting-edge thinking
and best learning practice to a global market.

It is our goal to create world-class print publications
and electronic products that give readers
knowledge and understanding which can then be
applied, whether studying or at work.

To find out more about our business
products, you can visit us at www.ft-ph.com

IT'S YOUR MOVE
DEALING YOURSELF
THE BEST CARDS
IN LIFE AND WORK

Cyndi Maxey

Jill Bremer

FT Prentice Hall
FINANCIAL TIMES

An Imprint of PEARSON EDUCATION
Upper Saddle River, NJ • New York • London • San Francisco • Toronto • Sydney
Tokyo • Singapore • Hong Kong • Cape Town • Madrid
Paris • Milan • Munich • Amsterdam

www.ft-ph.com

Library of Congress Cataloging-in-Publication Data
Maxey, Cyndi.
  It's your move : dealing yourself the best cards in life and work /
Cyndi Maxey and Jill Bremer.
      p. cm.
  Includes bibliographical references and index.
  ISBN 0-13-142481-5
  1.   Success. I. Bremer, Jill. II. Title.
BJ1611.2 .M348 2004
158.1--dc22   2003016154

Vice President, Executive Editor: *Tim Moore*
Editorial Assistant: *Rick Winlder*
Editorial/Production Supervision: *Pine Tree Composition, Inc.*
Full Service Production Manager: *Anne R. Garcia*
Manufacturing Buyer: *Maura Zaldivar*
Art Director: *Gail Cocker-Bogusz*
Cover Design Director: *Jerry Votta*
Cover Design: *Anthony Gemmellaro*
Original Card Design: *Neil Bremer*

© 2004 by Cyndi Maxey and Jill Bremer
Published by Pearson Education, Inc.
Publishing as Financial Times Prentice Hall
Upper Saddle River, New Jersey 07458

FT Prentice Hall offer excellent discounts on this book when ordered in quantity for bulk
purchases or special sales. For more information, please contact:

U. S. Corporate and Government
Sales 1-800-382-3419
corpsales@pearsontechgroup.com

For sales outside of the U. S., please contact:
International Sales
1-317-581-3793
international@pearsontechgroup.com

Printed in the United States of America
First Printing

ISBN 0-13-142481-5

Pearson Education LTD.
Pearson Education Australia PTY, Limited
Pearson Education Singapore, Pte. Ltd.
Pearson Education North Asia Ltd.
Pearson Education Canada, Ltd.
Pearson Educación de Mexico, S.A. de C.V.
Pearson Education—Japan
Pearson Education Malaysia, Pte. Ltd.

FINANCIAL TIMES PRENTICE HALL BOOKS

For more information, please go to www.ft-ph.com

Business and Technology

Sarv Devaraj and Rajiv Kohli

The IT Payoff: Measuring the Business Value of Information Technology Investmen

Nicholas D. Evans

Business Innovation and Disruptive Technology: Harnessing the Power of Breakthrough Technology...for Competitive Advantage

Nicholas D. Evans

Consumer Gadgets: 50 Ways to Have Fun and Simplify Your Life with Today's Technology...and Tomorrow's

Faisal Hoque

The Alignment Effect: How to Get Real Business Value Out of Technology

Economics

David Dranove

What's Your Life Worth? Health Care Rationing...Who Lives? Who Dies? Who Decides?

John C. Edmunds

Brave New Wealthy World: Winning the Struggle for World Prosperity

Jonathan Wight

Saving Adam Smith: A Tale of Wealth, Transformation, and Virtue

Entrepreneurship

Oren Fuerst and Uri Geiger

From Concept to Wall Street: A Complete Guide to Entrepreneurship and Venture Capital

David Gladstone and Laura Gladstone

Venture Capital Handbook: An Entrepreneur's Guide to Raising Venture Capital, Revised and Updated

Erica Orloff and Kathy Levinson, Ph.D.

The 60-Second Commute: A Guide to Your 24/7 Home Office Life

Jeff Saperstein and Daniel Rouach

Creating Regional Wealth in the Innovation Economy: Models, Perspectives, and Best Practices

Executive Skills

Cyndi Maxey and Jill Bremer
It's Your Move: Dealing Yourself the Best Cards in Life and Work

Finance

Aswath Damodaran
The Dark Side of Valuation: Valuing Old Tech, New Tech, and New Economy Companies

Kenneth R. Ferris and Barbara S. Pécherot Petitt
Valuation: Avoiding the Winner's Curse

International Business

Peter Marber
Money Changes Everything: How Global Prosperity Is Reshaping Our Needs, Values, and Lifestyles

Fernando Robles, Françoise Simon, and Jerry Haar
Winning Strategies for the New Latin Markets

Investments

Zvi Bodie and Michael J. Clowes
Worry-Free Investing: A Safe Approach to Achieving Your Lifetime Goals

Harry Domash
Fire Your Stock Analyst! Analyzing Stocks on Your Own

David Gladstone and Laura Gladstone
Venture Capital Investing: The Complete Handbook for Investing in New Businesses, New and Revised Edition

D. Quinn Mills
Buy, Lie, and Sell High: How Investors Lost Out on Enron and the Internet Bubble

D. Quinn Mills
Wheel, Deal, and Steal: Deceptive Accounting, Deceitful CEOs, and Ineffective Reforms

John Nofsinger and Kenneth Kim
Infectious Greed: Restoring Confidence in America's Companies

John R. Nofsinger
Investment Blunders (of the Rich and Famous)...And What You Can Learn from Them

John R. Nofsinger
Investment Madness: How Psychology Affects Your Investing...And What to Do About It

H. David Sherman, S. David Young, and Harris Collingwood
Profits You Can Trust: Spotting & Surviving Accounting Landmines

Leadership

Jim Despain and Jane Bodman Converse
And Dignity for All: Unlocking Greatness through Values-Based Leadership

Marshall Goldsmith, Vijay Govindarajan, Beverly Kaye, and Albert A. Vicere
The Many Facets of Leadership

Marshall Goldsmith, Cathy Greenberg, Alastair Robertson, and Maya Hu-Chan
Global Leadership: The Next Generation

Management

Rob Austin and Lee Devin
Artful Making: What Managers Need to Know About How Artists Work

J. Stewart Black and Hal B. Gregersen
Leading Strategic Change: Breaking Through the Brain Barrier

William C. Byham, Audrey B. Smith, and Matthew J. Paese
Grow Your Own Leaders: How to Identify, Develop, and Retain Leadership Talent

David M. Carter and Darren Rovell
On the Ball: What You Can Learn About Business from Sports Leaders

Subir Chowdhury
Organization 21C: Someday All Organizations Will Lead this Way

Ross Dawson
*Living Networks: Leading Your Company, Customers, and Partners
in the Hyper-connected Economy*

Charles J. Fombrun and Cees B.M. Van Riel
Fame and Fortune: How Successful Companies Build Winning Reputations

Amir Hartman
Ruthless Execution: What Business Leaders Do When Their Companies Hit the Wall

Harvey A. Hornstein
*The Haves and the Have Nots: The Abuse of Power and Privilege in the Workplace…
and How to Control It*

Kevin Kennedy and Mary Moore
Going the Distance: Why Some Companies Dominate and Others Fail

Robin Miller
The Online Rules of Successful Companies: The Fool-Proof Guide to Building Profits

Fergus O'Connell
The Competitive Advantage of Common Sense: Using the Power You Already Have

W. Alan Randolph and Barry Z. Posner
*Checkered Flag Projects: 10 Rules for Creating and Managing Projects that Win,
Second Edition*

Stephen P. Robbins
Decide & Conquer: Make Winning Decisions to Take Control of Your Life

Stephen P. Robbins
The Truth About Managing People…And Nothing but the Truth

Ronald Snee and Roger Hoerl
  Leading Six Sigma: A Step-by-Step Guide Based on Experience with GE and Other Six Sigma Companies

Susan E. Squires, Cynthia J. Smith, Lorna McDougall, and William R. Yeack
  Inside Arthur Andersen: Shifting Values, Unexpected Consequences

Jerry Weissman
  Presenting to Win: The Art of Telling Your Story

Marketing

David Arnold
  The Mirage of Global Markets: How Globalizing Companies Can Succeed as Markets Localize

Michael Basch
  CustomerCulture: How FedEx and Other Great Companies Put the Customer First Every Day

Jonathan Cagan and Craig M. Vogel
  Creating Breakthrough Products: Innovation from Product Planning to Program Approval

Al Lieberman, with Patricia Esgate
  The Entertainment Marketing Revolution: Bringing the Moguls, the Media, and the Magic to the World

Tom Osenton
  Customer Share Marketing: How the World's Great Marketers Unlock Profits from Customer Loyalty

Bernd H. Schmitt, David L. Rogers, and Karen Vrotsos
  There's No Business That's Not Show Business: Marketing in Today's Experience Culture

Yoram J. Wind and Vijay Mahajan, with Robert Gunther
  Convergence Marketing: Strategies for Reaching the New Hybrid Consumer

Public Relations

Gerald R. Baron
  Now Is Too Late: Survival in an Era of Instant News

Deirdre Breakenridge and Thomas J. DeLoughry
  The New PR Toolkit: Strategies for Successful Media Relations

To my mother, Freda, who rode her bike ten miles each way on country roads to become the first in her family to graduate from high school. She didn't let one day in her life pass by without movement.

To my father, Kenneth, whose loving, intelligent support has propelled me forward my entire life. He doesn't let one day in his life pass by without thoughtfulness.

—C.A.M.

To my father, W. Jay, our inspiration for "Harry," who turned retirement into an art form. Teacher, author, Web marketer, reunion organizer, and master storyteller, he continues to inspire me and the countless others he touched during his lifetime.

To my mother, Jean, who taught me the essentials of style and deportment from an early age. An aficionado of language and grammar, she also instilled an appreciation for the written word. Thank you for heading me down the right paths and supporting me every step of the way.

—J.H.B.

CONTENTS

Contents

ACKNOWLEDGMENTS

The authors gratefully acknowledge...

Our husbands, Rob Maxey and Neil Bremer, whose creative, funny, outgoing personalities and witty minds have been a joy to be around for years and whose loving support made this book come to life.

Our children, Evan Bremer, and Ryan and Phelan Maxey, all young teens, who probably got tired of seeing their moms in pjs for five months. We love you.

Our agents, Jay Poynor and Erica Orloff, The Poynor Group, who seem to have found the perfect blend of optimism, talent, and savvy to make every conversation with them a joy and every goal achieved a celebration.

Our publisher, Tim Moore, whom we respect and admire and thank deeply for developing this idea with us during these times.

Our editors and designers, Russ Hall, Cleo Coy, Gail Cocker-Bogusz, Pine Tree Composition, and Neil Bremer, who cared about this book as much we did in their attention to detail and tone.

Our friends and colleagues, Deb McBride, Anne Hunt, Ed Gordon, Jerilyn Willin, Phil Orlandi, David Boylan, Catherine Johns, Ed Rodham, Pat Ewert, Jeri and Dick Church, Cheryl Perlitz, Christine Corelli, and Lori Klinka, who listened to our ideas in those early stages when it takes patience to listen to authors' dreams.

Our connectors and counselors, Brad Bushell, Sonia Choquette, Rita Emmett, Mark Partridge, and Anne Bayse, who put us in touch with movers and shakers in the publishing business.

Our colleagues, business associates, clients, mentors, neighbors, friends, and family who agreed to be interviewed herein.

The creative arts of music, interpretation, and theatre that brought us together more than twenty years ago.

INTRODUCTION

ARE YOU READY?

It's your move. Are you ready? Of course you are! There's nothing more stimulating than change, and this book is about making positive changes in your life and work. Too many people think about what they could do someday. You're ready to do something today. You're ready to make a winning move, and we're here to help you make many of them in lots of different ways. You'll get to know yourself better as you meet others in this book who are like you. You'll also learn from those unlike you. Keep their point of view in perspective as you move along in the game. You will be energized and up to date with the latest information on successful work and life strategies.

You'll tap into what we've learned throughout our twenty-plus-year careers as speakers, seminar leaders, consultants, and coaches, working with thousands of people whose goal is self-improvement. You'll share in the lessons about how to play the game successfully that our clients have learned. You'll follow the footsteps of the people we've interviewed specifically for this book and learn from their moves as they share their honest insights, mistakes, and wins. We'll help you find the life and work success you're looking for with practical, experience-based moves that have already been proven to win. We're glad you're ready!

Who are we and why did we write this book? First, we are longtime friends and colleagues who share a common love for people, communication, creative work, and learning. Years ago, we met in a commercial acting class in Chicago, later worked together as singing "wenches" in a medieval theme restaurant, and along the way established busy seminar and consulting businesses in the image and communication fields. We've learned a lot as professionals, and we've developed a network of savvy folks who have graciously contributed to this book. With all of this help, along with years of work and life experience, we joined forces to write this book on how you can make the right moves.

1

About Cyndi

Cyndi's creative, outgoing husband, Rob, and two active teenage children, Ryan and Phelan, provide both balance and chaos in her life. Writing about the courage to make moves strongly echoes her personal belief system; she has always respected and admired those people who take initiative. She has changed careers in life, balanced two careers simultaneously, and managed a successful home-based business for fourteen years. She's also had many opportunities to reevaluate moves and challenges in her personal life, having bounced back from a fire that destroyed all of her belongings, from being fired, and from stress as a high school overachiever.

Professionally, Cyndi has a master's degree in communication studies from Northwestern University and a bachelor's degree in theatre education from Illinois State University. She is a speaker and seminar leader who helps people become stellar communicators. For the past twenty-two years, she has presented workshops across the United States and Canada. Cyndi holds the National Speakers Association's Certified Speaking Professional designation, the group's highest earned designation. She has owned and operated Maxey Creative Inc. since 1989. Her articles have appeared in many professional journals and magazines, and she is co-author of two books, *The Communication Coach* (Coloring Outside the Lines, 1998) and *Training from the Heart: Developing Your Natural Abilities to Inspire the Learner and Drive Performance on the Job* (ASTD Books, 2000). She has held leadership positions in the Chicago Chapter of the American Society for Training and Development, Chicago Chapter of the National Association of Women Business Owners, and National Speakers Association–Illinois.

About Jill

A resident of Oak Park, Illinois, Jill is married to Neil, an art museum director and professional singer and mother to Evan, an emerging teenager and future movie director. Jill has made numerous major moves in her career. In her previous life as a professional actor, it happened on a daily basis. Combining her experience on stage and in film and as a corporate spokesperson, image consultant, business trainer, presentation skills coach, and professional speaker, Jill has combined all of those skills and built a successful business that prepares others to make their best moves.

2

Professionally, Jill has a bachelor's degree from the University of Cincinnati and holds the Association of Image Consultants International Certified Image Professional designation. She founded Bremer Communications in 1986 and began offering consulting services to individuals seeking to improve their professional presence. The company expanded in 1990 to offer Image Insight® corporate training programs, SpeakAbilities® workshops, and Executive Image Coaching. She is the author of *Image Insights*, a leading image eZine that has subscribers worldwide. Jill's articles have been published in a variety of trade journals, and she is an in-demand expert sought by business periodicals and major metropolitan newspapers. Jill's chapter on professional image appears in the book *Rude Awakenings: Overcoming the Civility Crisis in the Workplace* (Dearborn Trade, 2002). A member of the Association of Image Consultants International, Jill currently serves on the International Board of Directors.

We hope you'll feel free to contact us at any point as you read this book at either www.cyndimaxey.com or www.bremercommunications.com.

We know you're ready. Let's get started.

Play the Game with Us

Success in work and in life is fun and rewarding. It's a great game, but a game that requires a very strategic plan, and we'll show you how to follow the plan step by step. As you read, you'll notice that you've become a player in a card game with us. You won't have any cards to start, but with each new chapter, you'll gain insight into a different hand of cards that will lead you to success. Each hand has a lesson—a strong suit that you'll have to play. At the end of each chapter, you'll be asked to draw at least one card to get actively involved in the game in your own life. This strategy will keep you in an active, doing mode and out of a passive, thinking mode.

After you complete each card's instructions in your own life, you'll record your results in your game plan at the back of the book. This is a game you'll be able to play throughout your life because, as your goals change, your game plan could also need to change. Without revealing the whole game, here is a brief preview of the hands you'll be dealt:

Begin Game Here

In Chapter 1 you'll get a glimpse of the big picture. You'll learn about others like you who are facing decisions and moves on a daily basis. You'll understand the overall important themes of the game: wisdom, courage, strategy, and timing.

The Preparation Hand

In Chapter 2 you'll learn to step back, take stock of your life, and find your passion. You'll define your values as well as clarify and write your goals. You'll be able to look inside yourself, plan in pieces, and make room for work and family.

The Attitude Hand

In Chapter 3 you'll get a healthy dose of the positive. You'll learn how to shine through, say yes, give more, allow failure, find the window, take risks, be a cheerleader, forget perfection, and embrace change.

The Visibility Hand

You'll learn in Chapter 4 how to be visible, have energy, talk to everybody, reach out, and follow up. You'll be able to maximize every networking opportunity.

The Style Hand

In Chapter 5 you'll enhance your know-how of style by understanding your special flair and how to use it. You'll learn to choose appropriately, understand perceptions, enhance yourself, know your buyer, entertain, give gifts, and celebrate you.

 ### *The Presentation Hand*

Chapter 6 will help you when you're asked to speak to others. You'll be inspired to write and speak often, to be unique, think globally, know your tools, build your case, and keep current.

 ### *The Listening Hand*

Chapter 7 is an important hand that is the center of every other play. You'll look closely at how you listen to learn, are accepting, and acknowledge mistakes. You'll also learn to listen for style, listen with your eyes, listen up, and listen to language.

 ### *The Learning Hand*

In Chapter 8 you'll focus on how to learn through being aware, asking for help, developing yourself, and taking responsibility. You'll learn from other generations and cultures.

The Balance Hand

Chapter 9 describes the all-important balance that you can achieve through addressing anxieties, simplifying, managing thoughts, saying no, and making a plan for family.

 ## *The Flexibility Hand*

Chapter 10 provides the last step in keeping you flexed for the future through simple strategies for change management from accepting to letting go to moving forward. You'll be inspired to take action.

Shuffle the Deck and Play against Yourself

In a card game, the cards are shuffled to challenge the players. Likewise, you are encouraged to shuffle the deck to get better and better at unexpected situations and mixed suits. By the end of the book, all fifty-two cards will have been on the table and you'll have played many of them. You'll have recorded the results in your Game Plan. We'll remind you to look at the results frequently to help you analyze what your game is about—and to keep playing. After all, you're playing only against yourself. You can't help but win. Play on!

CHAPTER 1

BEGIN GAME HERE

Read the Rules

If life is a game, how do you play it? The rules seem to change on a daily basis. You're not even sure who the players are. You work and live in an economy where job turnover now averages less than 3.5 years and frequent news headlines announce layoffs of 7,000 people at a time. Your car salesman this past weekend was last month's airline pilot. Your financial planner is now in chef school. Your organization is being led by its third chief executive officer in two years. Stress levels are high. Your competition is working harder to grab your best customers. Your organization is asking you to do more with less. Your school and community are asking for more of your time. Your family life is out of balance. As you struggle to get a grip on the rules, you wonder what your next move should be.

Want to Win

You're at a turning point. You know you want to make a change. You've thought about the direction you want to go, but for some reason you haven't taken action. Do you want to move up, in, sideways, or even out? Or do you want to make a subtler move—one to simply enhance your current position? Whichever you choose, you know that every move you make is important if you want to succeed. It's important because there's not much time to test your ideas. Life is moving fast. You'd prefer to be on the next promotion list rather than the layoff list. You'd like to be more visible. You'd enjoy bigger challenges. You're searching for a boost, for meaning, for happiness. Whether you're a seasoned manager, entrepreneur, recent retiree, salesperson, stay-at-home parent, outplaced executive, recent graduate, immigrant, or part-time professional, you want to make the right moves for you. You want to be an impact player in the game.

Use Your Strengths

It might be difficult to think of yourself as an impact player. When you look at the playing field, it seems large, cold, and lonely. The players look different, too. If you're a Baby Boomer or a retiree, you could be feeling too old to play well. If you're a recent graduate or immigrant, you could be feeling inadequate on new turf. If you've been out of work for a long time, you could be feeling lost. If you're a full-time parent, you could be feeling isolated. All of these feelings could deter you, but you won't let them because you will use your strengths to overcome your fears.

Perhaps you haven't thought much about what makes you strong. Chances are, however, when you make moves in life, you're operating from an innate sense of what you do well. Everyone has unique ways to reach their goals. That's the reason people make moves differently, and that's all right. As an adult, you've collected unique life experiences to take out on that field with you. Use those strengths as well as your heart and mind to get comfortable on the playing field. Be a genuine player. You'll soon see that any game played successfully is played for real—with wisdom, courage, strategy, and timing. There are no false moves: There are only moves that are true for you.

Play with Wisdom

The first time through a game, you're often testing your skill, but by the second and third time, you've learned from earlier mistakes. With experience, you win more frequently. As you plan your future in a fast-paced environment, trust your personal wisdom. Traditionally, society gives people credit for being wise when they are very old. Why not break from tradition and use your wisdom now?

There is indeed a wisdom for every age. The college student has new wisdom with each class, the parent with each child, the employee with each project, the senior with each year. It's important to listen to the wisdom of the experienced people in your life and to be energized by the wisdom of each day's growth.

Melissa, a registered nurse and graduate student in nutrition, keeps a journal of things she learns from her patients as she makes her internship rounds. Different from the official, required medical reports, her journal entries remind her of the humanity of her patients. She doesn't want to forget that. Ralph, an art gallery owner and father of two, is learning daily from the different behaviors of his two sons: One an introspective, thoughtful child, the other a nonstop talker and instigator. Ralph applies his learned tolerance to his difficult art buyers. Penny, a vibrant marketing director for a medical specialty clinic, brings eight years of marketing experience in pharmaceutical sales to her job. Her daily learning, though, comes from listening to the patient services staff members at each clinic who teach her what it's like to be on the inside.

Betty, a retired homemaker, combines the experience of both years and days in her life philosophy. When she rises each morning, she says out loud, "Well, new day, what am I going to do with you? What will I learn from you today?" At day's end, she takes her answer to heart as she looks forward to the next one. Ken, a widowed part-time worker in his early seventies, reads a daily prayer or spiritual poem every morning at the kitchen table while his toast browns and his coffee perks. People who know Ken say that he lives the words of his poems. Betty and Ken have ageless wisdom.

Your wisdom grows in unexpected moments: Your child turns to you and offers an insight on your mood in a way no adult ever has. Your most difficult client offers a critical comment that illuminates a flaw you've been avoiding too long. Your spouse tells you something that you cherish at the end of a long day. Your newest employee solves a problem on the shipping dock because you finally took a moment to really listen. Your reflection in a mirror tells you the truth. When you add the moments together, you realize that wisdom doesn't involve much talking at all. Wisdom involves a lot of listening.

Play with Courage

The right move is not always the easiest move. Today's winners are making choices in challenging surroundings. Seldom in our history has the workplace been more unstable or the home front more frantic, thanks in large part to lightning-fast shifts in the economy and technology. You want to be able to meet the challenges with courage and confidence.

If you look, you will find people playing courageously everywhere. Robin, a sixty-two-year-old career strategist, realized that she needed a rest after working at a high pace for twenty-two years helping others find direction. She had helped clients take time off and now thought about taking a year for herself. Robin remembers, "At first, I was afraid a year would be too long—that people would forget me and that my business would die. I had so much of my identity tied up in my work. What would life be like as an unemployed middle-aged woman in the suburbs?" She chose not to listen to that frightened internal voice and courageously took off a full year. She decided to do the things she had long yearned to do: She visited national parks, appeared as a movie extra, and took cooking classes. Afterward, she felt renewed and enthusiastic about returning to work.

Gary, 45, a small town stockbroker, needing a new client base, bravely accepted a position miles away from his Midwestern home to work in the financial field with a commission-only base. The new location in the southern United States was both a cultural and distance shock for his close-knit family, but his charm and knowledge helped the new community warm to his financial advice. He became active in the Rotary, the church, and the arts council. His family is now one of the most popular in town, and his business is thriving. With a newfound southern lilt, Gary laughs, "There's a fine line between courage and desperation. As a native in my small town, people were slow to share their financial dealings with me. I was someone they grew up with. But to take the new job, I had to leave behind my wife and baby for a few months while I found us a place to live. That took the most courage. Once there, working in a cloud of anonymity was an advantage; I wasn't a threat. In the new location, I didn't do anything differently than back home, but the strange environment helped me position myself as an expert."

J.J., twenty-four, a motivational speaker, played hockey with a passion until an accident during a game caused him to be quadriplegic at sixteen. Although he broke his neck, he overcame the odds not only by living but also by gaining more movement than the doctors ever believed he would. His will to walk again was strong and buoyed him for some time. His defining moment, though, came when a specialized hospital in Colorado deemed that there was no more it could do for him. Doctors told him to go home. Outside the hospital that day, he saw a dog running with his master; for a long moment, he felt that the dog was better off than he was. The dog could run and play. On a final goodbye trip to Pike's Peak, however, he adjusted his thinking. The majesty of the mountain renewed his perspective on life, and he courageously accepted life in a wheelchair. He'll tell you that he never really considered himself courageous. He will say, "I just kept thinking, this is what I have to do to move forward. This is what I have to do with my life. I won't let being in a wheelchair get me down." J.J. is attending classes to professionalize his motivational speaking career. Everyone in the class has more work experience, but his energy and courage shine through, and he motivates them all.

Play with Strategy

Perhaps you're contemplating a major move, as Gary did. Maybe you, like Robin need a long break, or perhaps you're restructuring your life after adversity, like J.J. You could also be like Melissa, Penny, Betty, or Ken—someone who wants to stay where he or she is but not stagnate. Like Ralph, you could be a busy parent who just wants to make the most of your current position or life situation and your chance to excel. Making a move doesn't always mean a change of career or locale. Many moves are internal strategies that propel you forward. For Robin, it was acknowledging that she needed a full year away, for Gary it was needing client trust, and for J.J. it was accepting his condition while atop a mountain. In every case, the inspiration to change began internally.

If you're like most people, you value the rewards of personal growth and living a fulfilling life. To reap those rewards, you don't want to flounder too long with trials and errors. Your best plan is to blend creative inspiration with solid guidance and strategy. Think about the strategies you've used in the past— the times you've been a major player in a change on the job or in your personal life. What was the change? What was your role? What problems did you encounter? Consider the times in your life when you were caught between the status quo and change. What did you do and why? Did you have a plan? Did you listen to that inner positive voice or the negative one? Did you think calmly through the change?

When nine miners were stranded in a collapsed and flooded Pennsylvania coal mine in July 2002, they survived through strategy—not panic. It was a strategy to work as one that kept them alive. When two of the men experienced chest pains, the others grouped together and calmed everyone so nobody would have a heart attack. They shared the meager remains of a lunch pail that they found floating in the floodwater. They used their strengths—humor, experience, and technical knowledge—to think and rethink their situation. It was strategy above ground that saved them as well; someone thought to bang on a nearby pipe to get an accurate count of trapped miners and to send oxygen down first before drilling a rescue shaft. Strategy is guided inspiration: it is an all-important part of a successful move.

Play with Timing

With today's fast-paced technology permeating every aspect of your life, you struggle to make the right moves quickly enough to make a difference. You no longer have the luxury of time to ease into change. You want to thrive without losing your sense of direction. If you remember the rotary telephone, the typewriter, or handwritten school papers, you've probably been amazed by the onslaught of handheld telecommunications and computer technology that have sped up the pace of just about everything we communicate.

Commerce, the economy, trends, travel, family life, and education—all of these aspects of life have new time frames. People take more twenty-four-hour getaway vacations than ever before. Families are eating many meals in restaurants. Fashion and dress codes change as rapidly as the stock market. Corporate decisions are based on the rapidly changing habits of the consumer or the global market.

Great moves happen with a great sense of timing. In the Pennsylvania mine incident, the quick thinking of one of the trapped men saved nine additional miners. In the first seconds of the turmoil and the flooding water, he picked up a phone to warn a second crew to get out. He knew what to do when. The fast pace of the world, just like the fast pace of the floodwater in the mine, doesn't have to get in the way of a clear, planned, intelligent use of time.

You can plan clearly and intelligently even when your routine is jarred by outside events. For example, Billie had been a line worker in a factory for thirteen years when the plant was forced into a major layoff and she found herself one of eighty-five employees without a job. She had been happy there; a little bored, perhaps, but she had never felt a sense of urgency to change. However, after losing her job, she knew she didn't want to do factory work any longer; she was thirty years old and wanted to make a move. Looking back on that period, Billie recalls that having no options made her brave. Even so, she remembers driving around in the parking lot of the local junior college, gathering up the courage to enter. Now an admissions adviser at that very junior college, she helps many who have been jarred out of their pattern as she once was. They have a choice about whether or not to do something different. Billie says now that she feels sorry for people who come to that moment of choice but don't take the step. They choose to stay in a life that they really don't want anymore. Billie firmly believes that the worst day in the professional life that you've *chosen* is better than your best day in a job that you hate.

Play Well with Others

Just as there are no false moves in a successful game, neither are there false players. Successful players are real people who are able to build lives and careers that are meaningful and rewarding. Throughout this book, you'll meet a number of people like yourself, learning with them in various situations. You'll also meet people who are different but who will provide valuable information from which you can learn. You'll learn from the first-hand experiences of the real people we've interviewed as well as from The Players who progress in their own unique game plans throughout the book. The Players represent composites of people like you who want to make moves.

MEET THE PLAYERS

Anthony Anthony is a fifty-five-year-old former sales executive who had worked his way up in the furniture business when the recession hit. With two grown children in college, it was tough. New jobs were not easy to find, and he encountered resistance to his age and experience. Luckily, a friend with connections in a large office products distribution company helped him get a job as an internal consultant. When you meet Anthony, he is without direct reports and a management position for the first time in twenty-five years. What should his next move be?

Kathleen   Kathleen is a "go-getter," a twenty-eight-year-old pharmaceutical sales representative with seven years of experience—a real dynamo who set sales records within her globally based company. She frequently travels internationally, working the key accounts with the latest products. A high achiever, she falls below her peers only in interpersonal skill areas. Highly independent, she loves to work alone and is motivated by money, honors, and travel. You'll find out if she's moving toward the promotion list.

Harry   Harry, sixty-six, retired two years ago from a forty-one-year career as a high school music teacher. He enjoyed his years as an educator and loved working with teenagers. He earned a number of awards from both the community and professional associations and was a respected teacher. As he neared the end of his teaching career, he looked forward to his retirement and having time to devote to his family, hobbies, and travel. After two years of active retirement, he found himself a widower and without direction. Harry wants to redefine himself and find a niche that will make him happy. What will he choose to do?

Linda   Linda is a forty-five-year-old female independent contractor who spent eight years working in the human resources department of a governmental agency. She enjoyed her work, having moved up quickly from nonexempt recruiting to senior recruiting. After marrying and having children, she took fifteen years off to stay at home. When Linda decided to go back to work, she weighed her options and realized that she wanted to manage her own small business so she could have more flexibility. What are her best moves now?

William   William, energetic but inexperienced, is a twenty-two-year-old Asian American who recently graduated with a bachelor's degree in computer science. While in college, he participated in many extracurricular activities such as swim team and jazz band, but honors math and science classes were where he excelled. He had several great job offers and now works with a well-known West Coast computer company. How does he play the game on his first job?

Juana   Juana, thirty-five, an immigrant from Mexico, is experiencing her first job in the United States to help her husband and family afford a better life and education. She is learning computer technology as a customer service representative at a garden center where her husband also works. Juana speaks some English and wants to excel at her job. What moves should she make, and when?

These players represent a few of the many people who will help you learn what moves to make and when to make them. Finally, we know you'll enjoy meeting the people in the Key Player Profiles, successful real people in different work and life areas who share how they've overcome challenges and made moves that led them to where they are now. They will inspire you through their personal paths to success.

Begin the Game

Take a deep breath. The air is clear and the day is calm. The field is empty. The board is open. The deck is crisp and new. The other players will enter soon. Are you ready? It's your move.

CHAPTER 2

THE PREPARATION HAND

SUCCESS
CARD **1**: *Step Back & Take Stock*

Step Back

To win at this game, first you're going to need to take a step back. Stepping back allows you to clear the clutter and noise of everyday life and begin to see the bigger picture. It helps you decide what you really want. To do that, you need to get away from the daily grind and find some solitude. You can't find the quiet you need by closing your office door or sitting alone on your bed. Get out of your typical, everyday environment. If you can, get out of town. George, a busy sales manager, climbs trees. He's not trying to relive his childhood; he's a deer hunter, and a number of momentous life and career decisions have been made in the solitude of a Michigan forest up in a tree stand at 4 in the morning. His wife retreats to a cottage near Lake Michigan's sand dunes. She also surrounds herself with nature, preferring to watch deer rather than hunt them. The majesty of the great dunes and their ancient history help her put things in perspective.

Your retreat might be on a beach, in a tent, or in a suite with twenty-four-hour room service. Cross-country flights can be a great time to do some deep thinking. A long plane trip, with phones, beepers, and computers turned off, can give you the space you need to strategize, process, and prioritize. Granting yourself "think time" periodically allows you to remove yourself from the all-too-familiar routines of life and work—which can easily overpower big-picture thinking.

It's Your Mo
It's Your Mo
It's Your Mo
It's Your Mo
It's Your Mo
It's Your Mo
It's Your Mo
It's Your Move

Anthony's Move   When Anthony lost his job in the furniture business, he spent long hours writing letters, scanning Web sites, and making phone calls. Finally, one evening, exhausted and frustrated by the lack of opportunities that were right for someone in mid-career, he heard his inner voice telling him to stop for awhile and breathe. He listened; he took a day off from his rigorous job hunt and called an old friend in Chicago. He purposefully did not bring up his job loss until his friend asked. A few days later, that connection led to another call from his friend's firm. That led to an interview, and Anthony finally found a good job. Someday, Anthony will realize that his best move at that time was to step back.

Think time is vital to starting this game and needs to be granted *by* you and *to* you several times each year. You'll know when you need it. You'll hear a little voice that says, It's time to make a change; I need to simplify; the stress is too much; or I'm not happy. Don't let the voice become a shout. People who ignore the inner signals can turn into unhappy people very quickly. It's not hard to look at those around you and see who has listened to the little voice and who has not.

"I listened to myself."

I always had an interest in the arts, but my mother pushed me into teaching. As a woman in the 1950s, you didn't have a lot of career options. You were a nurse, secretary, or teacher. My mom wouldn't pay for me to study the arts; she didn't want me to become a starving artist. She told me I should find some way to incorporate arts into my teaching. So I got my education degree with an art minor. I taught third and fourth grade for twenty-two years. It was a secure income, but I was really miserable. At the end, I was unhappy, stressed, and my physical health was going downhill. I thought I would end up in a hospital if I didn't do something to change my life. One day, I found myself standing in front of a real estate office staring at the pictures of condos for sale. And a little voice said, Maybe I should unburden myself. Maybe it's time to simplify. So I downsized into a small condo, took a leave from teaching, and went back to school to study interior design. And here I am, later in life, working in a bur-geoning field where I help people create living spaces that are both beautiful and livable.

Betty, self-employed professional organizer

Take Stock

Now that you're quiet and secluded, you need to determine what things bring you joy and what do not. In other words, take time to develop your personal "joy sensor." Think in simple terms, and try not to edit. Ask yourself: What has made me happy? What has made me unhappy? Theresa Welbourne, Ph.D., a performance specialist, researched employee happiness in many organizations and found that people change only when they convince themselves that they're dissatisfied with something. So it's important to think about the answers to both questions.

Examine all the facets of your life: work, love, friends, community, family, spirituality, and so on. Do this exercise on paper, not just in your head. This is brainstorming, and it's important for the game that you capture all responses. Start by making a list of what you were doing when you were struck by either your delight or displeasure.

> I enjoy working with little children.
> My boss makes me unhappy because he is so negative.
> I enjoy competition.
> I'm happiest speaking in front of groups.
> I'm unhappy when work pulls me away from my family time.
> I'm good at being in charge.
> I enjoy being the breadwinner and providing for my family.
> I love to take classes and learn new things.
> I hate feeling unorganized and overwhelmed.
> I enjoy spending time with my friends.
> I like being with older people, like my grandmother.

This is the same process that Rodney used years ago when he decided to retire from professional football. He struggled at first, believing the only things he knew how to do were running and tackling. It took some soul-searching to realize he had developed other skills along the way. His many years as a professional athlete had taught him self-discipline, the value of teamwork, and the ability to inspire others to do their very best. These skills became the foundation of his postretirement career as the owner/developer of youth leadership summer camps across the nation.

Give yourself permission to dig deep and be honest. No one will ever see what you write here. If you find this exercise difficult, start a journal and note each time you feel real happiness or unhappiness. It won't take long to develop your joy sensor to determine what brings you joy and what does not.

"I longed for the front line."

I thought I had really made it when I became the vice president of learning and development. At first it was exciting managing other trainers and the training budget for the entire company. But as months passed and I continued to observe our technical trainers in action, I realized that I wanted to be back in the classroom. I don't think I would have realized this had I not had the opportunity to look back at the work I once loved from my loftier position. A friend encouraged me to write down everything I loved about training vs. managing. Guess which list was longer? Since I knew my company wouldn't let me go back, I began to look for the front-line position I have now—in a larger organization with lots of people who want to learn.

Daniel, trainer for a Fortune 500 technology company

Roger had a ten-year track record in the advertising business before he left to form his own consulting business. For three years he tapped into his sizable network and built a respectable business as a meeting marketing consultant. At first he was enthused, but over time he seemed increasingly unhappy. When he checked his joy sensor, he found that his independent work was creatively fulfilling, but he felt out of touch. Finally, he realized he just wasn't connecting with the large projects he loved, and so he closed his small business. He took a position in public relations for a large firm with large clients. He feels part of the mainstream again.

George Bernard Shaw wrote, "The people who get on in this world are the people who get up and look for the circumstances they want, and, if they can't find them, make them."[1] If you've followed Shaw's advice and made yourself get up, look, step back, and take stock, you've taken the first steps to moving your game ahead successfully.

SUCCESS CARD 2 : *Dream Again & Define Values*

Dream Again

Now ask yourself, What would make me *happier?* Some people have become so stuck in the life they've created for themselves that they've lost sight of what they truly want to do. This could be the very reason you're reading this book; you're stuck. You've become stagnated in your job, or you're feeling lost or burned out. Maybe you've plateaued in your organization. You're feeling a need to "unstick" yourself and find a new game to play. Your best move could mean getting out of the workforce altogether or getting back in. But you won't find the answer without allowing yourself to dream.

Close your eyes and think back to your youth or childhood. What thrilled you? What was your dream for yourself: to be a firefighter, a teacher, a movie star? It's important to travel back mentally to your youngest days. Dreams were easier to dream and some of you knew even then what you really wanted to be when you grew up. If you don't go back that far, you might not identify that moment of clarity. John Updike wrote, "Dreams come true; without that possibility, nature would not incite us to have them."[2] Betty, the professional organizer, has memories of childhood days spent rearranging furniture in her dollhouse. Louisa, an actress, was teased as a child by her siblings about performing every time the refrigerator light went on. Tom, a video game designer, spent his youth playing board games. You need to determine whether there's still any truth to those early dreams for you. How serious were you about becoming a business executive or fashion designer? Does something down deep still tug at you when you remember those dreams? If so, it's time to step back and take stock again.

"I found my place."

All my life I thought I wanted to be a vet. I can't remember ever wanting to do anything else. But during high school, I realized I didn't really want to take all of those college science classes and extra years to graduate. But I knew I loved animals. I took a summer and, for the first time, didn't do anything related to animals for three months. I did a lot of soul-searching and realized that I didn't feel the need to work with all different types of animals; I just loved horses. I'd been a nut about horses since I was a kid, taking riding lessons and competing in horse shows. Why was I trying to force myself to be a vet? I felt reconnected with my dream and more focused than I ever had been before. I'm now in the process, with a partner, of starting a horse stable and riding school.

**Lesley, owner
of a riding school**

Sometimes, as you mature, a new dream reveals itself. Often, a great teacher, volunteer colleague, or trusted co-worker helps turn on the light. Perhaps you know someone who floated through life, bouncing around high school activities or college degree programs, and then suddenly realized what he or she wanted to be. Many men and women start new businesses after other less satisfying careers. Sari is a perfect example of such a person; although her earlier jobs were high-profile executive positions in financial companies, her real love was health and wellness. She found herself attracted to those programs whenever she could participate and believed that companies should do more about such issues for their employees. So she began her own health and wellness consulting firm, distributed ancillary products, and grew it to a successful small business.

Are you living your dream now, or has it been overshadowed by the minutia, chaos, and responsibilities of everyday life? You could be a basically happy person, but if your life lacks passion, it's time to do some more dreaming. Perhaps nobody has examined passion as thoroughly as author Richard Chang, who, in his book, *The Passion Plan: A Step by Step Guide to Discovering, Developing, and Living Your Passion*, provides a seven-step model to finding passion. He stresses that passion is a natural part of you—that it is unconditional and evolving all of the time.[3] Take a moment right now to look within and ask yourself this tough question: "If my life ends tomorrow, am I doing what I love to do?" You could be pursuing your passion outside of work, and that's all right. Just look for the passion somewhere. Follow a dream, even if it's not your original one.

Define Values

There's a difference between valuing something and having values. We can value possessions, big paychecks, or power, but lives based on principles are lives filled with meaning. What are your fundamental values? What principles guide you through your day, week, and life? Take a blank page and list your personal values, the ones you currently hold and those you'd like to develop. Here are some to start with, but add your own as you go.

Honesty

Courage

Tolerance

Integrity

Selflessness

Compassion

Sensitivity

Family

Religious belief

Health

Stability

Friendship

Home life

Intelligence

Education

Spend the next few days thinking about your personal list of principles and values. Catch yourself in the moments of action and decision. What guides you during these times? Do you get caught up in the here and now, the quick fix? Or do you see the higher purpose? You can choose how to live your life and play the game. Make the choice to live a life and build a career based on sound values.

"My values finally matched."

As I was growing up, my life revolved around soccer. I played on the national youth soccer teams, traveled to Europe, and at age fifteen, spent a summer training with a professional team in England. I always knew I was going to be a professional soccer player. I had a full soccer scholarship to a top Midwest university, but when I got to college, things began to change. I started to see everything I had missed along the way. My high school years had been filled with practices and games and I didn't get to do a lot of the other things my friends were doing. I got to college and longed to be "normal." I was feeling burned out and unhappy, so I just walked away from soccer and my scholarship. I kicked myself for a while because soccer was the only thing in my life for which I ever had a passion. But I finished school at another university and then bounced around between a few jobs. I worked in the financial industry, then for a dot-com company. I still wasn't happy. And looking back, I can see that these jobs weren't based on the values that were important to me: honesty, stability, and family. Then an old soccer coach of mine called and presented an opportunity—teaching soccer and other sports to little kids. I thought, Could this be it, my calling? I've been teaching now for a couple of years and really love it. I'm working with kids, whom I enjoy, and I'm playing soccer again, albeit with shorter opponents.

Jerry, coach at a sports academy

Paul has learned through mistakes and missteps along the way that integrity is a value that is important to him. Earlier in his career, he may not have confronted a colleague or client whose ethical standards he questioned. Now he does. He takes a deep breath, calls the person, explains his stance, and asks for feedback. He knows that he is taking the risk of ending the relationship; however, he prefers fewer, more trusting relationships. He creates written agreements for contracting, not only with clients but also with colleagues to keep standards clear in all types of business relationships. He is more confident living that value now.

Linda's Move When Linda was struggling with the decision of whether to return to work after fifteen years at home with the children, she found herself weighing her values more than ever before in her life. Yes, she valued family and stability, but she also valued courage and professional growth. She knew that her life would not be complete without returning to the stimulating work in recruiting that she once loved. To her surprise, her teenage children wondered why she'd waited so long to return to work. "Gee, Mom," they said, "You're always at those meetings with your old friends on Tuesday nights. Why don't you work anymore? It seems like you really miss it." Linda returned to recruiting in her own style with her own small business. It was the right move and it probably could have been sooner.

SUCCESS
CARD **3**: *Write Your Goals & Plan in Pieces*

Write Your Goals

If you are like most people, you're not jumping at the chance to write your life and career goals. It's just not a popular pastime, but it must be done. Goal writing is easier than you might think. If you played the first cards in the Preparation Hand, you're prepared to write. Long-term goals—for example, where do you want to be in five, ten, twenty years and short-term goals such as what do you want in the next six to twelve months—are vital steps to this game because they clarify your sense of direction and purpose. You've probably heard that goals aren't goals unless they're written down and that they need to be specific, measurable, and action oriented. Goals also must be tied to your passion and values.

Your goals could include moving up in the company so that you fulfill your potential, taking early retirement to work as a community activist, or starting a new business that will grant you the freedom to spend more time with your family. If you create goals that are fixed to hollow principles or written without your dream in mind, you're not going to like the results and could lose out on a life filled with meaning. Take a moment now to think about the behaviors and actions that can make your passion visible. Don't forget your personal values. Any actions you take to reach your dream must also be true to your values.

Harry's Move   It was a tough decision, but Harry decided to move out of the house he had shared with his late wife of forty-five years and into a retirement community for active seniors that was closer to his children and grandchildren. He didn't enjoy the yard work anymore and couldn't cook very well. The house was too big for one person. The retirement community offered lots of activities, friendly faces, and two meals a day in the beautiful dining room. He spent months downsizing his furniture and belongings and moved into a one-bedroom apartment with a view of the pond. The first few weeks were a blur of unpacking, errands, and impromptu get-togethers with the new neighbors. As Harry began to feel more settled, the reality began to sink in. What do I do now? he thought. He had plenty of solitude in his new environment. He decided to reexamine his life and come up with a game plan for the future. He took out a ledger pad and started to list what was important to him and what he thought he could accomplish with the rest of his life. He knew he valued family, friendship, and music, but as his list got longer, he was surprised by the ideas that popped into his head for the future. Why couldn't he start a men's chorus or bell choir for the retirement community? He'd often toyed with the idea of writing a music textbook or even articles for the music educators' associations. Perhaps retirement wouldn't be as boring as he'd feared.

Karen, a registered nurse and speaker, cites writing her goals as a key to her success. She asserts that she achieved every goal she listed, whereas she forgot every goal-related thought left unwritten. She attests to meeting her career achievement goals, her business goals, and her relationship goals by writing them down. She continues to work on new goals: To earn the highest professional designation in her field and to serve her association in a national capacity. Why not follow Karen's plan? Writing produces thought. Thought produces action. Action produces success.

"I realized my goals."

I'd already been working in the field of museum management for about ten years when I had the opportunity to go to graduate school to earn a master of arts degree in arts administration. I had mixed feelings about it. I was entering middle age and had years of museum experience under my belt and would be part of a classfull of college-age kids with no experience. But I thought I probably needed this degree to be able to advance in my career. Part of the application process was to write my long-term and short-term goals. I realized it was the first time I had ever done that in my life. Seeing my goals on paper, clearly defined, made me confront what I really wanted to do with my career; I wanted to be a museum director. I balanced my years of experience against what this program had to offer and promptly left. I started my job search, and it wasn't long before I was hired to run a beautiful mid-size art museum.

Bob, executive director of an art museum

Close the book, take out some paper or your laptop, and start to work out your long-term and short-term goals. Do they move you toward your dream? Are they true to your values?

Plan in Pieces

Turning goals into daily activities is a crucial card to play in this hand. You can become a slave to your daily to-do list instead of keeping your eye on the prize—your dream. Sure, you need to get to the cleaners or mow the lawn, but you also need to take time every day to work on the really important stuff. Here's how you do it. Instead of jumping right from the long- and short-term goals into your daily tasks, take intermediate steps. For each goal you've written, list the tangible action steps you can take to reach it. Each long-term goal can take you a number of years to achieve. Your shorter-term goals can take months. Action steps usually take days or weeks to accomplish and are the stepping-stones for turning dreams into reality.

Example 1

Long-term goal = To manage the marketing department in five years.
Short-term goal = To be a team leader in nine months.

27

Action steps = Tell my supervisor about my desire to be a team leader.

Enroll in the team leadership course my company offers.

Do extra work on the next assigned project.

Example 2

Long-term goal = To start a consulting business in two years.

Short-term goal = To quit my current job within twelve months.

Action steps = Learn how to create a business plan.

Save more money from each paycheck.

Join an association for professional consultants.

Example 3

Long-term goal = To become a published author in three years.

Short-term goal = To write a book proposal in the next ninety days.

Action steps = Take a writing class.

Develop list of possible topics.

Research how to write a book proposal.

Select the top three or four action steps for each goal; then start working them into your daily to-do list. For example, you can call local colleges this week and inquire about their writing classes, buy a book tomorrow during lunch that explains how to write a business plan, or schedule a meeting with your supervisor. Your daily list will have many other tasks, but try to do something related to one of your goals each day.

KEY PLAYER PROFILE: MARILYN MIGLIN

"The 'lightbulb' went on for me at a point in my life when I was occupied with raising children, being a corporate wife, and taking care of a home. The mail kept piling up and I had trouble handling all of the things I was supposed to be doing. Everyday I would find myself thinking, "Oh, if I only had one more hour." I loved reading books about successful people and there weren't a lot of them written about women at that time. But there was one common thread that went through all of those books—successful people got their best work done early in the morning. Then it hit me. All I had to do was get up one hour earlier each day and I would have five extra hours each week—almost a whole day! I started getting up just fifteen minutes earlier each day, and very soon, waking up at 5 A.M. was really easy. And now, 4 A.M. isn't even a problem. As a result of this enlightenment, I was able to create a very balanced life and have been able to accomplish everything I wanted.

"Do I set goals? Absolutely and without question. If you don't, you're on the road but don't know which way to point your car. I have been in the habit of setting goals ever since I was very young. I write annual long-term goals during a trip to Hawaii I take at the end of each year. Any short-term goals I make are done on an ongoing basis and filed away mentally. I write daily to-do lists and use colored folders and colored pens. The urgent, awful, terrible things are in red and I work on those items as soon as possible so they don't gnaw away at me. Blue is for happier items, green is for projects that involve deals and new opportunities, yellow is for personal matters. And once I begin one of the activities on my daily list, I do not allow anyone to interrupt me, whether I'm writing nineteen thank-you notes or twenty-three proposals. I don't permit people to steal my time."

. . . Marilyn Miglin, founder of the Marilyn Miglin Institute, a world-renowned beauty authority, author, speaker is among the nation's top 500 women business owners. She is a founding member of the University of Illinois advisory board for the Craniofacial Center and has received, among many other honors, the Raoul Wallenberg International Humanitarian Award.

Juana's Move Juana had dreamed of putting her high school computer classes to use some day. She had often told friends that her goal was to have a job where she could use the database management skills she had learned in high school. One Sunday morning, an ad in the local newspaper for a customer service representative at the same garden center where her husband worked attracted her. When she wrote the phone number and the words, "Call Monday morning," she took a step she hadn't taken before—the first action step toward her goal.

With each action step you accomplish, add a new one under that goal so that you always have three or four to focus on under each heading. Breaking your goals into smaller, reality-based tasks is the best way to create the life of your dreams. Author George Morrisey, a researcher on goal setting since the early 1960s, stressed in his book, *Getting Your Act Together,* that reducing goals to bite size helps create mental pictures of tangible results.[4] What better way to make a dream reality than to visualize it?

"I sat on the back burner."

I've never been very good at turning big goals into daily steps. I always get too bogged down in the everyday stuff. My sister and I run the family supplies distribution business. She's good at the big-picture things, like doing cost analyses, studying the facilities capabilities, and so on. I'm the short-term thinker, always worrying about what needs to be done *today* to keep the business going. She and I recently did some brainstorming about ways to grow the business and came up with an exciting idea for increasing sales. It was an invigorating process for us, but we still haven't broken it up into all of the little steps we need to do for this idea to take off. And this great idea is still on the back burner.

Sandy, vice president of an industrial supplies distribution company

---

SUCCESS
CARD 4 : *Know Their Goals & Define Yourself*

Know Their Goals

Now that your goals and action steps are set, you need to know the objectives of the people in the positions of power around you. To get ahead in this game, you must be clear about their goals because they can influence your rate of success. A good place to start is by looking at the mission and vision statements of both the organization and its customers or constituents. What do the statements tell you about the organizations' goals and values? Do the leaders "walk the talk"? We hope that they do and that their fundamental values match yours. If not, your next move could be to look for employment elsewhere.

> ## "I realized it was time."
>
> I've been a physician for about twenty-two years. The medical field was different when I started my practice. It used to be more personal and performed at a slower pace. I had time to get to know my patients and provide more personalized care in the old days. But now, everything has changed. To reduce my costs and overhead, I joined a group practice that I thought would allow me to practice medicine in the way I was accustomed. But this practice is actually owned by a company that is interested only in the bottom line. It pushes us to see more patients every day and to spend less time with each. I'm working really long hours and am not in control of my schedule. I'm seeing less of my family and miss quite a few of my kids' activities. It's time for me to move.
>
> **Barry, family practice physician**

What other goals do the organization and customers have? Is the company looking for someone to head its first international office? Does your professional association need a new chairperson? Do you have a customer who needs someone to handle the largest order it has ever placed? Your skills and expertise will be important considerations, but you also need to *look* like you can handle the job.

At the most basic level, organizations have a goal to employ and do business with people who are trustworthy, honest, and capable. To get the position and keep the customers, you must convince them that you are all those things. The most direct way to do that is through impression management. In *You Are What You Wear*, William Thourlby writes that people most often like and trust others who are comparable to themselves, people who hold the same basic ideas and values.[5] Thourlby comments that if you want to have people like you, you should present a visual image that is similar to those very people. Managing your impressions so they reflect the goals of those who are important to your future is an important move in this game.

Kathleen's Move   Kathleen had been with her pharmaceutical company for three years when she read on the company intranet that a new international office in Tokyo was in the process of being staffed. She was eager to move into a position that would allow her to travel the world and work with international customers. She decided it was important to her career for the Tokyo office to get to know her. First, she did her homework, learning everything she could about the people in charge there, as well as Japanese business practices. She learned that the Asian headquarters would be run by a team who were very conservative and traditional in their beliefs, dress, and management style. She learned some basic Japanese phrases, studied Japanese business etiquette, and invested in a new, conservative navy skirted suit. When a representative came to her division to conduct interviews, she made a positive impact and was offered a position.

Define Yourself

The next move for you is to define your personal image. *Image* comprises a number of elements: wardrobe, grooming, behavior, attitude, and communication skills. Each element of your image needs to be developed, examined, and reexamined periodically. The goal is always to communicate a cohesive image to others with no mixed messages. A solid, consistent image will help you achieve your goals as well as survive difficult times. It should also be a true reflection of who you are in the inside.

William's Move   William had no idea how to dress when he started his first job. He'd been hired by a software company and was very confused. People wore just about anything to work, and he didn't know what direction he should take. He went to a clothing store first that tried to outfit him too traditionally. Then he went shopping with his girlfriend, but she picked out clothes that were too trendy. He talked to his mother, but she didn't understand the computer industry. Finally, he decided to call his future manager and ask his advice about dressing for work. Sensing that William wanted his new co-workers to think of him as capable and knowledgeable, his manager suggested he invest in quality, tailored business casual clothing, to iron his clothes before work, and to bring a jacket along in case a situation warranted one. William did just that. Armed with his new wardrobe and the latest in personal technology tools, he entered his new workplace with confidence.

Try this simple exercise for determining your image. Make a long list of adjectives, and then select the five that best describe you. One person might choose friendly, knowledgeable, relaxed, articulate, and honest. Another might select creative, flexible, caring, optimistic, and cooperative. Other words to consider include organized, unconventional, reliable, neat, mature, efficient, conservative, experienced, powerful, assertive, liberal, intelligent, capable, passionate, spontaneous, and responsible. Add any additional words, and then choose your five.

How can you turn those adjectives into your image, so that when someone simply looks at you those words spring to mind? Examine each word, one at a time. If you chose friendly, think of all the ways you can communicate that quality. You can certainly convey friendliness verbally. You can also convey it through body language, attitude, manners, and wardrobe. What is a friendly wardrobe? Colors such as browns, greens, and lighter shades of blue are not overpowering and send messages of approachability. Unmatched jackets and bottoms are less intimidating than matching suits. Consider the word *reliable*. You can convey reliability by arriving on time, speaking honestly, and following through on promises you make as well as by dressing appropriately for every situation. Examine the words you chose for yourself. It's also helpful to list synonyms. Then record every possible way you can communicate that adjective. Your answers to this exercise become the foundation of your personal image.

"I expressed the real me."

My second job after college was working at a Fortune 100 industrial manufacturing company. In 1979, I was the first degreed woman to be hired in my department. I found that I had no role models as a woman in management. I looked at the administrative staff, but they were all wearing simple skirts and blouses; there wasn't a suit anywhere. I decided that I wanted to dress both comfortably and distinctively. So from that moment on, I had all of my suits handmade. I felt that custom clothing would give me a beautiful fit and would look very professional. It was also a way to express my creativity. I've always thought of myself as creative, resourceful, flexible, adventuresome, and curious. I knew that to survive in this male-dominated industry I would have to appear authoritative and conform to a certain standard of dress. But I had this inner need to express my creativity, which I could fulfill with the dressmaking process. I loved selecting the fabric and buttons and working with the seamstress to design the suits. If I couldn't have something custom made, I would take great care in selecting interesting accessories with an eye toward creative detail.

Margaret, self-employed image consultant

SUCCESS
CARD 5 : *Make Family Room*

Before you finish this hand, revisit the goals and actions steps you listed earlier. Are they all career related? Be careful that you don't create goals for only one or two aspects of your life. Family, however you define it, is an important element and can keep you grounded and balanced. List goals that make room for your family life along with other relationships, financial comfort, self-development, and spiritual growth as well as your career. A balanced life is a healthy life. Remember the values you thought about earlier? Do your goals reflect them? Winners win because they play a balanced game.

Just as Jackie discovered, it is possible to "have it all." A life that balances fulfilling work with happiness at home is a life everyone can aspire to. You've started that journey with the Preparation Hand.

"I have it all."

I always wanted to be a teacher and did that for a number of years before I got married. But when I met John, I quit my job, got married, moved back to my hometown, and promptly had a baby— then another one. I became a full-time mom and loved it. My life was filled with family activities, especially on Saturdays. My husband was a mail carrier and worked on Saturdays, so that was the day I would take my kids to visit family members. We had aunts and grandmothers to spend time with, even an elderly woman who babysat the kids when they were younger. I loved being home and not working. But as my eldest neared college age, I started to worry about money. I knew I loved teaching and had a passion for working with kids but also knew that teaching could consume all of my time with functions in the evenings and weekends, papers to grade, and so on. I didn't want that. I thought about my goals. If I just needed money, I could bag groceries at the supermarket. Did I really need to have meaningful work? My answer just fell into my lap. One day at church, the head of Christian Education approached me and shared that she was retiring soon. She told me she thought I'd be great in that job and wanted to recommend me to the church leadership. I had to think about it for awhile but eventually saw that this could be my dream job. And it is. After being a wife and mother for seventeen years, my passion for kids and teaching has been rekindled, but in a way that balances my 'other' life, too. It's part-time work with great flexibility. I'm still home for my kids when they need me. I can have lunch out with friends. I even read a book during the afternoon once in a while. I'm also taking classes again on topics that relate to my new responsibilities. It's funny, I never used to like taking classes, but I'm running out the door these days to learn more. This is the balance I've been looking for.

Jackie, homemaker and director of Christian education

Play the Game: It's Your Move

You've now played the Preparation Hand. You've done good work to get the game off to a solid start. To help turn your thoughts into action, draw one of the following cards for your first move. How? You can close your eyes and point to one. You can roll some dice and let them tell you your next move. You can ask your child or friend to pick a move for you. Perhaps the first one is already clear in your mind. How you choose isn't as important as choosing and choosing now. Write your choice in your game plan at the end of the

Step Back & Take Stock

Success Card 1

If you draw this card, you must do *one* of the following:

Schedule two hours of uninterrupted time into your calendar this week for some think time. Required: Get out of your office or home.

Spend one evening connecting with intermediate and extended family members. Talk with them about the qualities that define your family.

The Preparation Hand

Dream Again & Define Values

Success Card 2

If you draw this card, you must do *both* of the following:

Spend an evening looking through scrapbooks and photo albums from your youth.

Ask three good friends to identify what in their opinion, you seem to value. Compare their responses, add your own, and select the top three.

The Preparation Hand

Write Your Goals & Plan in Pieces

Success Card 3

If you draw this card, you must do *one* of the following:

Write thee long-term goals and three short-term goals for yourself.

List three action items you could accomplish for one of your goals. Do one of them tomorrow.

The Preparation Hand

Know Their Goals & Define Yourself

Success Card 4

If you draw this card, you must do *one* of the following:

Become familiar with your organization's mission statement this week. Discuss it with two other people at work.

Spend time tonite selecting your wardrobe for tomorrow. Make choices based on qualites that tie you to the organization's value.

The Preparation Hand

36

Make Family Room

Success Card 5

If you draw this card, you must do *one* of the following:

1 Reschedule your after-hours commitments this week so that you have at least one full evening free. Spend that time alone, with friends, or with family.

2 Write three new goals for yourself that are not career related.

The Preparation Hand

book. When you've completed the move, return to the game plan to fill in the results.

End Notes

1. Sandie Byrne, "Mrs. Warren's Profession," *George Bernard Shaw's Plays*, 2nd ed. (New York: W. W. Norton, 2002), p. 37.

2. John Updike, "Getting the Words Out," *Self-Consciousness: Memoirs* (New York: Alfred A. Knopf, 1989), p. 98.

3. Richard Chang, *The Passion Plan: A Step by Step Guide to Discovering, Developing, and Living Your Passion* (New York: John Wiley, 2000), p. 19. This material is used by permission of John Wiley & Sons, Inc.

4. George Morrisey, *Getting Your Act Together: Goal Setting for Fun, Health, and Profit* (New York: John Wiley, 1980), p. 71.

5. William Thourlby, *You Are What You Wear* (New York: Forbes/ Wittenburg & Brown, 1978).

CHAPTER 3

THE ATTITUDE HAND

SUCCESS
CARD 6 : *Shine Through*

Frances was a single woman in her early forties, a large woman with a giggle that children loved. Although she lived at home with her parents, she maintained a large, active network of former business school friends and their families, whom she visited often. When their children would ask her why she wasn't married, Frances would laugh and say that the right man hadn't come along. Visits from Frances were greatly anticipated. She always brought small toys, her own hand-crafted items and, best of all, pastry samples from the Lucky Boy Bakery where she worked as a secretary. On summer visits, she found time to make sand pancakes with the kids in the sandbox, infecting everyone with her humor and positive attitude about life. During Frances' visits, busy mothers relaxed, sat down, conversed, and laughed more too. To her friends, Frances was an angel of sorts—a giver of laughter and love.

Then one day, Frances announced that she had met someone, a bachelor sheep farmer named Richard, whom she immediately dubbed "Dickie Lee" because in her world, everyone had a nickname. A new chapter of Frances' life began, and, although the farm was small and poor, her attitude prevailed. She named each newborn lamb and cried over any that died. Her letters to friends were filled with lists of newborn lambs by name. During those years, Frances and Dick invited the friends' children to visit and help with the lambs; the children loved their visits because of the attention they received and the grown-up responsibilities of farm chores.

They were married only ten years when Dick died of cancer. Alone on the farm, Frances faced invading raccoons, weather tragedies, and a changing market for the sheep. Finally, after many years of adversity, she moved back to town and painted ceramics to earn extra income. Many of the grown-up children who visited her during that time observed that, even as an old woman, she still had a "shine": the same great giggle and the attitude that infected them years ago. What was it? Frances' shine was a sincere, unstoppable positive approach to life.

If you had met Frances, you would not have had to guess about her life philosophy. It was evident in simple, observable ways. There was just no doubt that she lived life with a positive spin. To play the attitude hand successfully— to communicate a positive, confident attitude clearly through your behavior so that it is immediately evident—is also your goal. Others will see it. You will gain momentum from it. Day in and day out, you will shine through, no matter how cloudy the weather.

Linda's Move   Energized by her decision to start her own recruiting business, Linda called a former co-worker who still worked at the agency where Linda had worked fifteen years ago. Expecting her friend to be happy and supportive, Linda was surprised when, instead, her friend cautioned her against it. The economy was awful, business was down, and hiring was also down. Linda had hoped her former employer would be her first client, but now her hopes were dashed. As the day continued, she called other old contacts; many said they were afraid for their own jobs and remarked how brave she was to be starting out on her own. Between each call, she would take a deep breath, drum up a smile in her voice, and proceed. After all, this was her dream, her goal! Finally, around 4:30 P.M., after several forwarding numbers, she contacted Joe, an engineer she had placed years ago on a development project. Joe had been busy. He now owned his own engineering firm, and yes, he would love to talk to her about recruiting because he didn't have anyone who could devote enough time to it. Thrilled, Linda set the appointment to meet with Joe the next week.

Like Linda, you too, could have faced a day when nothing seems to go right. These days often start at home. You forget to set your alarm. You spill jelly on your shirt. Your child needs three permission slips signed immediately. You get all the red lights on the way to work. You arrive to find you're late for the early bird meeting. Later, on voice mail, your internist's nurse has called to say that the doctor would like to schedule more tests. Then your supervisor steps in to say, "Due to cutbacks, we'd like you to take on Donald's workload this week until we figure something else out." Or worse, "I'm sorry, but due to cutbacks, we're not going to be able to keep you."

How, you could be wondering, can I possibly have a positive attitude at the end of a day like that? Or maybe you're remembering a day that was much like it. Actually, it's not as difficult as it seems to adjust your attitude if you can get in the habit of taking specific mental, physical, and even verbal actions throughout the day. To shine through all your days, no matter how tough they are, try these simple steps:

1. *Pause and take a deep breath while counting to ten.* This brings oxygen to your brain so that you can think; counting helps control your emotions.

2. *List either mentally or out loud all of the things you're thankful for in your life.* Begin with the most immediate and keep going as long as you can.

3. *Stand up and walk or stretch.* Physical activity distracts you from mental trauma.

4. *Do something positive for yourself.* Call a friend, hug a child, write a quick note, look at a cherished photo—anything immediately easy to do.

5. *Begin again.* This step is perhaps the most important for successful attitude adjustment. You've got to consciously begin again, or feelings of self-pity will reemerge. It's like trying to hold a beach ball under water; you have to keep applying pressure or it bounces back.

This five-step process helps you put your situation into perspective with what's really important to you in life. Putting things in perspective gives you a more realistic sense of comparison. It helps you adjust your attitude.

"I appreciated clutter."

The other evening I caught myself. I came home from a long day and paused in the entryway—not because I wanted to but because I could barely get into my house. There were two skateboards, ten pairs of shoes, three scooters, five types of balls, three backpacks, a lunch bag, a coat, and three T-shirts. Now, I have only two children. I was just about ready to yell when an older neighbor's words went through my mind. "They grow up so fast," she said, as she reviewed their college choices with me. She even went as far as saying she missed the Lego blocks of their childhood lying around. So even though my entry was more like an "enter-at-risk" way, I paused, exhaled, moved a skateboard, and called out, "I'm home!"

Sarah, public relations executive

Frances, Linda, and Sarah each adjusted their attitude so that their behavior reflected their most important values. Deceptively simple everyday activities—attending to others' children, making one more phone call, or pausing in a doorway—allowed them to shine through life's difficulties. You, too, can adjust your thoughts and behaviors to make your life more positive every day.

SUCCESS CARD 7: *Embrace Change & Allow Failure*

Embrace Change

Change is like the weather. No climate on earth is totally predictable. When you were little and a rainy day ruined your play, your mother said to you, "Cheer up. You can't do anything about the weather." You'd go outside and splash in puddles or play inside with your blocks. Now that you're bigger, are you still able to cheer up when change ruins how you want to play? Do you adapt as quickly? Change is often unpredictable, so your best choice is to embrace it as your mother taught you. Turn a cloudy, rainy day into opportunity.

"I observed and positioned."

Though my degree is in management, and it's all I ever wanted to do, I needed technical skills to get my foot in the door in the insurance industry, so I took twenty-one hours of computer science. I came to the company with the intention of doing systems development work. I did that for seven years, but I worked hard to get the management role I had always wanted. I gained an understanding of the people I worked with. Also, I was working with information security and, in learning a significant amount of specialized administration, I became the only person who knew what was going on. I convinced the company to promote me and get a technician to replace me so they wouldn't have to be dependent on me for everything. I also knew that I didn't want to get overspecialized.

Well, I got promoted to be an information security manager with about six reports. I positioned myself to manage other areas so I could advance and make more money. At one point I managed ten people. But, after a significant layoff due to a political change, I saw technicians in high demand while managers were scrambling to keep their jobs. In fact, one of our managers who was laid off ended up selling me a life insurance policy from a competing company. I bought it because he needed the work and I needed a good policy. Still on the job, I worked to develop expertise in our new email system. Now, I'm an expert technician in this area. I don't manage others anymore, and I really think management is the harder job.

**Clay, technical consultant
providing email for a large
insurance company**

Transitions at work and in life cause some people to spin out of control, but other people such as Clay don't let that happen. In fact, one trait of a successful executive is to manage change and transitions well. You don't have to be an executive, though, to do what Clay did: to observe what's going on around you, make mental notes, and come up with a personal plan to get you through. Listen to and learn from your observations. Do you feel you are working harder but accomplishing less? Are you getting more irritable, angry, and short tempered with people around you? Do you feel more cynical about your life or work? On the other hand, are you energized and positively challenged by the unpredictability of each day? Does a change in the status quo add interest to your life? Are you ready to take on new activities?

If you're out of work and want to be employed, you're probably an active soul searcher; change is a part of your day now. You're considering things that you may not have considered before. If you're a Baby Boomer, you may be feeling a bit like a "has-been." Maybe it's just time for your "second calling," and, if so, you can follow the lead of many who've found happiness in second careers later in life. John Mahoney, a Steppenwolf theater, television (*Frazier*), and movie actor, began acting in his thirties. Grandma Moses started painting in her eighties. Student teachers can be any age.

Dr. Norman Vincent Peale, in his classic book, *The Power of Positive Thinking*,[1] interviewed many everyday people who overcame adversity. Each person had a story to tell about a lesson learned on how being positive and having strong beliefs changed his or her life. Over the years, many of their lessons have developed into well-known adages, for example, "If you expect the best, you will get the best."[2] Before the word *self-talk* was widely used as an internal technique to help people build confidence, Dr. Peale was building his case against defeatism. He encouraged people to see that unexpected change is not insurmountable; he helped them take control of their lives and embrace change with specific actions. Well worth reading, Dr. Peale's book has sold seven million copies and is still available in paper, hardcover, audio CD, and cassette.

Juana's Move The first day on the job surrounded by English-speaking customer service reps, landscape architects, and wealthy customers was overwhelming to Juana. She smiled a lot, said little, and listened as hard as she could. Once, in the ladies room, she wiped back nervous tears and bravely walked back on the customer service floor where she resumed her training. At lunchtime, she called home, reveling in the soft Spanish tones of her mother who lived with the family. She heard the pride in her mother's voice when she talked about her new job. That soft voice soothed her through the rest of the day.

Juana faced extreme change: a full-time position in an environment with a different language. Even though she doubted her ability, she was doing many things right. She committed to a job with an early morning schedule in spite of her young family; she arrived early for training and kept a smile on her face, although inwardly she was losing confidence. Calling her mother was a good idea; it reinforced her family's support, but Juana can keep working to maintain her self-esteem without checking in at home. After all, she was an A student in computer science in high school. She should give herself credit for being able to learn the new system, keeping in mind that the experienced workers have just used it longer.

Most stress in your life is caused internally—by your own perceptions of and reactions to life's events. Only a handful of major life crises—death, injury, illness—are external stressors. In other words, your judgment of a situation is what creates most of your stress. Managing your response to life's challenges takes discipline and often lots of self-talk so that you can keep them in perspective.

"I talked to myself and others."

In a one-and-a-half-year period, I lost four key people in my life. My mother died, then my husband, of pancreatic cancer, his mother died the day of his funeral, and my father-in-law died five months later. I'm a firm believer in reaching out for any kind of help that is available, and so, during that time, I attended the support groups of the Cancer Wellness Center and my church and got professional help with stress and depression. Talking to my friends was a much-needed connection to my husband. They'd say something like, "Boy, if Stuart could see the mess you've made with your checkbook," and I would have to laugh. I talked to myself all the time. I would say things like, "Life is going to go on with you or without

you; you can either be out of the picture or go on. The world is going to go on." People say things like, "Time goes quickly," and "Life is short," and now I know it really does and it really is.

Today, I'm more impulsive. I've been to Tahiti, swimming with Beluga whales, hiking the Canadian Rockies, and I'm planning a trip to the Southern Arctic—things I may not have done before. It helps to have something to look forward to: a concert, a play, something on the calendar. I remind myself every day that I don't have the right to feel sorry for myself. I am able to feel more compassionate toward others now.

Jean, operations manager of a medical specialty practice

Though you may feel overwhelmed by the amount of change in your life, you can take action to accept it. Rather than hold on to the past, you can let go and move on, like Clay, Juana, and Jean did. Each found ways to live positively while facing major change.

Allow Failure

When people are asked what they've learned most in life, they'll frequently say things such as, "I wish I'd committed to my passion sooner" or "I shouldn't have listened to the people who said, I couldn't do it." If you are employed, you know that in your job, you are constantly being evaluated. If you aren't employed, others judge you on a daily basis in different ways: What are you doing with your life? Do they agree with what you're doing? How do you measure up? People will always judge other people; it's in their human nature to do so. It helps them make sense of the world. It's a given: You will fail to measure up to someone else's expectations at some point. That's all right. If you want to be better at failing, you simply have to adjust your attitude.

"I struck out before I got the home run."

As a professional speaker, I'm evaluated on every speech I give. It's part of a meeting planner's job, understandably, to conduct evaluations of the speakers they hire. For large conferences, they rank all of the speakers to provide a summary report for their meeting client. The rankings are mailed to us also. It's always a little nerve racking opening that envelope to see how you did. Once, after speaking to a conference with fifty-three other presenters, I received the mailing. I opened it and stared at it with horror and disbelief. I had given two presentations and one of them was ranked fifty-fourth—last place! The other was also in the bottom half. After reality settled in, I called the client and offered his money back; he refused, attempting to assure me that it was just the wrong topic fit for the group. But I was disheartened. I was an experienced professional, not a beginner. As a speaker, you have to have guts to keep going; but I just couldn't find anything good in that experience. When my next booking arrived, I was more nervous than usual; it was an annual meet-

46

ing for two hundred employees, and I was being videotaped as well. I listened to the president introduce me, took a deep breath, and plunged in. Happily, the speech went well; people laughed when I hoped they would and interacted when I asked. Afterward, the client telephoned me. I held my breath. She said, "Ce-leste, there were absolutely no bad evaluations for you; we've never had that happen with a speaker. You were a 'home run.' A home run! Amazingly, the fifty-fourth ranking and the home run happened within thirty days of each other.

Celeste, professional speaker

Perhaps you've heard the adage, "He who never makes a mistake probably isn't doing anything." Top salespeople don't close every prospect; top athletes don't win every game. Certainly top speakers aren't always ranked number one. People who are able to allow failure in their lives without being paralyzed by it are busy people. They have so many places to go and so many things to try!

One of the most difficult things parents do is watch their children fail at something, but lessons learned from failure are some of the most meaningful ones. The same is true for adults. Failures should be seen as gifts. Great things can come from failure—character development, self-confidence, and innovation. Mistakes are often big wins in disguise.

"I played on."

All throughout my childhood, I took piano lessons at our community's music conservatory. Just about every weekend, there was a recital of some kind in the concert hall. At age 12, I was playing in a piano recital along with other students, when I experienced one of those character-building events that I will never forget. I was slog-ging through Chopin's "Minute Waltz," taking considerably more time than the composer had intended, when my mind went completely blank. I froze right in the middle section of the piece, with no clue as to what my fingers should do next. I sat there, alternating between staring at the piano keys and replaying the previous few bars. My parents, of course, were in the audience; and, in this large hall packed with other parents, grandparents, and siblings, the silence was overwhelming. I felt myself getting angry because my father was not jumping to his feet and coming to my rescue with the music, which he was holding in his lap for just such an emergency. He let me crash and burn in public and I was embarrassed and humiliated. But seeing that my only other option was to run out of the hall, I kept taking a stab at the piano, trying to find a way out of my dilemma. I eventually hooked on to some later part of the piece, which ultimately got me to the end. I don't remember walking back down the center aisle, but I'm sure everyone applauded, at least out of sympathy. I walked right out of the hall and outside the building with my father close behind. At this point, I completely broke down. As we walked, he let me vent my tears, anger, and embarrassment. But then, he told me what a good job I'd done, and how proud he was of me. He explained how important it was for me not to be rescued, to persevere and get myself out of the tough spot. I have never forgotten that lesson.

Joan, retail store manager and amateur pianist

William's Move William soon discovered that IT projects were competitive events. He often sat in heated project meetings with his colleagues, each trying to be the best programmer on the project. As the team leader, William was positioned to manage the team so that all members looked good. It was the perfect opportunity to attain the high achievement standards expected by his family. His parents would want to be proud. There was little room for failure, even though this was his first real job. He worked day to day for perfection, cherishing the few words of congratulations from his new boss on a job well done. Then one day after a grueling week of deadlines for a high-maintenance client, William entered some essential information incorrectly, sending the entire project in the wrong direction. His team rebelled; what little loyalty there had been vanished, and William was called to the boss's office. As he walked down the hall, he was already agonizing over how to explain his impending demotion to his parents. Surprisingly, the busy boss gave William a quick reprimand, asked him to correct the error, and thanked him for coming. The world did not end. William returned to his cubicle, vowing never again to be hammered by a mistake. For the first time, he realized that failure was part of work life.

If you've ever been in a position similar to William's, you know what it's like to try to avoid anger and panic in the face of failure. You don't want to be like other people you know who whine, blame others, and refuse to own up to the problem, but it's difficult to admit a mistake. During these times, it's important to remember that, in spite of a poor decision or an error, you're still a good person who overall does well. You're a good employee, a good spouse, and a good parent. Whatever your overall goodness role is—give yourself credit.

SUCCESS
CARD 8: *Find the Window*

You've probably heard that every cloud has a silver lining or that when one door closes, another opens. Everyone experiences pain, loss, and adversity. It's difficult to see the silver lining and the open door during these times. When your life is cloud covered, it's important to find the window that lets in the sunshine. There is always a window.

A morning television talk show once ran a human-interest story of a small beagle trapped in a culvert pipe with a porcupine that he had unknowingly chased too far into the pipe. After hours of rescue attempts, the beagle emerged, covered with quills. More than sixty caring human rescuers immediately surrounded him. They will never forget the sight of the poor dog, covered with the souvenir prickly quills across his snout, tail, and entire small body. The pain of the dog's situation illustrated that even when you feel trapped while trying to pursue a goal, there is always hope at the end of the tunnel.

Of course, you need to develop the attitude and action plan to get you through. Others can't do it all for you. Life today seems to be filled with tunnels and traps at every turn. If you've weathered six job cuts in seven months at your organization, you're probably tired of holding your breath. If you've been looking for new work for over a year, you'd probably like a group of sixty kind humans waiting at the end of your tunnel. First, you have to examine your own attitude. People who are successful at finding the window share these characteristics:

A personal sense of commitment in life.

A feeling of control over their life.

An ability to let go when the time is right.

A strong support system of family and friends.

A belief in a higher power or strong value that guides them.

Knowing this, rate your own commitment to what you're doing. Theodore Roosevelt once said, "No man needs sympathy because he has to work. Far and away, the best prize that life offers is the chance to work hard at work worth doing." Have you won the prize? What do you enjoy doing? What gives you personal satisfaction? What brings balance to your life? How much time do you spend doing what makes you laugh and feel happy and good about yourself? When do you feel in control? With what parts of your support system are you happy? Who can you count on to be there for you? Do you really have a positive attitude? Do you laugh easily and often? How easily do you accept what happens to you and then deal with it?

As you examine your attitude and your sense of commitment, here's a short list to help adjust your attitude:

Things you *can't* control

Traffic

The number of hours in a day

Your failing eyesight

Your age

A client's whims

A team member's lack of follow-through

The number of vacation days the company gives

Spilled milk after you've cleaned the kitchen

Death and taxes

Things you *can* control

How you treat others

When you leave for work

How you spend your evening

How you talk about yourself

How often you exercise

When to share your feelings

How you let your family know you're stressed

How old you act

How often you praise your children

Did you find yourself smiling as you read the can't control list? It's a little absurd to realize that we think we can control all those things. The can control list is full of ways to turn attitude into actionable behavior. That's the key to attitude adjustment. Take action. If you're in work transition, get involved with your organizations. Exercise more so you don't end up overindulging in food and drink. If you feel stuck at home with children and all you see is doors—slamming as the children run from room to room—get out and treat yourself to some "me" time. Call others who could be feeling the same way. Host a lunch for nearby parents with children who are home during the day. Start a block club to get to know others in the area. Flip the negatives into positives. Richard Carlson, author of the best-selling *Don't Sweat the Small Stuff,* stops a block away from his home before arriving at the end of the day to give thanks in his car for having a family and home to come home to. There might not be sixty caring people waiting for you at the end of the tunnel, but you're rarely really trapped. The window is always there somewhere.

You could find your window differently than the people you live and work with find theirs. You will most likely repeat strategies that work, learning along the way. Each day of your life, depending on your background, personality, and environment, you will discover what works best to get you through the day successfully. As you gain confidence, you will also discover how to help others find their window.

KEY PLAYER PROFILE: JIM DESPAIN

"I had an intense fear of failure. I always worried when I fell short; the hardest person on me was me. If I felt uncomfortable with something or someone, I read books and I tried to figure out what it was that they had that I didn't have. I sought approval from peers and people in higher positions and reacted favorably to positive encouragement. I believed in myself and that there was nothing I couldn't do. I thought that running into a brick wall only meant that you could hit it harder next time. I was extremely competitive—always wanting to raise the bar. I always believed that I could figure out a way. Progressing in the organization didn't drive me. I was driven by a desire to accomplish.

"I always had a deep appreciation for others and what they brought to the table; I had the greatest feeling of reward or good when I was helping somebody. To this day if I see one person helping another, I get emotional about it. There's nothing more human than for people to give to each other. It's important to let people know you care for them and that they did an excellent job. As a manager, I would ask around and figure out what was important to them. I would learn to ask them, 'How would you prefer to do it?' and I'd say things like, You can't screw up something we can't unscrew together. That went a long way to having people tell me the truth."

"Leadership is one of the highest forms of giving. I think that people who are stuck are stuck because of their leaders. If you feel you're doing what you were meant to do, and if someone else encourages you to feel that way, you're not stuck."

. . . *Jim Despain, former vice president of Caterpillar Inc., now retired, started sweeping the halls at night, went all the way through the ranks, and brought a new leadership culture to one of the organization's largest manufacturing facilities, the Track-Type Tractors Division of Caterpillar headquartered in East Peoria, Illinois. The most innovative thing about his management style was that he believed that everyone in the company had worth, and he treated people that way.*

SUCCESS
CARD **9** : *Say Yes & Give More*

Say Yes

When your attitude is at its lowest is often the best time to say yes to things you've said no to before. Give yourself new challenges. Do something to distract you from your current state. You could even want to call someone back who had asked you to participate in something that you previously declined. You can change your mind without a lengthy explanation. You can say, Joe, y'know, I've reconsidered, and I would like to help you with the girls' basketball team. Do you still need an assistant coach? You can approach your boss again, Diane, last week you asked me to consider learning the new database program; is it too late to get in the class?

Here are some other activities you might want to consider saying, yes to:

Agree to be on the board of your association.

Try team leadership.

Take on extra responsibilities in a new area at work.

Babysit a neighbor's children or pets.

Go on the company's outward-bound adventure.

Sign up for the management class your training department offers.

Sign up for a class in a new area of interest: art, writing, photography, and so on.

Treat yourself to a new kind of cuisine.

Partner with someone on a time-share basis.

Barter your services for another's (legal help for painting a room, for example).

Give More

Swami Satchidananda, a spiritual teacher, was once asked to explain the difference between illness and wellness. To answer, he silently walked to a chalkboard and wrote the word *illness* and circled the *i;* then he wrote the word *wellness* and circled the *we*. There is a "we" in wellness. Feelings of caring, love, and connection keep us well. To avoid too much self-focus, give more. Here are some ways you could give:

Take your kids to the zoo.

Sign up to be a docent.

Write a column for your school newsletter.

Host a networking group in your home.

Spend more time with an elderly parent.

Volunteer for the company picnic committee.

Donate an hour of your professional services to a worthy cause.

Volunteer to teach an after-school children's class.

Kathleen's Move Overhearing two co-workers talk about her ego was a wake up call for Kathleen; in official meetings everyone smiled and interacted respectfully, but obviously this was not the case in the parking lot afterward. Driving home, Kathleen decided that she was becoming too focused on money and advancement. When she sorted through her mail that evening, the inspiration came with her church newsletter. People were needed to teach tennis to underprivileged children in a summer camp program. She played tennis well, and although she had never considered herself much of a teacher, she signed up. The next month, at the two-hour training session, she made an incredible realization; for the past two hours, she hadn't thought about the week's quota once.

A "halo effect" comes with volunteerism. Being in the right place at the right time produces unexpected positive results in other aspects of your life. More than half of all adults in the United States volunteer three to four hours a week. Of those who don't, 68 percent say they would if asked. Why wait for someone to ask you? Seek causes and groups of which you'd like to be a part. Call the chair of a committee or the organizer of an event to get started. Watch your attitude adjust accordingly.

SUCCESS
CARD 10 : *Take Risks & Be a Cheerleader*

Take Risks

A Chinese proverb states, "Man who says it cannot be done should not interrupt man doing it." With the fast pace of life today, the proverb holds true now more than ever. How many times have you had an idea only to find that someone else took it to market faster? Think of all the Amazing successful ideas that naysayers said would never happen. How about shopping on the Internet? Do you remember the early pioneers in the industry, perhaps even saying to someone you knew, "Amazon.com? What's that?" Now it's nearly a household name around the world. Jeff Bezos, the CEO of Amazon.com, is a risk-taker and innovator. He believes that one of his most important roles as a leader is to make sure that his people know that things that seem impossible only seem impossible. They're often very doable.

"We took risks in different ways."

I was working at a large law firm with a nice salary when the firm offered marketing training. The workshop showed me that I enjoyed the creativity that marketing offered even more than the practice of law, and I felt that somehow I needed to change my profession from lawyer to marketer. However, there was no place to do this at my firm. I decided to leave, but to leave a steady, respected, well-paying job to try a field that was in its infancy was scary. My wife had recently given up a thriving costume and clothing design business to be a stay-at-home mom. I finally did find a firm that was interested in me, but it meant taking a severe pay cut. I tried to negotiate a creative salary structure for the new marketing position. I asked the employers to evaluate my performance in three months and, if they felt I was worth more than what they were paying me, to give me a raise. I also asked to be reviewed for an additional merit raise at six months, which would have brought me back to my original salary at the previous law firm. I worked hard and received both raises, which meant that I was able to support my growing family. If my wife hadn't been supportive and believed in me during this time, then I could not have made the change. Making the change was the best thing I've ever done.

Joe, marketing consultant to the legal industry

Don't get stuck in a state of toleration. The status quo can be just as demoralizing as some types of change. When you're tolerating something, your energy is in a negative place. You feel drained. You start attacking yourself, and your self-esteem suffers. Why not put all of that negative energy in a much better place? Turn it positive and take a risk!

Taking risks is part of managing yourself. Nobody else will take the risk for you; it's up to you. Management professor and author Peter Drucker once said that he no longer teaches the management of people at work because he no longer thinks that learning how to manage other people is most important. Now he teaches, above all, how to manage oneself. Self-management is the skill for successful game players today. If you're employed, try to remember that, above all, you're in charge of you. Work for yourself, not your employer. If you're at home, work for your own goals, not everyone else's. Do you have too many rules and not enough freedoms? Creative life and work decisions require the removal of pressure, fear, and judgment. Assess your attitude toward your work and life frequently. Don't be afraid to carefully examine these questions:

What parts of your work or life do you love?

What parts are least enjoyable?

What changes in your physical environment do you need?

What would make work or life more fun?

Do you feel happy nearly every day?

Earlier, when you played the Preparation Hand, you looked at your joy sensor. Your attitude is reflected in the outcome of your assessment. If you'd like to increase the happiness and positive moments in your life, here are some ideas to help you every day:

1. *Focus on one task at a time.* A busy entrepreneur calms herself by hand washing the dishes in warm soapy water. She focuses on the dish, the soap, and the feel of the water.

2. *Set limits when you need to.* Saying no doesn't mean you have a bad attitude; it means you care enough to say yes at a better time.

3. *Allow extra time for tasks and appointments.* When you know your child's orthodontist appointment includes an hour wait, make room for a full hour and a half in your calendar. Take a good book or balance your checkbook while you wait.

4. *Get help with jobs you dislike.* Cleaning help, database entry, phone calling, or dog walking—all can be contracted or bartered.

5. *Set realistic expectations for yourself.* Don't try to do everything on your to-do list every day. Be happy when you check off some key items.

6. *Express your feelings.* A group of overworked computer programmers surprised their managers when they asked for a day off to be with their families instead of their typical monthly bonuses.

7. *Schedule more fun and breaks in your day.* Read the "funny papers" in the morning. Get to know one of the cartoon families, and it will help you laugh at your own situation with your work, teenager, or romantic life.

Be a Cheerleader

Frances, the lamb farmer with the shining attitude, always signed her letters "Francie," beside a scribbled self-portrait. If you looked closely at the scribbled portrait, you would notice that she gave herself a halo every time. Perhaps that's one reason her friends and their families believed that she was an angel. She believed it herself.

Frances's cheerleading began within. Yours should, too. If you can't support yourself, you can't support others. Dr. Carl Hammerschlag, an expert psychologist and author on wellness, says that you can't pour from the cup to share if your own cup is empty. Who can you cheerlead for if not yourself?

Harry's Move Harry quickly found that the retirement community could be negative. A good sense of humor about aging could easily turn into unfounded, morose sarcasm. He realized that if he were going to make it through this time in his life without severe depression, he had to be his own cheerleader. He made a pact to respond positively to every comment made by his retired friends, no matter how Pollyannaish it seemed. When someone complained about an ache or pain, Harry would say, "Well, at least you're vertical today!!!"

Harry responded beautifully to a negative environment. He took action. If people who whine and complain have ever surrounded you, you know how hard it is to try to be different. Try cheering others on, too. Recognizing others' accomplishments and good deeds can do wonders for your own sense of peace and well-being. Sometimes, shifting the focus from yourself and to others can be a springboard for a fresh outlook on your own life.

SUCCESS
CARD **11** *Forget Perfection*

Actually, what is perfect? Have you ever heard the perfect speech? Have you managed the perfect project? Have you raised perfect children? Is your marriage perfect? Is your job perfect? Why do we perpetuate the myth that we have to be perfect to be successful? If you're employed, you can easily get caught up in the stress of your workplace to make perfect decisions. If you're at home, you can get caught up in the stress of whether you're managing your home according to standards others have that aren't really yours. You get caught up in unreal life rules such as these:

I must never fail.

I must always look smart.

I must work very hard at all times.

I must never get angry.

I must always look thin and attractive.

I must always play it safe.

Perhaps you learned these rules as a child, directly or indirectly. Incorporating them into your value system only sets you up for stress. You can't possibly live up to these rules; instead you run away from people and problems; you become aggressive; you remain passive. If family or friends who seem to demand perfection surround you, talk to them about how those standards affect you. Let them know if you feel more stressed than challenged by their standards. They won't know how they're affecting you unless you tell them. In fact, authority figures such as managers or parents often share how difficult it is to find the right way to create a motivating climate for those they care about. Not knowing what else to do, they often end up modeling behaviors that their own managers or parents used with them. Traditions die hard.

Real-life rules are more like this:

> You can't have everything.
> Things won't always go your way.
> Life is unfair.
> Some people will never understand you.
> You can't please everyone.

Strive to follow the real-life rules and forget the unreal ones. You'll be much happier more of the time.

Anthony's Move Far flung from his known world of sales, Anthony worked hard on a daily basis as an internal organizational development consultant to say the perfect thing and to provide the perfect advice to his internal clients who knew more about the business than he did. After all, they were looking up to him; he was the expert. He listened carefully, paraphrased perfectly, and chose his words with care. Daily he developed a raging headache that stemmed from trying to be a guru to all. The headaches continued throughout his first months on the job until, finally, he admitted to a colleague that he just didn't know how to advise an overworked IT department because it wasn't part of his experience. When the colleague suggested that he simply ask them what they would do first, he tried it. Amazingly, he found that he didn't have to have as many right answers as he thought.

Like Anthony, you could find yourself trying to be a guru. You too could try to figure out the perfect answers without asking enough questions. If you're in a new situation, start asking questions right from the very beginning. Don't assume that you're the only one who doesn't know. Chances are, the right questions haven't been asked in a long time. Many times, people don't ask questions because they think it makes them look less skilled or knowledgeable. Consider this: Highly esteemed lawyers have been paid to ask good questions for centuries.

Find out as much as you can about the people with whom you interact. Know what they typically expect. Who is a stickler for details? Who thinks in big pictures? As you get to know others, you'll be less concerned about being perfect and more concerned about adapting to their specific needs in different ways. The focus will be where it should be: on them, not on you. As you build relationships, mention your past experiences and prior knowledge, such as, Kate, I'm looking forward to hearing about your work with ABC Office Products; I used to know someone there. Or Joe, I heard about your new venture award. Congratulations. Small gestures or compliments usually can't hurt if they're short and sincere. You're establishing yourself as a real person—a person with a life, a past, flaws, and lessons learned along the way.

If you're in a situation with a demanding boss or manager, remember that perfection is rarely a manager's ultimate goal. Overall, your manager knows you're not perfect. Your manager just wants you to make his or her job easier and meet production goals. Managers don't want to be embarrassed, and they want to be able to give employees feedback easily. Instead of thinking about perfection, think about how you can take initiative. What can you add to your to-do list that will make you more valuable? Seeking feedback is one of the strongest messages that you can send that you are confident in what you do. You can say something like, I know you want to meet your objectives, so here are some issues I am wrestling, or I need your help with this project if we're going to meet the deadline that I know is important to you. If you confront difficulties with your boss, it's difficult to let a negative attitude fester.

Honest feedback and understanding also hold true for parents at home with children. Each child is different; you can't be the perfect parent in one broad stroke. Perfectionism and child rearing just don't blend well. In fact, children can teach you a thing or two about the freedom that lies in creative failure and mistakes. As the adult, you're the one who can most easily say you're sorry or that you made a mistake. A key in eliminating perfectionism is owning up to your errors and working together to move forward.

Play The Game: It's Your Move

You've now played the Attitude Hand. To reinforce all of those positive thoughts you've been having during this chapter, draw one of the following cards for your first move. Remember that how you choose isn't as important as choosing now. Write your choice in your game plan at the end of the book. When you've completed the move, return to the game plan to fill in the results.

End Note

1. Dr. Norman Vincent Peale, *The Power of Positive Thinking* (Englewood Cliffs, N.J.: Prentice-Hall, 1952), p. 154.

Shine Through

Success Card 6

If you draw this card, you must do *one* of the following:

1. List or say out loud everything you have to be thankful for today.

2. List all of the angels in your life.

Attitude

Embrace Change & Allow Failure

Success Card 7

If you draw this card, you must do both of these today:

1. Write or say out loud three changes in your life that have resulted in positive directions for you.

2. Write one thing you would do if you were guaranteed success. Tape it on your bathroom mirror.

Attitude

Find the Window

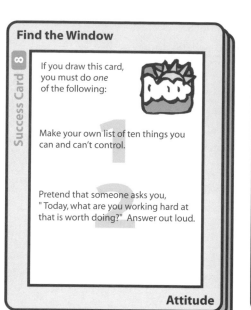

Success Card **8**

If you draw this card, you must do *one* of the following:

1

Make your own list of ten things you can and can't control.

2

Pretend that someone asks you, "Today, what are you working hard at that is worth doing?" Answer out loud.

Attitude

Say Yes—Give More

Success Card **9**

If you draw this card, you must do *one* of the following:

1

Sign up to help serve dinner to the homeless in your area.

2

Sign up to tutor a child in your school or community.

3

Find a volunteer agency in your community that needs help. Do something.

Attitude

Take Risks—Be a Cheerleader

Success Card **10**

If you draw this card, you must do *one* of these this week:

1

Contact someone who is tackling a difficult project and express your support.

2

Write a motto for your family or business, that represents the risk taker and cheerleader in you.

Attitude

Forget Perfection

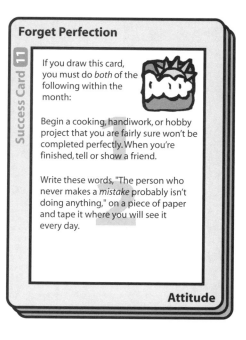

Success Card **11**

If you draw this card, you must do *both* of the following within the month:

Begin a cooking, handiwork, or hobby project that you are fairly sure won't be completed perfectly. When you're finished, tell or show a friend.

Write these words, "The person who never makes a *mistake* probably isn't doing anything," on a piece of paper and tape it where you will see it every day.

Attitude

62

CHAPTER 4

THE VISIBILITY HAND

SUCCESS
CARD **12**: *Show Up & Be Visible*

Show Up

Winners show up. If you've ever planned a meeting or event, you know how grateful you are when people actually arrive. You remember them. Showing up is the basic step to visibility. You will never be noticed if you're not there, even if it's not always a comfortable place to be. Stepping outside your comfort zone is instrumental to finding your potential.

Think of all the opportunities you have to show up. If you're employed, required meetings and events are part of your job. Everyone has an abundance of association meetings as well as educational and social events of your profession or hobby. Finally, community, church, and school events outside your work or hobby are within your reach. Attending these can help you reach your potential. Don't worry at this point about whether the program topic relates to your needs. You will always learn something or meet a new contact. Chalk it all up to your personal and professional development.

Anthony's Move Anthony missed the old days when the sales gang went out every Friday to the local German restaurant, drank great dark ale, and entertained each other with exaggerated imitations of customer objections they'd faced that week. As an internal consultant, he was indeed inside the corporation, yet he felt like an outsider to all of the other departments. For weeks, he went straight home from work to the safe haven of his family. One day, a memo popped up on his intranet announcing a company-sponsored business book club that met on Wednesdays after work. The group was currently reading a book that Anthony had thumbed through recently at the bookstore: the life lessons of the CEO of a global company. Expecting the book's lessons to be helpful to his consulting work, he hit the reply button and joined the group. When Wednesday evening arrived, he was tired, but he had already bought the book; he couldn't back out now. When he entered the conference room where the club met, he nearly turned around because he didn't recognize anyone. Silently, he took a seat, wondering why he was putting himself through this. However, the facilitator was skilled, and after a round of light-hearted introductions, Anthony was able to speak up about the first chapter's message. Someone agreed with him. His energy returned, and the hour went quickly.

It's easy to talk yourself out of showing up, especially if the event isn't required. If you're a free agent, a telecommuter, or unemployed, it's doubly hard to pull yourself out of the friendly confines of the home or home office. For example, if you're starting a consulting business after years as a salaried employee, you could feel a bit fearful about joining groups where you don't know anybody. But cocooning yourself in your office won't help your business grow. Try to turn your negative self-talk into a positive push out the door.

Be Visible

Seek opportunities to be visible. An old Spanish gypsy proverb states, "The dog that trots about finds a bone." You have daily, weekly, monthly, and annual opportunities to be noticed and meet others.

Look at your daily to-do list and check to make sure that it includes a nonrequired personal contact, perhaps to check in with a former client or to make a new connection with an old friend. People notice when you do things that aren't mandatory. Who do you know who just got married, had a baby, got a promotion, graduated, or experienced a loss? Take a moment to contact the person in some way. You can send a short note such as these: Thinking of you during a difficult change; Enjoyed your presentation; or Best wishes in your new position. Our friends tell us repeatedly that it's those unexpected contacts that people remember. Attending a family's meaningful event such as an Eagle Scout ceremony or a funeral shows caring, consideration, and opens the door for future contacts.

Linda's Move   Linda realized that she had opened a recruiting business but nobody knew about it. Business cards were being printed, but the rest of the transition process was a blur. One afternoon, while her daughter shared her A+ school essay paper with her, the teacher's cute, motivational stick-on notes gave Linda an idea. She called the printer and asked to have custom stick-on note pads designed. Then, instead of sending a standard new business announcement, she sent handwritten notes on the note pads—customized to each contact. She included business cards and sent them in a hand-addressed package to her friends and former customers. It took several days to complete the process, but she got many calls and emails congratulating her and thanking her for the notes.

Weekly Plan

Check your calendar, giving special attention to any meetings. Confirm the time, date, and location of each with the meeting planner. Priorities change quickly in today's fast-paced environment, so it never hurts to check. Ask what you can bring or what you should do to prepare. Most people won't take this step. It will surprise the meeting planner and give you added visibility.

Monthly Plan

Plan to attend regular events in your industry or area of interest on a monthly basis. Attend both large and small group events. You reap different rewards from each. One of the smallest networking groups in the Chicago metropolitan area is one of the most powerful. The attendees have fabulous credentials and experience, and one of the few ways to break in to the group is to speak to them. Size doesn't always equal power in the networking world. Monthly industry meetings also provide great opportunities to invite a client as a way to say thanks or to build a relationship with a potential customer. Make it your goal to bring a guest to every other meeting.

Quarterly Plan

On a quarterly basis, write something that will get your name in a byline. It can be very short and simple. You can report on a garden club meeting for your neighborhood newspaper. You can review a new restaurant in the neighborhood for your block newsletter. Get in the habit of sending letters to the editors of your favorite magazines or newspapers. Readers often contact people who write letters to the editor.

You can also send a quarterly update letter to your clients, prospects, or general network. Make it personal. It could be email, but a regularly mailed letter might be a pleasant change for people who are on the Internet all day. Make sure it includes more content and tips for them than it does news about you or your business.

Every few months, attend an event outside your field or interest area. In Japan, some executives are required to have lunch with someone in another industry at least once a month. Paula, a financial consultant, once attended a conference on telemarketing, and, because she was the only financial person there, was able to make a valuable, life-long client contact. She stood out because there was no competition! Jeff, a meeting planner, convinced his widowed father to attend a senior dance at the center near his home. Jeff succeeded and was pleased to see his dad develop an entirely new network of friends based on one night's venture out of his comfort zone. Gary Hoover, the founder of Barnes & Noble, often speaks about how his stores became successful because they stepped outside the traditional bookstore paradigm and offered other services for busy people. Stressing that all successful people are curious, he challenges, "What might happen if a doctor went to a dentist's convention?"[1] He has a point. Be curious.

Consider getting involved in the organizations to which your clients and trusted friends belong. Those meetings can bring you more contacts and keep you well versed in the happenings of their industry. John, an IT professional and part-time speaker, was asked to speak at a large logistics industry conference in the personal development track. He found it interesting that the person chairing that track was not part of the industry directly but an executive recruiter who specialized in placing people in that industry. She belonged to the association to stay visible to the movers and shakers, find new talent, and stay knowledgeable about industry trends and challenges.

Annual Plan

Yearly, attend at least one conference in your field. Conferences bring you national and international visibility, which is difficult to get in your office. They also provide valuable relationship-building opportunities. The keynote speeches and breakout sessions are certainly worthwhile, but the real benefit comes from working the hallways. You can usually find the stars of the industry engaged in informal meetings and socializing outside the session room doors. Plan on attending every breakfast, reception, and dinner; you will meet the largest variety of people. Plan your budget so you can travel and attend.

SUCCESS
CARD 13: *Arrive Early & Have Energy*

Arrive Early

The average person is on time. Winners are early. The winner arrives early for many reasons. If you're presenting at the event, you can review your notes and check the setup so that you can focus on mingling later. You also have a chance to select a good seat. Depending on the room size and the meeting intent, the best seat could be near the door where you can greet and chat with almost everyone who enters. Key information, which often passes before a meeting starts when people aren't on an agenda, could include facts and news items. It could also be impromptu observations of people and events that will really help you understand the politics of the situation.

"I met the key players."

I learned to arrive early at any new association meeting because board members are usually there at that time. The first time, it happened accidentally. I had the meeting start time wrong and arrived half an hour early. However, there were the main leaders—preparing the registration table and checking with the hotel, and I was able to take a few extra minutes to present a card and clarify my interest in the group. Then I asked if there was anything I could help with. They asked me to help people find the coatroom. It was a great way to meet people. Later, I could refer to our meeting in my follow-up note.

Julie, sales representative for a graphics firm

Kathleen's Move   An achiever, Kathleen arrived early to meetings whenever possible. She would grab a choice seat and then return calls on her cellular phone until everyone else arrived. She used the time to make important sales contacts, enjoying the envious looks from less experienced reps who had fewer calls to make. After realizing that she needed to build her people skills to be fully successful, however, Kathleen changed her tactic. She still arrived early, but she turned off her phone. Instead, she established eye contact with everyone who walked in, said hello, and made small talk. She noticed that the climate around her began to warm up, not only before but also during the meeting. Other salespeople built on her ideas more easily, and she just had more fun during what had been mundane, boring sales updates.

You can make a positive impression on any group when you act like a host instead of a guest. Even if you don't know a single person, you can still be helpful with directions to the coatroom, restrooms, and food table. Connie, an active meeting-goer in the retail industry, has often been mistaken for the program chair because she always helps other attendees get comfortable and settled at meetings. Superiors notice this kind of personal effort and could ask you to take on a more significant role at the next meeting.

Have Energy

How many times have you yawned at the end of a day and dreaded showing up at the meeting you registered for that evening? Winners take a breath, grab an energizing bar or drink, and go anyway. For example, in the competitive world of acting, beginners learn the value of manufacturing energy early. Spending their days fighting urban traffic to go to back-to-back auditions, "look-sees," classes, coaching sessions, and agency rounds, actors can often find their energy at low ebb when they need it most. They often have to tell themselves they're wide awake (or talented or beautiful or interesting) to make it through the next round—and the ones who succeed have that energy.

KEY PLAYER PROFILE: DAVID J. ROSENBERG

I wanted the opportunity to take risks—to live on the edge. I quit my job before I even thought about starting my own company. I wanted to be the top salesperson and I didn't get the support from the old company that I wanted on a big account. All I knew was the mail business; I knew that I could take mail, sort it, and build my own company. I turned in my Porsche and paid off my debts. I read *Think and Grow Rich* by Napoleon Hill. He talks about storage of negative processes in your brain; if you let the negative stay there, you dwell on it. I don't let negative thoughts interfere. Your lowest point is only for a moment. Once you hit the bottom, it's always up. Everything that hits you provides that road to recovery. You've got to pull from every situation. If you have a bad month in profits, you say, 'That was over; let's move forward.' If I look at a forest, I'm the first one to say, Have you tried this path? Owning your own company or being independent is not the only answer. Success comes in many forms—faith, love, and contentment are others. If you want financial success, you have to create something out there—an image, a concept, a belief, or a product. If you can find one other person to believe in it, you're on your way to success. We all are a little insecure—we need assurance that what we did is good. In order to be successful, somebody else has to see it as success. Somebody has to believe!"

. . . David Rosenberg is the president, founder, and chief executive officer of World Distribution Services, an international mail services company handling more than 10 tons of mail daily for over 700 clients throughout the United States.

If you show up, show up with energy and the right attitude. Take a deep breath before you open the door, put a positive expression on your face, and walk in with verve. Use your body language to communicate energy. Using your predetermined goals for the event as your "motivation," walk briskly, smile, make eye contact, extend your hand, and introduce yourself. Before you know it, the yawns are gone.

SUCCESS
CARD 14: *Start Talking & Talk to Everyone*

Start Talking

Susan RoAne, the networking maven, discusses conversation in her book, *What Do I Say Next: Talking Your Way to Business and Social Success*. She says that most of us try too hard to be perfect, when, in reality, great conversations "start very simply where you establish commonality."[2] An intriguing gem of a book *1,001 Ways to Improve Your Conversation and Speeches* by Herbert Prochnow, published in 1952, quotes Frank McKinney Hubbard, a popular American humorist of the time, "Don't knock the weather; nine-tenths of the people couldn't start a conversation if it didn't change once in a while."[3]

The wisdom of the 1950s holds true today. It's all right to talk about the changes in the weather. Simple beginnings uncover uncommon conversations. Joe, a middle-age actor, was meeting with his mortgage broker to adjust his mortgage during a recession. He struck up a conversation about what the broker did, and before long, the broker was recommending that the actor try being a loan officer. "It would be a great opportunity for an outgoing person like you with flexible time," he said. The actor was intrigued and began loan officer training. Simple questions ignited a new career.

When you go to meetings, make a point of talking not only with people you know but also with people you don't know. Don't automatically seat yourself with your best friends; check in briefly with them, but grab a chair next to some people you don't know. Make a point of meeting and talking with three new people each time you go. If you listen and ask lots of questions, they'll remember you as a great conversationalist. You'll probably learn something, too. It never hurts to have a couple of good opening lines ready to go. Comments about the event or location or even a genuine, positive observation about the other person can open the conversation. Listen carefully to his or her response for clues to your next question.

Be prepared to speak the language, whatever it may be. In the United States, for example, Spanish is the second most commonly spoken language; there are about 17.3 million native Spanish speakers. After English and Spanish, French is spoken regularly in U.S. homes (1.7 million) more than any other language. More than a million Americans also regularly speak German, Italian, and Chinese. If you're a globally oriented person, you're used to being surrounded by different languages, and you're probably well equipped to make simple conversation in several of them. Second to knowing a person's name and pronouncing it correctly, being familiar with his or her native language will score many interpersonal points for you. You don't have to be fluent; the basic phrases of travel, dining, and sports will get you started in a conversation. What would you like to drink? Do you enjoy golf? and How was your trip? are some questions that most beginners can learn. Once you've opened the conversation, you can always admit your limitations.

"I was inspired at the company party."

When my client, the president of a small manufacturing company, invited me to the annual company party, I was thrilled at the chance to solidify our relationship. Of the two hundred employees, I had met many managers and supervisors but hadn't seen the warehouse workers often. I knew they were a diverse group, and I was interested to see how everyone related.

The event was a crowded affair, and due to a reservation seating snafu, my husband and I volunteered to sit at a table with some of the warehouse employees. Throughout dinner, our tablemates spoke Spanish, graciously including us in any simple exchanges in English about the food and drink. We progressed through the dinner with a few words and smiles and gestures, but I regretted not knowing more. I would like to have asked the man next to me about his family and his work. After dinner, the president spoke and handed out awards, several of which went to warehouse supervisors. From my vantage point among the warehouse employees, it was evident that if he had known a few phrases in their language, he would have won their attention immediately.

After that experience, I was inspired to enroll in a Spanish class and to encourage my client to learn some phrases for next year's awards banquet. I enrolled at my local adult discovery center and learned how to order eggs and ask for a bus. With the help of my workbooks and several bilingual employees, we coached the president, and the next year, when he said "Thank you" in Spanish, Hindu, and Polish, he received applause.

Joan, a benefits consultant

More immigrants are entering the U.S. workforce than ever before. At a Wal-Mart store in the Washington, D.C., metropolitan area, employees are from forty-five countries and speak one hundred languages. In the Chicago, Illinois, public schools, more than sixteen different languages are spoken frequently. The voting instructions for Chicago elections are written in ninety-eight languages. It's becoming more and more evident that language capability is a real strength for anyone wanting to be more visible.

If you are an immigrant, be sure to assess your skills so that you are capable in your new country. If you are a native born-speaker, learning other languages will help you make connections. For example, if you happen to work or volunteer in an industry or area that is primarily Asian, French, Polish, Turkish, or Hispanic, learn the basics of that language. Most major cities have language training schools, and many programs are available on the Web, some for free!

Janet, a homemaker considering full-time work, made some great business connections while brushing up her French at a local French alliance organization. The class she took happened to attract many global businesspeople as well as energetic fans of the country and the cuisine, and they stayed in contact with each other after the class. She went to a cocktail party for all of the students, got a chance to practice French there, and happened to meet the director of the alliance. It was the perfect event, giving her a chance to socialize in French and meet savvy, generous people. The director later donated a class for her school's auction fund-raising event.

Language can either bond you or bar you from inclusion. Judge yourself. Which way do you feel most often? It's your move to increase your chances of being included. No one else can learn the language for you.

Talk to Everyone

Robert Kelley, author of *How to Be a Star at Work: Nine Breakthrough Strategies You Need to Succeed,*[4] discovered that peer-nominated stars at work were people who knew where to go to get answers. They were admired because they made the whole team look good. How did they know where to go? They knew many people across hierarchies, departments, and locations.

Schmoozing is not a bad thing. You should know the people you work with and stay in contact with former co-workers because they're important resources. A recent University of Cincinnati study of eighty employees and twenty-two supervisors revealed that people who are successful make friends with everyone. They get higher ratings on reviews. They reach out and make contacts with a diverse network of people. One example cited in the study was an upper-level marketing manager with specific ties to the assembly line. According to University of Cincinnati Professor Ajay Mehra, "People who serve as bridges by connecting people tend to outperform those who don't and are therefore seen as more valuable by their supervisors.[5] Most organizations are less hierarchical today and rely more on employees to build bridges to get the job done.

Sandra, who worked as a salesperson at a high-end clothing store, learned a valuable lesson about the importance of talking to everyone. Early in her retail career, she often walked past the women who were not well dressed, assuming they didn't have the money to spend lavishly. Later, however, she saw fellow associates accompany those same women to the register to ring up huge sales. She learned never to make assumptions about anyone.

In your personal life, talking to everybody is also important. You probably know people who are great conversationalists. They seem to be at ease talking to just about anybody—on the phone, in person, at work, and at social events. If you live or work with people like this, it can even be frustrating to have them constantly fraternizing while you're trying to get something done. But it's important to keep in mind that while they're fraternizing, they're building valuable networks.

An old Chinese proverb says, "A single conversation across the table with a wise man is worth a month's study of books." Here are some things you could use to approach your personal network:

High school selection

Movie passes

Where to find a good loan officer

Vacation rental advice

Math tutors

Laser eye surgery recommendations

The best hardware store in a one-mile radius

Family-friendly restaurants

A good tailor

How to get involved in your block club

Dining spots near the airport

Halloween costume sewing tips

A reliable place to get your car tuned

Here are some things you might discuss with your professional network:

Sources for a list server for your new electronic newsletter

The best version of a software program

Association management resources

A good speaker for your next event

Other respected IT system vendors

How e-learning or e-commerce is working in their organizations

Where to go for budget advice

Recommendation for a medical insurance plan

How to book travel

Leadership advice for serving on a new board

A good place to study workplace Spanish

An inexpensive location for a meeting

Whom do you contact when you need something?

SUCCESS CARD 15: *Sign Up & Reach Out*

Sign Up

Average players attend required meetings. Winners attend not only required meetings but also others. You may wonder why would you want to add to your already busy schedule? The answer is that you will benefit greatly from other perspectives. This is the reason that cross-training and job shadowing are time-tested job enrichment techniques. They force increased understanding of what it's like to do another person's job.

"I went to every off site I could observe."

I was always intrigued by what was going on in the marketing arm of my division. Even though I have a heavy IT background, if I heard about a company-sponsored marketing retreat, I'd ask to attend as an observer. I was rarely turned down. I did that for the first few years at my company. Things changed; departments merged and evolved. When they needed a manager for the organizational development area of marketing services (which is really a lot of IT work), they asked me because of my strong marketing interest. Now I'm in charge of all of the education for the division. I'm glad I pushed my way into those retreats.

**Laura, manager,
organizational development
of a large financial services
organization**

If you're currently working, think of all the meetings you could attend at your business location: department meetings, virtual meetings, client meetings, management meetings, orientation sessions, benefits briefings, and safety briefings as well as lunchtime learning sessions, e–learning, and Web chats. If you're new, you have a great reason to request attending and observing other meetings. If you're a seasoned veteran, you can make up a reason. Volunteer for a special project or design one of your own. Chair a committee. Conduct a survey. Interview for an article or write one yourself. Volunteer to take notes or be the recorder.

Today, having experience with virtual meetings is essential in most large organizations. Virtual meeting participants can live in different time zones, speak different languages, receive materials in different formats, and are often uncomfortable with the virtual interaction. To stand out in virtual meetings, observe your first one, participate in the next, and when it's your turn to lead a virtual meeting, you'll be prepared and confident.

A great way to sign up for meetings is to offer to be the speaker. You might find this idea challenging, but, if you're like most people, you have something to share. Think of what your life experience has taught you. You can share that experience in many formats. At work you could present an overview to the board about a conference you attended. You could outline the newly developed five-year plan in a department meeting. Outside of work, you can speak at many places. Churches, schools, and community groups are always looking for speakers to present topics that range from the benefits of low-fat cooking to help with taxes. There are lunchtime learning series, evening workshops, and Sunday sessions. Find out who's in charge and extend the offer. If the need is not immediate, send a note or your card now and then to remind the person of your interest in speaking.

Reach Out

Volunteering is another good way to become known. When you selflessly volunteer for causes you believe in, such as giving blood or helping with a company- or church-sponsored tutoring program, you earn a halo of recognition. It's the best kind of halo because you've volunteered for the cause first; the recognition is simply the bonus. When you become a resource to others, you help yourself and revitalize your spirit.

One-on-one coaching, mentoring, and guidance also keep you visible among your colleagues. You could be thinking, Me? Mentor someone? You'd be surprised to know that just about everyone can mentor someone on something. If you've been on the job a while or know your craft, you have skills to share. If you're retired, your wisdom can be of great benefit to new workers. Mentoring is gaining in popularity as companies watch their employee development budgets. It's a low-cost way to use internal and former talent. If you're a consultant, an entrepreneur, or a former skilled employee, you can coach people who want to do what you do. People don't forget a good coach.

Juana's Move Juana had been on the job as a customer service rep at the garden center for a few months when her supervisor asked her what she and others were discussing in Spanish over lunch. When Juana explained that her co-workers from Mexico were unsure of how to register their children for public school, her supervisor asked if she would be willing to bring in some forms and help them during an extended lunch hour. Juana, in a valiant effort to overcome her insecurity, said yes. The following week, she caught her supervisor smiling in the doorway as Juana walked her co-workers through the process of kindergarten registration.

Volunteer for your professional organizations and be more than a *good* volunteer—be *great*. Average players are semicommitted. Winners can always be counted on. You can do simple things such as volunteer for a phone-calling tree, shake hands at the door, or clean up afterward. When you're ready, chair a committee. Run for the executive board. Be the president. Organize the annual conference. No matter what your volunteer role, it's important to be dependable. The friendships you make with people who share your profession are special. Stay in touch with your professional friends forever.

"I volunteered."

In the early stages of my career, going to my association's meetings taught me valuable skills. I learned leadership skills through my volunteer involvement. I learned how to think strategically, how to motivate others, and how to communicate persuasively and effectively. I also gained confidence in my abilities. I discovered a vast network of professional colleagues—peers and associates I can call on to discuss issues or serve as resources from time to time. And I now consider many of these colleagues my personal friends.

Peggy, vice president and chief financial officer of a health system

---

You might want to consider volunteering first for the membership committee of an association. Membership gives you the opportunity to become the front line for the organization. You usually get to work the registration table, which is a great spot for seeing and being seen. You get to know everyone and can gain insight into how the group works behind the scenes. Working at check-in also allows you to become the master connector, orchestrating important connections for people who may not have done so themselves.

SUCCESS
CARD **16** : *Re-ignite Supports • Refer Work • Advertise •*
Make Dinner

Re-ignite Supports

Stay in touch with every contact who has supported you—*forever.*

Refer Work

A proven phenomenon is that strength lies in weak ties. This means that people who don't know you quite so well will tend to recommend you and your services before your best friends and acquaintances will. Recommending someone you don't know well involves reduced risk. Think about it: Every tie in your network is important. You could find that you will receive referrals from people whom don't know you at all. They've heard your name somewhere or know someone who was familiar with your skills. This is the strength that lies in weak ties. Refer work to others. They will remember.

Harry's Move   One morning, sipping his coffee, wondering what to do next, Harry received a call from Sean, a former student. Very apologetic, Sean thanked Harry for his time, revealing that he had gotten his number from an old neighbor. Sean had been a tenor in Harry's choir in high school and was now a recent graduate looking for a teaching job as a choral director. It was a smart call on Sean's part. Harry had met many teachers and administrators during his years teaching high school. His choir had competed throughout the nation, and his networking contacts in music education were vast. Pleased, Harry told Sean that he needed to think about his current connections and would call him back. Within a few hours, Harry had the names of several music department chairs throughout the region. Sean was grateful and invited Harry to be a guest conductor at his first concert.

Don't be afraid of your competitors. Find out who they are and make sure they know you. If you're a good sport who enjoys being in the game, you'll soon see that there's enough work to go around. Many association members use each other as strategic alliances, referring them to clients who need their related products or services. You can partner with a competitor in many ways: on presentations, on proposals, on resources or travel—even on passing jobs along when you're unable to take them.

"I had the best partner."

When I first met Debbie, we were both outside consultants contracted separately to complete a major management training initiative for a telecommunications company. We shared lunch, eyeing each other cautiously at first since we shared the client as well. Over many lunches, we found that we had a lot in common; our children were about the same age and we were both inspired by our consulting work. Then one day the client announced that she needed someone to provide intense training for one of the company's suppliers. Its entire employee population needed to be prepared for a team-based work structure. Deb looked at me. I looked at her. We knew that together we could complete the job beautifully. We did; it was a great success, and now, eight years later, we still share the materials we developed. She was definitely the best partner I ever had.

Janet, training consultant and corporate coach

Advertise

Advertising gets the word out about good people, products, and services. Get your name in print as much as possible. Place an ad in your clients' trade journals or those you read monthly, send out postcard updates, or create a brochure that can be used for customers. If you're within an organization, consider developing a marketing piece that could be used internally for cross-selling purposes. If you're independent or based at home, a newsletter is a good way to stay in touch. Electronic newsletters and e-zines are becoming more and more popular and easier to produce with some set-up tools and basic training. You can also advertise in fund-raising programs and marketing pieces or calendars.

Get your photo out in as many places as you can. Putting a photo on your business or calling card can give you a lot of recognition. The more that people see your photo, the more often they will recognize you. A good headshot is priceless and important for almost anyone to have because you can use it for programs, family events, and all sorts of church, community, and work needs. Photographers who specialize in taking actor's headshots are often the best at capturing your personality. Their entire business centers around taking photos that show faces at their best. They also can recommend good make-up artists and wardrobe stylists. Many larger urban areas have a photographer with a related background. If you have a Web site that includes a photograph, you will notice that people you meet in person or on the phone seem to know you. The Web inspires countless opportunities for advertisement and visual recognition.

"I ran an ad."

Before I really had enough money to advertise, I put a small ad with my photo in our professional trade directory. That was 20 years ago. The ad has changed over the years, but I have maintained a presence. People often meet me at meetings, saying, "I've seen your photo. I've heard of you." I'm happy to know I built the visibility I wanted.

**Carol Ann,
career consultant**

Make Dinner

Most people are honored to be invited to someone's home for dinner. Restaurant meetings are nice and coffee at the corner shop is great, but dinner at home is more personal. Whether or not you are a great cook, you can provide a meal with the help of deli-prepared food as long as you showcase one homemade item. Why make one item? You can discuss the heritage of the recipe!

Men as well as women can invite clients home. Tom, a single man who lives in a large urban area, hosts an annual holiday party for ten co-workers every year using take-out deli trays from the local gourmet grocer. His single homemade item is the shrimp sauce—a simple mixture of ketchup and horseradish.

Everyone has a great time, and he gets to show off his inherited family collection of holiday decorations.

Extend an invitation to co-workers, friends, or clients, and don't forget the boss. If you don't typically socialize with the boss, you will feel more at ease if you also include a few others from work. You can mix up your dinner guest lists and invite people outside work to blend with the business crowd. This eclectic combination of people can allow more interesting dinner conversation. Tom once hosted the first two clients to hire him when he opened his business. They had never met, and he thought they would get along beautifully, but he had another motive as well. One of them was in job transition and the other had a large network in sales. As a result of the dinner, the two brainstormed some good job leads and still stay in touch.

A dinner club is also fun. You can get together with four to six couples and start your own modern version of a tradition started in the 1940s and 50s. When everyone brings a dish to share, the pressure of preparing an entire meal is off the host or hostess. This, paired with gathering in someone's home, offers a way for everyone to relax and discuss things that might never come up in a restaurant or at another type of social event.

William's Move   William was new in town and to the workforce. He knew only a few people at work and had no outside friends at all. Tired of all work and no play, he decided to do something about it. He sent customized email invitations to people in his department inviting them to a potluck dinner at his apartment. He realized he wasn't a very good cook, but he could throw together his mom's recipe for shrimp fried rice. Almost everyone was able to come, bringing a multitude of foods and a willingness to get to know each other better. It was such a hit that William has turned it into an annual Chinese New Year party, an event that his co-workers look forward to each year.

SUCCESS
CARD 17: *Follow Up*

Most people forget. Winners follow up. Years ago, after attending a presentation by a panel of experts for her professional association, Wanda, a real estate saleswoman, followed up with letters to each panel member thanking them for their presentations and expertise. She then called them all later to follow up on her letters. Although two never returned her messages, one did. That one return call from a vice president of a large financial services company resulted in a meeting, igniting the beginning of a ten-year client relationship for her. Think how simple this follow-up was: three letters and three phone calls. Cost = less than one hour of time and $1.00 postage. Value = thousands of dollars of profit, priceless relationship, and years of career support.

Face-to-face contact is the best type of follow-up, although it's not always possible. Follow-up via email gives the impression of "work-as-usual" and is uninspired. Phone calls, notes, and letters make more of an impact because they take some time and effort to accomplish. If you don't have personalized stationery, have some made. Whether you're an employee, a homemaker, or an entrepreneur, people will recognize your personal touch when they receive your note. Many believe that one of the things that helped elect George H. W. Bush as the forty-first president was his use of thank-you notes. He carried his personalized note cards wherever he went and jotted a few quick lines to every person who had been involved in the campaign stop he'd just left. Hundreds of people received these personal notes and remembered his thoughtfulness on voting day.

Follow-up can also include clipping and sending articles pertinent to the discussion you and your contact had together. Send the restaurant guide to Paris for a client's vacation in France or research related to drugs and depression to a pharmaceutical client to use on her calls to physicians. If you ever see contacts' in print, clip and send that, too. Alert them to Web sites you've unearthed that will help them with their projects. Invite them to a different meeting you're attending or speaking at. Ask if they'd be willing to review some written material you're currently working on such as your brochure or an article.

The follow-up is a winning move that many people consider but few actually make. Some are afraid of rejection; others just don't take the time for details. Consider this popular adage: "Successful people do what others don't want to do." Remember that follow-up steps complete the positive impression you want to make.

Play the Game: It's Your Move

That sums up the Visibility Hand. How will you play it? As before, draw a card and play it this week. Record your results in your game plan at the end of the book.

End Notes

1. Gary Hoover, speech to the National Speakers' Association Winter Workshop, Philadelphia, PA, 2000.

2. Susan RoAne, *What Do I Say Next? Talking Your Way to Business and Social Success* (New York: Warner Books, 1999), p. 42.

3. Herbert Prochnow, *1,001 Ways to Improve Your Conversation and Speeches* (New York: Harper and Brothers 1952), p. 1.

4. Robert Kelley, *How to Be a Star at Work* (New York: Times Business, 1998), p. 75.

5. Ajay Mehra, Ph.D. University of Cincinnati. Conversation with the author, January 18, 2003.

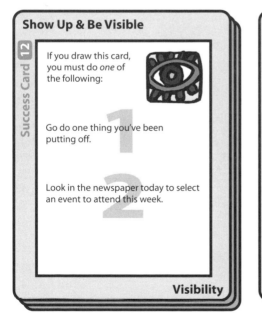

Show Up & Be Visible

Success Card **12**

If you draw this card, you must do *one* of the following:

Go do one thing you've been putting off.

Look in the newspaper today to select an event to attend this week.

Visibility

Arrive Early & Have Energy

Success Card **13**

If you draw this card, you must do *both* of the following:

Locate the next meeting on your calendar and plan a way to arrive fifteen minutes early.

Plan your opening greeting so that it conveys energy and a positive attitude.

Visibility

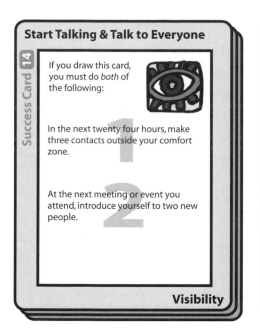

Start Talking & Talk to Everyone

Success Card 14

If you draw this card, you must do *both* of the following:

In the next twenty four hours, make three contacts outside your comfort zone.

At the next meeting or event you attend, introduce yourself to two new people.

Visibility

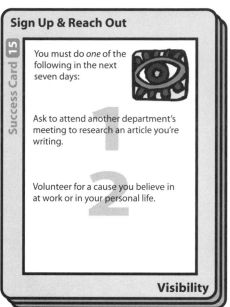

Sign Up & Reach Out

Success Card 15

You must do *one* of the following in the next seven days:

Ask to attend another department's meeting to research an article you're writing.

Volunteer for a cause you believe in at work or in your personal life.

Visibility

Reignite Supports—Refer Work—Advertise—Make Dinner

Success Card 16

If you draw this card, You must do *two* out of the three activities:

Send a handwritten note to your oldest client or friend. Don't ask for anything.

Call a long-time client or friend and recommend the services of another long-time client or friend.

Invite a client or co-worker to dinner.

Visibility

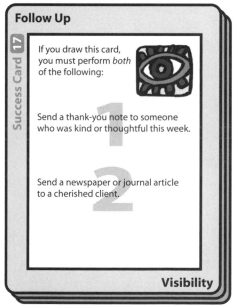

Follow Up

Success Card 17

If you draw this card, you must perform *both* of the following:

Send a thank-you note to someone who was kind or thoughtful this week.

Send a newspaper or journal article to a cherished client.

Visibility

CHAPTER 5

THE STYLE HAND

Know Your Buyer

The Preparation Hand discussed the importance of reflecting the goals of the organization and clearly defining the personal image you want to convey. The Style Hand will give you the tools you need to dig deep and build an image that will serve you well in all situations. It has to do with crafting your appearance to influence how others perceive you. It's about thinking ahead of time to the messages you want to convey and to customizing your clothing, color, and grooming choices to communicate those qualities.

Now, wait a minute, you're thinking. Are you saying that I have to become some sort of clone to get what I want? Do you want me to try to fool people into thinking I'm something I'm not? Not quite. In the course of a single day, you play a variety of roles, and each role calls for a different "costume," a different way of speaking, and a different way of behaving. Dressing to watch a child compete in a volleyball tournament is different than dressing for a sales call. You speak differently with your siblings than you do with the chairman of the board. Behavior is different, as well. Gulping down a burger from the drive-through window looks different from the way you eat in the company of clients or on a blind date. You subconsciously make adjustments throughout your day to feel comfortable and accepted. Why not make them consciously? Being aware of your image choices and plotting them out ahead of time

87

can affect how you are perceived and, therefore, impact your success. It's true that most people like to do business and develop relationships with others like themselves, people who reflect the same values, background, and experiences. This is not to suggest that you change who you are and what you value. Simply adjust the outer choices to reflect the qualities that will work to your advantage in each situation. Political media adviser and former TV producer Roger Ailes summed it up in his book, *You Are the Message:* "It's that important for you to accept that *you* (the whole you) are the message—and that message determines whether or not you'll get what you want in this life."[1] Help each audience see you through *their* eyes. Think of it as product packaging.

Businesses spend millions each year on product design and packaging. Should our cars be available in bright red or burgundy? Should the new perfume bottle be tall and slender or short and wide? Should we make computer components in black as well as almond? Companies take great care selecting the shapes, styles, and colors that will appeal to the buying public and move their products off the showroom floors. Try thinking of yourself in the same way. What would appeal most to your buying public? From just a visual standpoint, your packaging consists of color, wardrobe, accessories, and grooming. Every choice you make—suit versus sweats, wrinkled versus ironed, black versus brown, nylon versus leather—sends a message to others.

Understand Perceptions

As much as you hate to admit it, perceptions *are* reality. It often doesn't matter what the truth is but what people believe. You could value orderliness and describe yourself as an organized person, but if you arrive late, are inappropriately dressed or disheveled, and are without the information or tools you need for the meeting, the perception is that you're quite unorganized. And perceptions can be very difficult to change. In their book, *Put Your Best Foot Forward*,[2] authors Jo-Ellan Dimitrius and Mark Mazzarella assert that perceptions are based on stereotypes and prejudices and that people harbor prejudices based not only on the large issues of gender or race but also on every conceivable human attribute or choice. Clean or dirty, tall or short, thin or fat, articulate or inarticulate—we each prefer one to another. A single trait can then lead to more sweeping assumptions about a person. If he is inarticulate, then he's probably also unassertive. If he's unassertive, he's probably lazy, and so on. You can begin to see how important it is to be in control of every choice you make.

You also have emotional or "gut" reactions to people. You could not know why, but you're usually drawn to or repelled by people within moments of meeting them. They, in turn, have the same reactions to you. You respond subconsciously to color, clothing, and body language and assign values to what you see. Like a cover on a book, people believe that the outer choices reveal something about the inside. It's a part of human nature to categorize people quickly; it brings order to the chaos. It's been this way since time began. Think of the caveman. He who sized up situations the quickest lived to hunt another day! Modern life has made it only more difficult. We live fast-paced lives with sound-bite mentalities. Television has conditioned people to believe that messages can be delivered in thirty seconds or less—and with the mute button on. You've heard this phrase many times: You never have a second chance to make a first impression—and it's true. Jobs are won or lost, opportunities offered or denied, and relationships begun or thwarted because of first impressions.

Harry's Move   Wanting to play a more active role in his granddaughter's life, Harry volunteered to pick her up after children's chorus rehearsals. He drove to the elementary school where the choir met to rehearse each Tuesday afternoon. He arrived early and settled in to wait for her in the car. When he rolled down the window, he could hear the beautiful voices of the choir. Harry ventured inside and followed the singing to the choir room. As he stood in the doorway to listen, his granddaughter caught his eye and waved to him. As he listened and observed the director work with the children, Harry realized that he could have something to offer this young group: the experience and proven techniques of a veteran music teacher. His mind worked fast, formulating ideas of how he could volunteer his services. He decided to introduce himself to the director right after rehearsal. As he moved through the crowd of children, the director came right up to him and said, "I'm Mrs. Baker. You must be Karen's grandfather. She's so excited that you've moved closer to her. It's always great to have our Grandpas close by. Nice meeting you." As the director walked away, Harry realized that, in his sweat suit and baseball cap, he looked more like a grandfather than a music professional and peer to the director. Fearing he'd already ruined his chances, he vowed to adjust his attire next Tuesday to make a better impression on Mrs. Baker.

Carol, a consultant, learned a valuable lesson about first impressions early in her career. The small consulting firm she worked for at the time had booked a presentation skills training program for all of the new managers of a Midwest airline. The training was to be held in a retreat atmosphere at a majestic, old oceanside inn in Maine. As part of the deal, Carol and several other trainers, including Carol's boss, would fly on the client airline to Maine. For comfort, they all decided to wear jeans on the early morning flight. To their dismay, as they arrived at the departure gate, they were greeted by the sight of all of their customers—the managers—in full professional dress with the airline's uniform: jackets, badges, suits, and skirts. Sheepishly, the casual consultants introduced themselves to the professional-looking clients. They believed it was more difficult to establish credibility as they began the sophisticated training program the next day. Carol says that to this day you will not find her traveling in blue jeans, even on family vacation trips. Her travel uniform includes tailored black pants that can adapt to any unexpected meeting.

Think of yourself as an actor at an audition. Actors continuously alter their outer image to project different qualities. Before they go to any audition, actors always ask their agents, "What are they looking for?" The agent's answer helps them determine whether to look like a powerful executive, novice assistant, or harried parent. The actors then select the clothes, accessories, and hairstyle that best fit that character. They know that producers and directors look for visual "types" first. The people whom you need to influence do, too. They could be your boss, neighbors, voters, professor, or clients, and they can't picture you in the position you desire until you *show* them that you belong there. "Dress for where you're going, not for where you are" is a good phrase to keep in mind when you're making your move.

"I wore the right clothes."

One of my early jobs was working in the buying office of a clothing store. Buyers were expected to dress in trendy clothes, so I did. At the time, oversized clothing was "in." A typical outfit for me was a padded shoulder T-shirt, chunky belt and long skirt, two sizes larger than my real size! I then moved from the buying office to the human resources department, with the responsibility for training managers and all new employees. I was now working on the same floor as all of the owners and conducting training three days a week—wearing the same clothes as I did as a buyer. One day during my lunch hour, I decided to do a little shopping and hooked up with one of our personal shoppers. Working with her in the dressing room, she was shocked to see that I was not a large person but a small person hidden under huge clothing. She pulled together a beautiful outfit for me, one that was the right size and right style for my line of work: black skirt, cream blouse, designer jacket, skin-toned hose and pumps. I wasn't sure about any of this at first, it was such a different look for me, but it didn't take long for the positive feedback to roll in. More people were noticing me and greeting me. The owners seemed to know who I was. I believed that I had more respect in the classroom and was receiving compliments on my appearance. The personal shopper taught me the concept of spend more, buy less: buy fewer clothes but invest in better quality clothing. The biggest payback came when I left that job. Interviewing in my new style of dressing, I was able to jump up a couple of levels. I was hired right onto an executive-level team.

Lisa, sales director of a major hotel chain

Take time before you walk through their door to think about what *they* want, need, and value. Confucius said, "In all things, success depends upon preparation, and without such preparation there is sure to be failure." Prepare for that all-important first impression. Do they need someone creative and energetic? Do they value people who are efficient and self-motivated? Here are some other qualities they may value:

Friendly
Knowledgeable
Youthful
Mature
Cooperative

Flexible

Relaxed

Unconventional

Reliable

Caring

Neat

Optimistic

Conservative

Powerful

Assertive

Liberal

Happy

Intellectual

Passionate

Spontaneous

Responsible

Control the perceptions they have of you. Prepare yourself to succeed by projecting the qualities for which they're looking.

KEY PLAYER PROFILE: YOSEF I. ABRAMOWITZ

Recently, my development director took me shopping so that I could buy my first suit in fifteen years. After choosing my new, conservative blue wool-silk combination, he asked me if I had dress shoes. 'I actually do,' I responded. 'My Edgar shoes.' The black leather shoes, nicknamed for one of my first philanthropic supporters, symbolize my first brush with compromise as I adjusted to dressing for a new role. After my initial meeting with the philanthropist in 1987, the foundation's director took me aside, glanced disapprovingly at my canvas footwear, and stated in a hushed tone, 'Here, you wear shoes.' I bought the shoes, but I also stowed them in my backpack until the very last minute before an Edgar meeting to minimize the disruption to what has been my standard uniform in nonprofit life for almost two decades: sports jacket, button-down shirt, slightly funky tie, ancient jeans, and the ever-present sneakers. The wardrobe was about comfort and class, meant to convey a message of independent activism for a fast-paced younger generation.

"My unorthodox style had seemed to be an asset, especially in the early years. But I have had to use the Edgar shoes a half-dozen times in the past four months, and only two of those times were with Edgar. The difference is that I am now a CEO. Not executive director or chairperson, or any of the other titles I've held during my twenty years of nonprofit work. Donors have changed, too. Now everyone wants a business plan or at least a strategic plan that incorporates business-minded thinking. And they want someone who dresses the part of CEO to sell it to them. I'm game. Since I have the responsibility of raising the money and protecting key assets and jobs, I can't let a dress code get in the way. If I am seen as a young activist and not as a maturing CEO, my organization will not be able to raise the money we need to succeed. So I suspect my uniform will continue to evolve."[3]

. . . *Yosef I. Abramowitz is chief executive officer of Jewish Family & Life (jflmedia.com), a charity in Newton, Massachusetts, that uses the Internet, magazines, and books to encourage Jews to make the religion's values and culture a part of their daily life.*

SUCCESS CARD 19: *Know-How • Choose Appropriately • Enhance Yourself*

Know-How

Now is the perfect time to take stock of what you have to work with: your personal coloring, body type, and current wardrobe. Every life transition or career move should be accompanied by a complete overhaul of your "look." This visual makeover signals to the world that you've done some self-examination, made a few changes, and are ready for the next phase of your life. Professionals in the image industry are the people to go to when you need an objective and expert eye. For example, certified professionals of the Association of Image Consultants International have been qualified through years of professional training and experience to give you the answers to your questions about how to dress, groom, and shop. Whomever you choose, call their references before you begin; you will be putting your trust in them.

Clothing should be the backdrop, never the star. Your use of color can aid in that effort. When you wear clothes that flatter your natural coloring, there's nothing to distract the observer from finding your face, making eye contact, and communicating. *You* become the focus, not your clothes. In very simple terms, people fall into one of two categories: those with predominantly cool tones in their skin, hair, and eyes, and those with predominantly warm tones in their skin, hair, and eyes. Cool-toned people usually look best in cool clothing colors and cosmetics; warm-toned people usually look best in warm clothing colors and cosmetics. To learn whether you're cool or warm, consider booking a color analysis consultation. A trained color professional can select a grouping of colors for you that, when matched in your clothing, will enhance your natural coloring. Armed with this information, you will be able to make informed shopping choices and select clothing in hues that add to your personal presentation.

"I looked good on TV."

Several years ago, I was invited to appear on a local cable TV show to talk about my experiences as a stay-at-home dad. I worried for days about what to wear on the show. My wife suggested that I watch the talk show ahead of time to see what other people wore. So I did, and what I started to see was very interesting. Some people looked great on the screen while others looked really bad. I realized that it had a lot to do with the colors they wore. A number of people wore black, which looked really dead on them. One woman wore a lime green top that made her look sick. One guy wore three different patterns together and they actually looked like they started to move on the screen! His clothing was so distracting that I couldn't even tell you what he was there to talk about. My wife and I set up my video camera and taped me in a few different outfits. We came up with a good combination for me—a blue shirt, navy blazer, and gray pants. When we played back the tape, the blues looked good both on me and on the screen. So that's what I wore to the show. I even got a compliment on my clothing from the show's director.

Jerry, stay-at-home father

You need to be aware of another aspect to color: how people *respond* to it. Color is a dominant element of your visual image and has the power to influence and affect people emotionally, behaviorally, and physically. According to the Wagner Institute for Color Research, color plays an important part in every decision people make. Color has the power to attract or repel, to make you eat more or less, and to buy or not buy a product. You have both involuntary and learned responses to color and subconsciously assign qualities to the colors you see. Whatever you *feel* about that color you also feel about the person wearing it. Blue is considered to be cooling and relaxing. Blue, especially navy, communicates loyalty, responsibility, authority, and respect, which makes it especially good to wear in conservative business environments. Red communicates courage, passion, danger, or love and can cause your blood pressure and respiratory rate to increase. Red lingerie is always a strong seller; red cars get more speeding tickets. Avoid wearing red when presenting in front of a group. After more than a few minutes, it becomes difficult to look at and makes audience members feel distressed.

Green evokes compassion, wealth, inexperience, growth, and balance. Darker shades of green can be worn for business; lighter or brighter shades are popular in casual and recreational clothing. Brown communicates reliability, stability, and honesty and works well when you want to be considered approachable and have others open up to you. Gray communicates stability, dignity, and possible negotiation. Black is the ultimate power color. Save it for the occasions when you want to appear intimidating, powerful, sophisticated, and aloof. Rapport is difficult to establish around black; wear it when you need to be seen as the definitive authority. President Ronald Reagan was a master at the art of pairing color with wardrobe. He chose navy blue suits when delivering the State of the Union addresses as leader of the free world. When he spoke directly to the American people from the Oval Office, however, he usually wore brown to communicate that he was one of us. You, too, can use color to your advantage. Color analysis and color response can be important tools in your image toolkit.

Choosing the best styles for your body is the next item on the know-how checklist. You could already have an idea of some of the styles that work well for your body type. You could have decided that open necklines are flattering to your neck or pants look better than shorts. The truth is that everyone has a few body challenges he or she would like to camouflage, and, thanks to age, gravity, and inactivity, several of them can be found at or below the waist. You probably have outfits right now in your closet that you look and feel great in and others that just don't work at all, but you're not sure why. The answer to your wardrobe dilemmas lies in a very simple concept of optical illusion: Horizontal lines widen and shorten; vertical lines narrow and lengthen. When you learn how to apply this concept, you'll be able to pull together ensembles that will look good on you at every stage of your life and body.

The next time you get dressed, look at the horizontal lines created by your clothes. You'll find them at the ends of your sleeves, at the waistline, jacket bottom, skirt hem, and pants and shorts bottoms. You can also have horizontal lines built into the design of the garment itself, as in horizontal stripes. The secret to successful dressing is never to place a horizontal line at the widest points of your body, unless, of course, you *want* to add width and weight to that area. Sleeves should not end at the widest point on the arm, don't accent a wide waist with belts and tucked-in shirts, and never let jackets end at the widest point of the derriere. Skirts, pants, and shorts should not be hemmed to hit the leg at the widest point. Simply choose or adjust items so they end above or below the widest points.

Place vertical lines on top of areas that need to appear longer and slimmer. If you have an outfit full of unflattering horizontals, strong vertical lines worn over them can often conceal them. Open jackets, coats, and cardigans create vertical lines and easily camouflage problem areas at the waist, hip, thigh, and derriere. Skirts with vertical interest and sharp creases in pants also draw the eye up and down rather than side to side. Neckties, shirts with vertical stripes, oblong scarves, V-neck tops, long sleeves, and one-color dressing are examples of other vertical lines. If you are tall and thin, you have the luxury of wearing horizontal interest anywhere you like; you don't need to create the illusion of vertical lines. For those of you with extra width in places, create the illusion of long and lean by wearing more vertical lines than horizontals.

Linda's Move Linda's recruiting business was starting to take off. She had made some good contacts through her networking efforts and had a number of inquiries to follow up. When Linda realized that face-to-face meetings with prospective clients were imminent, she started to get worried. She wasn't worried about selling her services; what concerned her was her wardrobe. She had been out of the workforce for a while and knew that styles had changed—and so had her body. She tried on all of her old suits and was shocked at how they looked. Skirts were too short, the jackets looked outdated, and everything was too tight around the waist. She was hoping to avoid investing in a new wardrobe until her business had brought in some money. So she dug a little deeper into her closet and found a couple of things that could work. She had a nice black skirt that was a little too tight and too short. She also found a burgundy jacket with black buttons—one-half of an old suit—and a white shirt. The jacket was too tight to wear buttoned, but she could see in the mirror that, if she wore it open, it looked presentable and seemed to hide her waistline. She set the skirt by the front door to take to her neighborhood tailor in the morning.

Choose Appropriately

Dressing was easy when there were clear-cut dress codes for every situation. Today, however, the rules have become fuzzy. The advent of business casual has brought comfort but also confusion. Some organizations have strict wardrobe guidelines; many others have looser dress codes that allow employees to use their own judgment.

Wardrobe has evolved to four different delineated levels—traditional, executive business casual, standard business casual, and basic business casual. Many people are able to select their clothing based on their activities for the day and the messages they wish to communicate. Before you dress each day, ask yourself the following questions: What are my goals for the day? In what activities will I engage? With whom will I be interacting? Where will I be meeting them? If you're part of the workforce, you need to consider your industry, your organization's written (or unwritten) dress code, and your position within the organization. You will also need to ask yourself, What will my customers/clients be wearing? What will my superiors be wearing? The answers to these questions will help guide you to the appropriate level of dress.

If your day includes making a presentation, meeting new customers, conducting negotiations, having a job interview in a conservative industry, or visiting conservative customers, you will want to wear traditional dress. This level of dress sends the message that you are an authority, credible, trustworthy, and professional. Traditional dress is the most formal and for men consists of suits, shirts, and ties and for women matching skirted suits or dress/jacket ensembles. Look for conservative styles in neutral colors. Pay attention to the amount of contrast between the different elements of your ensemble. High contrast combinations (i.e., a charcoal gray suit with a white shirt or blouse) communicate formality; medium contrast (i.e., a brown suit with a blue shirt or blouse) conveys a more relaxed and approachable image.

Each of the three levels of business casual has its own messages, criteria, and components. Industries such as finance, law, accounting, health care, and insurance have a conservative, traditional image; business casual dress is often limited to Fridays only. Employees in real estate, travel, manufacturing, computers, high-tech industries, publishing, and education usually wear some level of business casual on a daily basis. Creative industries, such as advertising, public relations, and entertainment, value a fashion-forward look. Try blending elements of traditional with some trendier business causal pieces.

Executive business casual conveys that you are professional and can also be a good choice for presentations, various leadership roles, and meetings with business casual customers. It features luxurious fabrics, such as wools, cashmere, silks, and linens, expert tailoring, and a contemporary flair that conveys influence.

This level calls for a structured jacket at all times but not necessarily a tie. Men can choose sport coats or blazers, pants in natural fibers and blends, and shirts, knit tops, or sweaters. Matched or unmatched pantsuits in natural fibers or blends are good choices for women, as are skirts teamed with unmatched jackets.

Standard business casual consists of a top and bottom teamed with a third piece. This level of dress, worn on a daily basis for less-formal industries and casual Fridays in some conservative industries, is appropriate for meetings when you know others will be similarly dressed or for off-site workshops and conferences. It sends messages of accessibility, practicality, and dependability.

The additional layer, which can be in the form of a casual unstructured jacket, cardigan, or pullover sweater, tie, scarf, or vest, adds a professional touch to tailored pants or skirts teamed with a casual shirt, knit top, or sweater. A collar is an important detail for men and should always be included in these ensembles, if not in the shirt beneath, then in a jacket on top.

Basic business casual, the most casual level, communicates a friendly and relaxed attitude and is appropriate for some informal off-site training sessions, retreats, company-sponsored sporting events, and, in some instances, in the office for those days when you'll be working without any face-to-face customer contact. Basic business casual can be appropriate on a daily basis for less traditional industries; it depends on the guidelines of the particular organization. This level consists of ensembles made up of only two pieces, a top and a bottom. No jacket is necessary, nor is wearing a collar of any kind. Men and women can team casual pants (jeans would depend on the organization's culture) with a short or long-sleeve shirt, knit top, or sweater. Women also have the option of wearing a casual skirt and top or a casual dress.

"I overshot and overdressed."

I've worked for professional associations for over thirty years, but it took some time for me to understand the unwritten dress code of the industry. Early in my career, I had to go to a special industry event, a formal ball. I was very excited and my husband and I got all decked out in the fanciest clothes we had ever worn. We arrived at the ball and were eager to start our wonderful evening. I was looking forward, particularly, to seeing my fellow co-workers dressed in their finest. But, as we worked our way through the room, I came to the realization that I had overdressed by a long shot! None of the staff or other executives was as dressed up as I was, but the female association members and male members' wives *were*. I was suddenly embarrassed at my extravagant look and the evening was spent, not on the dance floor, but sitting at our

> table. I learned that evening that I should never outdo the members of our association. It's just like what they say about weddings: Never outshine the bride.
>
> **Patricia, vice president of membership for an international medical association**

Patricia learned one of the pitfalls of choosing the proper attire—overdressing—but one can also underdress. Never make the mistake of dressing *too* casually for any business situation. Dressing down too far can cost you customers, jobs, promotions, and opportunities. It's better to exceed wardrobe expectations—short of a ball gown!

Juana's Move Juana's income at the garden center was a welcome addition to her family's finances, but there was not any surplus in their bank account for her to invest in a wardrobe for work. She was frustrated and a little embarrassed by her clothing. She often had to wear the same pieces two and three times in one week, and they weren't holding up well to the constant laundering. Then one day in the lunchroom, she came across a catalog for uniforms and began leafing through it. There, in front of her, was the answer to her problem. She talked with the other CSRs about her idea that afternoon, and they urged her to bring it up to their supervisor. Juana scheduled a meeting with her boss and showed her the pages she'd marked in the catalog. Juana suggested that the company invest in knit shirts and cotton pants for all of its employees. She told her how the uniform would provide a consistent and well-groomed image for the garden center and could provide much-needed assistance to entry-level workers with little expendable income. The supervisor loved the idea and promised to personally escort it through the proper channels.

Enhance Yourself

There is more to wardrobe than just pairing tops with bottoms. Accessories complete an outfit and provide a way to express your personality. Like your clothing, they need to be appropriate to the situation and consistent with the level of dress you've chosen to wear. Wearing a cartoon character necktie with a conservative navy double-breasted suit throws a kink into your image and sends a mixed message. Traditional and executive business casual accessories consist of gold, silver, or pearls, dress watches, no more than one ring per hand, post earrings instead of drop styles, silk ties or scarves in conservative patterns, and leather belts, handbags, and briefcases. Select the best pieces you can afford. They could cost as much as some of your clothing items but should last for many years to come. Standard and basic business casual ensembles need accessorizing, too. Sport watches, fashion-forward ties, cotton scarves, woven belts, nonleather purses and briefcases, novelty pins and necklaces, and fashion earrings are consistent with the business casual image. These accessories project a trendy, creative look. They will not cost as much but can go out of style quickly.

William's Move   William was feeling more and more comfortable with how he was dressing for work. He believed that he'd made a successful leap from his college wardrobe into the business casual look—but something still felt wrong. For his graduation, he had received an expensive gold watch and a very conservative briefcase, leather with a handle and latches on top. He felt good in his clothes but these accessories made him feel self-conscious. One new friend at work even teased him about adding wing-tip shoes to his wardrobe. William decided there was probably some middle ground for these accessories—something better than his college look but not overly traditional. He took a shopping trip and, with the help of a young but experienced sales clerk, invested in a sportier watch and attractive nylon backpack-style bag.

Your visual image also extends beyond the top of the shoulders. Grooming habits are an important part of your image. Conservative organizations appreciate hairstyles that are neat and controlled. Creative groups accept trendier hairstyles. Most traditional or popular ethnic hairstyles are acceptable in the workplace but should not be extreme in length, height, or color because any radical choice communicates eccentricity. No matter the style, hair should always be clean, flattering to your face shape, and easy to maintain. Once a year, plan on updating your hairstyle. Peruse hair magazines or the hairstyle books at your salon or barbershop. Talk with your stylist about ways to change your look. It could be as simple as longer sideburns or the addition of bangs.

Don't let yourself get stuck wearing the same hairstyle for many years. Out-of-date hair projects out-of-date attitudes and rusty skills.

"I cut the ponytail."

When I graduated from college, I didn't go far. My first job was right here at the university working for the alumni association. I helped create events and services for our most recent graduates and also worked closely with our collegiate members who were current undergrad seniors. There was really no reason to dress any differently than I had when I was going to classes; everyone I worked with looked pretty casual, just like a student. I loved wearing long hair and usually tied it back into a ponytail, which was not an unusual look for a guy like me. After about a year, though, I was promoted to work with the university foundation in gift procurement. Then my job entailed working with the older and influential alumni and encouraging them to give back to the university through private gifts and endowments. My "audience" had definitely changed. My supervisor took me aside one day and shared that she had followed up with one of the alumni I had recently met. When she mentioned my name, the man said, "Oh, the one with the ponytail. No, I don't think so." I cut off my ponytail the next day.

Brian, university foundation staff member

People often notice your teeth and breath before any other detail. Straight, white teeth and fresh breath are the hallmarks of good hygiene. If your teeth need attention, don't wait. Dentists offer a number of fast, discreet tooth-straightening and whitening services. Discuss them with your dentist at your next six-month appointment. Keep a toothbrush handy for between-meal attention. Look for mints and sprays without alcohol or sugar. Alcohol and sugar can dry out mouth tissues and bring back bad breath with a vengeance. Hands and nails need attention, too. Hands should be smooth with no dead skin or dry patches. Men's fingernails should be clean, short, and smooth; women's nail polish needs to be well maintained.

Clothing also needs grooming. Clean your clothes frequently and iron them often. The best way to care for your professional clothing pieces is to have them cleaned and pressed routinely by a dry cleaner you trust. Regular cleaning can remove stains and eliminate odors created by perspiration and body oils. Between cleanings, wool garments should be hung out overnight before being put back in the closet. Wool is a resilient fabric and will return to its natural shape if allowed to breathe. A laundry service is the best choice for men's business shirts and cotton pants. A combination of light or medium starch and pressing creates a crisp appearance. Alterations done by a professional tailor can make clothing bought off the rack look custom made. Sleeves and hems are common alterations; however, don't overlook the benefit of tweaking the waist, back, seat, and thigh of other garments.

SUCCESS
CARD 20 : *Entertain with Flair & Give Gifts*

Entertain with Flair

Entertaining provides a way for you to be in the spotlight. You have the opportunity to showcase your skills in organization, time management, marketing, communication skills, and, in some circumstances, housekeeping! You get to show your creative side, as well. Anytime that you step out of the everyday and take on a special project, such as entertaining, you have a chance to be noticed and make an impact. Once a year, take out your calendar and set a date for one event you'd like to host. For instance, it could be an informal potluck with friends, a baby shower for a co-worker, a thank-you breakfast with your best clients, or a holiday cocktail party. If you're feeling more adventuresome, plan to do all four! All don't have to happen at your home; some can take place at a restaurant or friend's house. Begin to think about one event that could become an annual affair, something that a particular group of people will plan on and look forward to every year. You could tie it into a holiday. Try celebrating something in a month other than often overbooked December: St. Patrick's Day, New Year's Day, or Fourth of July, for example.

The secret to successful parties lies in the planning. Your to-do list can seem overwhelming at first, but it will get easier once you've done several parties. Whether the event is formal or informal, the basic list is the same: objective, theme, guests, invitations, food, seating, music, and decorations. An event in a restaurant won't give you control over a few of those items, but for other events, pay attention to every aspect. An event's objective can be as simple as celebrating a birthday or completing a project. Its purpose could be to solidify a business relationship or to finalize an important deal. Once the objective is clear, the rest of the planning should be fairly easy. An event doesn't have to have a theme, but it's fun if it does. For an easy theme, center it around a type of food or past common experiences. High school reunions often feature "blast-from-the-past" themes with attendees dressing as they did in high school. Potluck groups often plan their meals around different ethnic foods or holidays. One particularly creative potluck group in Chicago threw a party based upon the "Dick Van Dyke" show from the 1960s. Attendees wore black and white, shared foods popular in the 60s, and each couple had to perform in the living room after dinner! For an offbeat theme, look through *Chase's Calendar of Events* at your local library. It lists all of the interesting—and sometimes wacky—days that Americans celebrate, such as National Sea Monkey Day (February 15), Northern Hemisphere Hoodie-Hoo Day (February 20), International Mirth Month (March 1–31), and Wonderful Weirdoes Day (September 9).

The guest list and invitations come next. Take care with the guest list; consider the different personality types. A mix of people can be stimulating, but avoid inviting feuding parties. Your event is not the place for them to make up. An invitation extended via phone is fine for informal business meals, but handwritten or printed invitations make an impact. Never use email to extend an invitation. Pull out your personal stationery or purchase fill-in-the-blank invitations and send them through the mail. Invitations need to be very clear and provide answers to every question your guests could have. Time and location are always necessary, but also consider including the theme, purpose, dress suggestions, parking information, whether to bring a guest, and how to RSVP.

Think through every aspect of the food and drink, including serving pieces, serving timetable, and how to keep food and drink at the proper temperatures. If you enjoy the chance to plan and serve multicourse meals and showcase the fine china and silver, a sit-down meal is the way to go. Just make sure you consider the number of guests you can accommodate at the table and the limitations of the kitchen. A buffet meal can be easier to undertake. It provides a more relaxed atmosphere for your guests; they can serve themselves and choose their dinner companions, too. You also have more time to visit with everyone because most of the food is prepared ahead of time. Because seating is more informal than a sit-down meal, you can usually accommodate a few more people. Cocktail parties work best when three or four satellite areas—drinks, cheeses, meats, desserts—are offered to encourage guests to circulate. Don't shy away from formality. Two young couples hosted a memorable holiday party for their friends a number of years ago. It took place in one of their homes and featured a bartender, live music, and formal attire. Their friends still talk about that party and the fun they had dressing up. Another group of friends staged a "Great Gatsby" party at one member's home, which bordered a lake. Attendees were asked to wear all white, a jazz band played music of the 1920s, and everyone had Charleston dance lessons!

To make the event complete, keep in mind that all of the five senses should be stirred, not just smell and taste but also touch, sight, and sound. Creative table settings, beautiful flowers, mood lighting, and interesting music will complete the experience. If the thought of these details makes you anxious, just light a few candles and pop in some of your favorite CDs; they can create instant party magic.

Anthony's Move   Anthony was beginning to feel more and more comfortable with his co-workers. He was enjoying the book club and the opportunity to get to know the other participants on an informal basis. But there were two internal consultants in the company who he thought felt threatened by him; they appeared to be good friends with each other, and neither of them seemed to acknowledge Anthony's existence. He decided to make the move to break the ice. Business meals had been a big part of his old job, but he hadn't taken anyone out for lunch in this new job. He called each personally and extended the invitation. He'd already asked around to get an idea of their food preferences and was able to recommend three restaurants he thought they'd like. They accepted his invitation, and Anthony set about to make a great impression on them. He made a reservation with the restaurant they chose and reconfirmed the plans with his guests the day before the lunch. Anthony arrived at the restaurant ahead of time and selected a desirable table. He also had the opportunity to speak with the server and explained that he was interested in great service and would tip accordingly. He met his guests in the waiting area and escorted them to the table. The food and service were great, and the small talk became more and more relaxed. Anthony listened intently as his guests talked, and, by the end of the meal, conversation flowed easily among the three of them. Although not yet "best buddies," they left the restaurant on warm terms. Anthony felt that the foundation had been laid for a more productive relationship.

Give Gifts

Gift giving is an often overlooked way to express your style. Too often gifts are ordinary and generic. Taking time to choose carefully, with the recipient's tastes in mind, is the way to do it right. Giving great gifts can also increase your visibility and set you apart as someone who is thoughtful and attentive. Gifts can be given at holidays, birthdays, and anniversaries, and to show good faith, to demonstrate happiness that an arduous process has ended, to demonstrate goodwill on an ongoing basis, or to celebrate a windfall.

Kathleen's Move The December holidays were coming, and Kathleen wanted to give a special gift to her best customer. She knew that this highly visible and well-connected individual was usually showered with gifts from people who wanted to make a good impression. Kathleen worried for weeks about what to give him. She decided that anything she chose would either be lost in the crowd or duplicated by someone else, so she decided to send him a personal note on notepaper that reflected his love of the outdoors. She spent a long time choosing just the right words to express how she valued his business and their working relationship. He called her immediately upon receiving the note. He told her how special it was to him and that he had passed it around to his colleagues. He said that it was the one gift that truly meant something to him that year.

The first step in gift giving is to do your homework. Investigate the recipient. Talk to the spouse, assistant, even his or her children to find out about his or her tastes, interests, and leisure pursuits. You are certain to find out something that will lead you to a great gift idea. Don't fall into the trap of giving food, candy, liquor, or flowers. Gifts of that kind can be seen as commonplace and are the worst choices for someone who has food or plant allergies, a weight problem, or an alcohol addiction! You also need to consider perceived value.

Gifts don't have to be large or expensive as long as they have a high perceived value. For example, a unique corkscrew can be inexpensive but could be a thoughtful gift for a wine collector. There is also the issue of hierarchy. The higher the person is on the organizational chart, the more valuable the gift should be. If you're giving gifts to an entire group of people, never give the same gifts to everyone. The chairman or CEO should get something more special than the vice president, and so on down the line. People appreciate gifts that are distinctive, creative, and original. They show that you took time from your busy schedule and didn't settle for something that was mass produced or overly promotional. Whenever possible, present gifts in person. If you must mail them, include a handwritten note.

"I gave the wrong gift."

When I was in college, one of my roommates was from Egypt. When his birthday rolled around, I wanted to give him something. I found a small wooden box with etchings on the top that could be used on top of his dresser as an organizer. Believe me, his dresser was a mess, as was our entire dorm room, and I thought it would be something he could really use. But when he opened it, he had a strange expression on his face that I couldn't quite interpret. He was very nice about it and ended up using it, but I wondered if I had done something wrong. Months later, I mentioned this to another friend of mine who was from the Middle East. She explained to me that wood has no value in their region because there are very few trees there. She went on to say that the air there is too dry for a gift made of wood; it would eventually disintegrate. I thought I had picked out a great gift, but it wasn't very good after all. I should have put more thought into it.

Dylan, systems analyst, computer company

SUCCESS
CARD **21**: *Celebrate You*

The Style Hand has asked you to look at your visual image very intensely. By doing so, you'll be able to control the perceptions others have of you and send the messages you want and need to make your next moves. You'll develop a wardrobe that fits your body type, enhances your personal coloring, and is appropriate for every situation. Don't ever get caught up in the concept of fashion. Fashion is fleeting; style is eternal. As you learn more about what looks good on you and what you need for your particular lifestyle, your personal style will begin to emerge, and you will develop your individual formula for visual success. Whatever your style is, relish it and express it with confidence.

To honor the new you, take time to celebrate. Treat yourself to a manicure, healthy food, exercise, a massage, a new hairstyle, and handsome clothing. Take a vacation. Let yourself breathe. Celebrate the *you* that is emerging.

Play the Game: It's Your Move

The Style Hand is now yours to play. What moves do you want to make? Choose a card right now and start developing your personal style this very week. Write your card choice in the game plan at the end of the book. When you've completed the move, return to the game plan to fill in the results.

End Notes

1. Roger Ailes, *You Are the Message: Getting What You Want by Being Who You Are* (New York: Doubleday/Currency, 1989), p. 26.

2. Jo-Ellan Dimitrius, Ph.D., and Mark Mazzarella, *Put Your Best Foot Forward: Make a Great Impression by Taking Control of How Others See You* (New York: Scribners, 2000).

3. Portions of this interview first appeared in *The Chronicle of Philanthropy*, May 16, 2002.

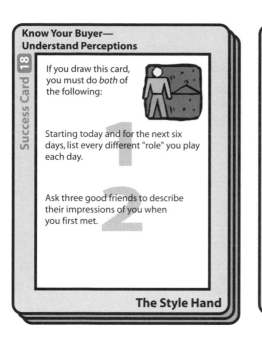

**Know Your Buyer—
Understand Perceptions**

Success Card 18

If you draw this card, you must do *both* of the following:

1. Starting today and for the next six days, list every different "role" you play each day.

2. Ask three good friends to describe their impressions of you when you first met.

The Style Hand

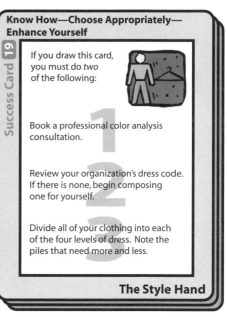

**Know How—Choose Appropriately—
Enhance Yourself**

Success Card 19

If you draw this card, you must do *two* of the following:

1. Book a professional color analysis consultation.

2. Review your organization's dress code. If there is none, begin composing one for yourself.

3. Divide all of your clothing into each of the four levels of dress. Note the piles that need more and less.

The Style Hand

Entertain With Flair—Give Gifts

Success Card 20

If you draw this card, you must do *two* of the following:

1. Look ahead to the next holiday on the calendar. Spend an evening planning an imaginary party based around that holiday.

2. List the most treasured gifts you have ever received.

3. Order a set of personalized stationery.

The Style Hand

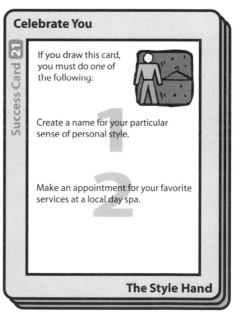

Celebrate You

Success Card 21

If you draw this card, you must do *one* of the following:

1. Create a name for your particular sense of personal style.

2. Make an appointment for your favorite services at a local day spa.

The Style Hand

CHAPTER 6

THE PRESENTATION HAND

SUCCESS
CARD **22**: *Write Often*

The ability to present your ideas clearly and concisely is vital to this game of making moves. Doors seem to open when you can stand and deliver a solid presentation. As a good public speaker, you're often sought out by others and showcased as a spokesperson or authority. Take Ned, for example. He is the associate director of an investment firm's security department and is continually asked by his boss to deliver presentations that the boss should be making himself. However, they both know that Ned's speaking skills are far superior to the boss's, so Ned is often called on to speak internally. As a result, he is gaining quite a reputation as someone who can deliver—on several different levels!

Studies show that most people fear public speaking with a vengeance. Are you someone who would rather have a root canal than speak in front of a group? Fear not. Most people who fear public speaking are actually afraid of impromptu speaking, being called on without warning to say a few words. With proper preparation, however, all forms of public speaking can become easier to handle.

Good presentations begin with good writing. The world's best speakers rarely "wing" it. They spend a long time crafting the perfect presentation before they ever stand in front of a group to deliver it. When you take the time first to compose a presentation in writing, you'll end up with a much better, more finished product. You'll be able to choose the precise words, double-check the grammar, create the transitions, and fine-tune the phrases until the meaning is just right. If you don't write it out completely first, you will surely stumble during the delivery as you reach for the right words.

"I learned I needed to find the time to prepare."

When I became CEO of a hospital, I dreaded one thing—public speaking. I've always hated public speaking because I never thought I did it very well. But in this high-profile position, presentations are a big part of my job. Just recently, I was the emcee for the ribbon-cutting ceremony of our new wing. I also spoke to the Rotary Club and was on the dais for our annual Gala where I handled toasts, introductions, and awards presentations. Soon after I took the job, my wife and I went to dinner with a married couple who hold top positions in their respective companies. As we ate, I started grumbling about how I had to do so much speaking, and Bob, the husband, said something that really made an impact with me. He said that, as a CEO, the most important aspect of my job was public speaking! The days of having to prove my skills in other areas were over; I had obviously done that to get where I was. Communication skills were all I needed now. And he was right. I realized I needed to make the time to properly prepare and practice for each speaking situation. So, I've done that. I now schedule time into my workday calendar to write and rehearse my presentations.

Mark, chief executive officer of a 600-bed hospital

You don't like to write? The good news is that the more you write, the better you get. Glenda, a self-employed consultant, had no writing skills when she started her business. In college, she dropped every class that required a written paper. The mere thought of composing a business letter or copy for an advertisement made her queasy. She kept at it, though, and became a good student of others' writing. Today she enjoys the writing process and is very comfortable handling all of her business correspondence, marketing materials, and stand-up presentations. She even has plans to write a book—quite a change for someone who didn't think she could write.

Write a little bit every day. If you've never written much before, start by writing in a journal. Writing down your personal thoughts each day can help you become more comfortable with the writing process. Journaling can be a safe way to explore your writing abilities because it is done privately; no one but you will ever read what you write.

Find new reasons to write. If you're in the workforce, work not only to improve your business writing but also to stretch yourself in creative genres. Try writing a letter to the editor. Experiment with short stories, poetry, or advertising copy. Try composing a toast to give at a friend's wedding, a "roast" to another friend, or a short commentary for a school or community newsletter. You'll gradually discover the type of writing you most enjoy. Your writing will most likely improve the more you write, and you'll end up with several pieces you can file away for future consideration. When you feel ready to get some feedback, sign up for a writing class at your community center or local college. A good teacher of writing will be able to help you hone your developing skills.

When you're ready to think about being published, consider writing an article. It's a fairly easy format for a beginning. Choose any magazine and try writing an article that would appeal to that target audience. Read your favorite trade or professional magazines thoroughly, and you'll be able to get an idea of what the editors buy. Article writing will help you organize your thoughts and tap into your creativity. The following are four keys to get you started writing an article.

Published writers can also make valuable contacts. People often contact authors of articles and letters to connect in some way. For example, JoEllen, a golf pro, was asked to review another author's book on golf for her favorite

Key 1 *List the things that are easy for you to talk or write about.* What topics are easiest for you to discuss? It could be because you absolutely love the topic, have lots of examples of the topic, or give others advice about the topic all of the time. Your easy-to-discuss topic could be as common as parenting or as specialized as selecting a grass seed for your lawn. Just make sure you love it.

Key 2 *Develop three to eight key points about that easy topic.* Don't make lists of twenty-seven or forty-two ideas. You can format three to eight points about something in many ways. Here are some ideas:

- Four keys to success
- Eight tune-up tips
- Six mistakes I'd never make again
- Five things I learned from my two year old

Key 3 *Consider a unique way to package the topic once you have your series of steps.* Here are some examples:

- *Inside information:* For example, What insurance salespeople know about policies that you don't, followed by five key tips.
- *Steps of a process:* For example, Networking: How to take a plunge, followed by an analogy to five steps of a dive.
- *Acronyms:* For example, HELP your customers win, followed by the H-E-L-P letters, which stand for your four key points.

Key 4 *Collect your stories and examples and write them down immediately.* Many speakers and authors keep either computer or index card files of stories. Stories, after all, are what audiences remember and connect with more than anything else about your presentations. Stories invite people to dream and visualize. They paint pictures for the listeners and take them on a journey. They illustrate important points and bring life's lessons to life. Start a file of your life's funny, sobering, and surprising experiences. Make notes of the various topics each story could be used for; the same anecdote can be used to illustrate different points, depending on the focus of the presentation. Glenda uses the same poignant story of her early struggles as an entrepreneur to illustrate perseverance to a group of independent contractors and time management principles to a group of first-time parents. Keep your story file open and active. Add to it whenever you remember stories or see them happening. If you don't have saved stories, perhaps these questions will inspire you to come up with examples:

- If I had a regular newspaper column, what would I call it?
- What have I spent most of my life doing?
- Where is my wisdom?
- About what do people ask my advice?
- For what topics do I have the most readily available examples?
- What are the strongest opinions I have?
- With what could I most easily fill a book about my experiences?

trade journal. As a guest reviewer, she would receive no pay, but she decided it would be a good learning experience. She read the book, enjoyed it, and her review was published a few months later. As a result, when JoEllen wrote her own book about golf for beginners a couple of years later, the author of the book she reviewed agreed to endorse JoEllen's own book. Without the book review, she would not have been aware of JoEllen, so it was a smart, winning move that paid off!

Anthony's Move   For a guy with a sales background, speaking was a lot easier than writing. Anthony knew, however, that the speaking he'd done as a furniture salesman was different than the speaking he was expected to do internally as an organizational development expert. He had to be in tune with global events and how they affected the company's future. He attended many meetings about corporate moves and policies. At one of the meetings, when the vice president of marketing asked for someone to write a column for the annual report, Anthony was not enthused, but when several seconds went by with no volunteers, he decided to give it a try. Putting together the column wasn't fun. He spent extra hours on the Internet at work and a few Sunday afternoons at home reviewing old annual reports—not exactly stimulating reading. His smartest move was asking for help from the corporate communications editor who knew how to structure information, and the tips she gave him got him started. Finally, he crafted a 1500-word article based on lots of global statistics and decisions. His reward came when the vice president asked him to present a summary to the executive committee. Many members had never met him before that day.

SUCCESS
CARD **23**: *Speak Often*

You need to find opportunities to get on your feet and speak if you're going to get good at playing the Presentation Hand. Many organizations in your community need speakers on a regular basis. Find out who they are and determine the composition of their membership. There are Chambers of Commerce, small business networks, church groups, professional associations, service organizations, senior citizen clubs, discussion groups, and clubs for every leisure pursuit imaginable. Call them and ask for the program chair, who will be able to fill you in on the group's needs and speaker selection process. Explain that you're in the information-gathering stage and could call back to get on their schedule at a later date. Then begin to create a presentation that would appeal to that organization. What do you know that you could talk about, demonstrate, or teach? Right now list three to five topics about which you could speak.

If you're employed, you can make internal presentations. Brainstorm the various speaking opportunities that exist there. Department meetings, client presentations, product rollouts, board presentations, after-hours events, and lunchtime programs are examples of some of the occasions that could exist. Some companies even have their own speakers bureau that makes employees available to speak to outside groups.

As with writing, your speaking skills will improve with experience. Don't bite off more than you can chew the first few times, though. Volunteer to speak in situations in which you don't have a lot to lose. A few smaller successes will build your self-confidence and prepare you for the bigger presentations to come. Keep your material concise and tightly focused. Don't try to cover too much; audiences would rather know less overall but in more depth. Panel discussions can be a good place to start. Each panel member usually presents a few minutes of formal content and then spends the remaining time fielding questions from the audience and moderator. Panels offer a safe environment for the novice speaker and can be a great way to build skills and visibility without much preparation or anxiety.

"I could see I made an impact."

I was very nervous for my first big presentation. I was actually a substitute speaker for someone who had to drop out at the last minute. He was able to give me an idea of the basic content that needed to be covered, but when I spoke to the program director, I was told I could put my own "spin" on it. So I did. I was flown to New Orleans to do a breakout session at a national association conference. My audience was filled with high-level executives from some of the top companies in America—which made my knees shake even more. I started questioning my content and myself. What could I possibly tell these people that they didn't already know? But the most amazing thing happened. I got through the opening remarks, and, when I launched into the first major point, every head in the audience snapped down to take notes on what I was saying! I think I actually stopped speaking mid-sentence, I was so shocked. The rest of the presentation was a breeze. I realized I was really ready for a presentation of that magnitude. I had "paid my dues" as a speaker and had the skills and material that could make an impact with this audience.

Jana, assistant manager of logistics services for a manufacturing company

When speaking to community and professional organizations, don't expect a fee unless they are established, large associations or happen to build a speaker fee into the budget for a specific type of event. However, most groups are able to offer an honorarium, which is a small fee to cover your basic expenses or to thank you for your time and effort. Remember your goals for speaking in the first place. Is money most important? Where else could you have a group of people giving you thirty to forty-five minutes of their undivided attention? You have the chance to try out a new training concept, a humorous story, or a marketing pitch. These opportunities are especially effective when you have something to sell because everyone in that audience could be a potential buyer for your product or service. Each person will leave with an in-depth understanding not only of your product but also of you as the seller. Pass out evaluations afterward and ask participants to comment on your effectiveness. Seasoned speakers will tell you that you'll know how well you did by the number of people who stick around afterward to talk with you and ask questions. This shows that you struck a meaningful chord.

Linda's Move   Linda decided that she should speak before the local Chamber of Commerce. She knew that many potential clients would be in her audience. Her first attempts at speechwriting were too unwieldy; she was trying to tell the audience everything she knew about the field of recruiting, and the speech got too long. She decided on her second attempt to think more from her audience's perspective. What could she talk about that would be useful to them, something that could help them do their jobs? The second speech was much better and focused on four major points that illustrated the benefits of hiring an outside recruiter. She would bring along her marketing materials and decided to create a half-sheet that listed her various services for audience members to check off for more information. She also decided to hold a raffle for a free book, a business best seller, so that she could gather everyone's business card.

Every public speaking opportunity has the potential of opening new and exciting doors for you. Audiences will naturally give you more credibility just because you're the one up front. It's an amazing phenomenon resulting from the fact that most people fear being up there themselves!

SUCCESS CARD 24: *Be Unique & Look Globally*

Be Unique

Audiences get tired of speakers and speeches that all sound the same. You've probably sat through plenty of speeches that could have easily been phoned in by the presenter: speakers stuck behind lecterns, heads popping up from reading notes only long enough to check that the next slide has appeared. No one likes to listen to a talking head. You need to find ways to be unique in this sea of presentation sameness. Being distinctive will set you apart and make both you and your message memorable.

Training workshops are different from speeches. Interaction and group activities are expected during training to ensure that learning has taken place. Be careful about adding unnecessary, gimmicky activities to formal presentations, especially if the audience is composed of high-level types. They're usually not interested in "icebreakers" or other types of frivolous exercises. They want solid content delivered by a knowledgeable speaker. That's not to say, however, that there can't be some creativity to the presentation. Audience participation can be part of your speech without asking anyone to move out of his or her seat. Asking questions, rhetorical or otherwise, can be a great way to involve the audience. One speaker during a post-September 11 presentation on home security asked for all firefighters and police in the audience to stand to be thanked publicly. Another presentation on twentieth-century military history asked audience members to call out their draft numbers. Simply asking for a show of hands can be an easy way to keep the audience involved and the juices flowing.

Harry's Move   The retirement home's activities committee invited Harry to give a short lecture to the residents on his life as a music teacher. He was flattered to be asked to talk about his experiences working with young people. He had many interesting and humorous stories to tell and he enjoyed reminiscing; he'd never before taken the time to review his life in teaching. He decided to format his speech into three sections: the beginning years, the middle years, and the final years. He would talk about his teaching principles and how he had to adjust them to the times. He would tell a story in each section that illustrated the various points he would make. But he was afraid it all might be too dry; the audience might get bored. So he decided to include a sing-along at the end of the presentation. He thought his fellow senior citizens would enjoy it, and he could demonstrate a few of his teaching techniques at the same time.

Write the opening of your speech so that it is as unique and creative as possible. The first thirty seconds of any speech are the most crucial. You're making that all-important first impression, and audiences are deciding whether they want to listen to you. Opening with a joke rarely works unless you're a professional comic; Tell a humorous story instead. Share a startling statistic. Use a famous quotation. Ask a thought-provoking question. Find your personal gifts and use them. Can you sing? Try a song. Are you good at drama? Tell a personal story playing two different characters from your life. One former convict opens his speech by pacing off the size of his death-row cell. Whatever opening you choose, make sure that it directly relates to the theme of your presentation. If it doesn't, your audience will be confused from the start.

"My opener was a complete flop."

I was invited to travel to a neighboring state and do a presentation for an association's state roundtable group. This was a big deal for me; I hadn't done many speeches outside my company. I thought I had pretty good content, but had no idea how to open the speech. Then I got this idea to use props. I've seen other people use props in their presentations, and it works well for them, so I thought, Why not? I chose a magazine, man's tie, and toy cell phone to make my points. As I opened the speech, I grandly presented each prop and, as I explained how I would dispel different myths, I tossed each prop, one by one, over my shoulder. They, of course, hit the ground with a thud and grabbed everyone's attention, except for the magazine cover, which I had ripped off before tossing. It floated around the room for a while, and then landed on one of the dinner tables. I had never practiced this before, so I hadn't thought about what would happen with the props once that they were on the floor. I looked at them for a minute and decided that I should retrieve them. So I stepped away from the lectern and crouched around the room picking up what I had tossed. It was a mess, and everyone knew it. I never recovered from that terrible opening. I don't think the audience listened to a word I said.

**Eddie, trust officer
for a bank/financial services
company**

Innovative speech titles can often fill auditorium seats all on their own. Take a well-known cliché or proverb and change it around. For a speech concerning personal accountability, try "If at First You Don't Succeed, Blame the Other Guy!" For a presentation about investing, the title could be "A Penny Saved Is a Nickel Next Week." Laurie, who speaks on customer service for the medical field, found that her bookings increased when she changed her title from "How to Achieve Service Success" to "Hold the Jalapeño Pepper, Please!"

As in article writing, creating your own acronym can be a good "hook" for a title. Invent a step-by-step system for solving a particular problem, and assign letters that correspond to each step: "K.I.D.S.—Four Proven Steps to Raising Happy Children." If you're in technology, think of the ways you can discuss software, "N-E-W—Needs Every Wizard" or " I T—Information Train." You get the idea. Go back to your list of possible speech topics and come up with clever titles for each.

Look Globally

Living, as we do in the twenty-first century, a global awareness has become part of everything we say, think, and do. Economics, business, politics, medicine, technology, and entertainment are seen in terms of the world rather than limited to a single country. The "big picture" must be considered in the presentations you make, as well. Your content and delivery style need to be assessed so that they are both valuable and appropriate for the diverse audiences to which you will speak. Your listeners' ethnic backgrounds will vary; the native languages will be numerous. Review your presentations with an eye toward cultural correctness. Be careful using slang words and idioms whose meanings could be lost on people from other cultures. Jokes to some can be insulting to others.

KEY PLAYER PROFILE: KATHY WOOD LOVELESS, MS, CSP

"I did my doctoral work in quantitative data analysis at George Washington University and was conducting research in water and energy resources. In 1987, I wrote a paper and submitted it for consideration to be presented at a world conference. I focused on six nations, specifically, looking at the comparison between the nations' economic development and water resource development. My paper was chosen and I was invited to present it to the U.S. conference in Reno, Nevada. I was then selected to represent the United States at an international conference in Morocco, Africa! Seventy-eight foreign countries would be represented at this technical conference. I would be the only woman in the U.S. delegation giving a paper and one of only a few women in attendance. I arrived in Rabat for my plenary session where I had the opportunity to review my presentation along with the other speakers. The primary language being spoken in the room was French, and while I speak a little French, I wasn't quite sure what the other people were saying. I could tell they were talking about me, though, because they kept saying, 'Madame Loveless.' I turned to the interpreter and said, 'I know they're talking about me. What are they saying?' He was hesitant to tell me, but said, 'Well, um, they are concerned because you are using Israel as one of the six countries in your presentation.' I paused for a minute and then it hit me. I'm in Morocco, Africa, a Muslim country.

"From a researcher's standpoint, this was absurd! I was talking about the relationship between a nation's economic development and its overall water resource development. It had nothing to do with any Arab–Israeli conflict. But I was told I had to eliminate any reference to Israel in my presentation. Now, all of my summary statistics were based on six countries, not five, and changing the content would also affect my conclusions, slides, and handouts. Changing the presentation would have been dishonest and damaging to the findings and was something I just couldn't do. But I was also thinking that I didn't want to start an international incident! I went to the leader of the U.S. delegation who then took it to the head of the entire world delegation for this conference. And the next thing I knew, I was told I could present the paper as it had been prepared and researched. This was such an eye-opener for me—to be able to see how people from different corners of the world see things and how our uncensored freedom of speech is often taken for granted."

. . . .*Kathy Wood Loveless, MS, CSP is president of Loveless Enterprises, Inc., a professional speaking and management consulting firm. She speaks extensively throughout the United States, Africa, New Zealand, Europe, Canada, and the Far East. She has been editor of the national publication* Reclamation Era *in Washington, D.C.; has served as vice president of a New York–headquartered investment banking firm; and is chair-elect of the board of directors of the California Independent Energy Association. She recently founded the Public Power Management Institute to provide leaders in the power industry with effective and timely management practices and strategies.*

A global perspective can enrich the content of any presentation. As Kathy discovered, even a scientific paper can be scrutinized for cultural sensitivity. It is important to be aware of trends and news events in countries other than your own. Include all that you can in your presentation, basing your information on solid research and interviews, and then do your best to strike a balance between truth and political correctness.

Although she doesn't make formal presentations, Eleanor feels that she is "on stage" in her job as a hotel concierge. She often interacts with people from around the world, and to keep herself sharp, pays close attention to international news stories on TV and goes to foreign films to learn more about different cultures. She has learned basic conversational phrases in ten languages and is well versed in the diverse etiquette and protocol for dozens of countries. She consistently receives very high ratings from the hotel's international guests. They say they appreciate her "presentation"; she always seems to know about their particular country and is able to offer smart suggestions for museums, restaurants, and nightlife.

Kathleen's Move Kathleen enjoyed her business trips abroad but had always tried to accomplish her work as quickly as possible so she could get back to the office, write her report, and leave again for another trip. Then she started trying to slow down a bit and add a day at the beginning or end of her international trips whenever possible so that she could see more of each country. She was trying to learn a bit of the different languages and often perused their local papers to get a sense of what was happening. One day while sitting in a sidewalk café in Portugal, Kathleen struck up a conversation with a local journalist at the next table, and they had an interesting talk about the growing aging population of the country. Kathleen was surprised at the insights she picked up and knew they could be helpful in her client presentation the next day and back at the home office. She decided she would make a point of becoming a better student of the world.

It's not necessary to be a world traveler to stay informed. Make a point of reading a variety of news and business magazines. They include news summaries and feature stories that will give you insight into events around the world. You can also find English-language versions of periodicals from other countries. Whenever possible, talk with people from countries other than your own. They can provide an insider's look, which you could never get from TV or periodicals. You, like Kathleen and Eleanor, can become a student of the world. It's a wise move to make.

SUCCESS
CARD 25: *Know Your Tools*

As a speaker, you have a number of tools at your disposal: voice, body language, notes, prompters, microphones, and audiovisual equipment. Learn how to use them all. Record yourself as you practice your speeches and listen for variety in inflection, pacing, pitch, and volume. Variety will make your presentation more engaging for the audience. Videotape yourself, too, and check for supportive gestures, active eye contact, and interesting facial expressions. Try not to lock yourself behind a lectern. Memorize your opening and closing remarks and deliver them to the side of the lectern; move behind it for the body of the presentation. If this all seems a bit daunting, consider hiring a presentation skills coach who can give you valuable feedback and guidance in a safe, nonthreatening environment. Working with a coach as your "audience of one" offers you a way to transition from talking out loud to yourself to speaking with confidence before many.

Using notes is an art form. Many people prefer writing speeches word for word and then rehearsing so well that they refer to the notes only occasionally. Others like to use outlines, key words, or mind maps (a graphic flowchart of the outline) for their notes. Try them all and see which works best for you. One word of caution: Use the latter only for material you know thoroughly. Otherwise, you run the risk of losing the audience as you search your mind for words and transitions. Notes should be typed in a large font size and on only one side of the paper. Lay the first two pages out side by side on the lectern, and then slide—don't flip—each page to the left as you read.

If you're speaking at a large meeting, you could use a teleprompter, but keep in mind that teleprompters take time and practice to master. Teleprompters project speech content onto clear panels placed to the sides of a lectern at eye level or along the front edge of a stage. Teleprompter operators scroll the lines as you speak, matching your rate of speed. The advantage of teleprompters is that your head will be up to make eye contact with the audience rather than looking down at notes. However, be careful that you don't become robotic as you move your head back and forth between the screens. Audiences are savvy to this technology and know that you are reading the copy. Adequate rehearsal is still necessary to be familiar enough with your material to speak directly to the audience.

Lecterns usually include a microphone, which may be permanently attached to or removable from its holder. Some mikes are hard wired; others are wireless. Lavaliere mikes are clipped to your clothing and can be wired or wireless. The best mikes give you freedom to move across the stage or around the room. Insist that a sound technician work with you before the presentation to set the volume and balance levels. Ask the technician to explain the various switches on the mike so you can operate it once he or she leaves. Whatever kind you use, hold the microphone at the same distance from the mouth for the duration of the speech; be aware of this as you gesture and move your head.

Computer-generated slides projected through a projection system onto a screen have become the technology of choice for most speakers. If you choose to use them, it's important that you understand how the equipment works and where each cord should be plugged. Once again, ask that a technician be present to troubleshoot any problems. Just because computer slide technology exists, however, you don't have to use it. You've probably sat through countless presentations that included slide after slide with too much text that the speaker read word-for-word from the screen. Slides should support your content, not match it. Create slides that convey your information in a different, more visual way. If you're talking about numbers, avoid writing out the numbers; create a pie chart or graph instead. Use photos, symbols, and line art as substitutes for text as much as possible. If you choose to use slides, keep in mind that audiences come to hear a speaker, not watch a slide show. You, the speaker, should always be the most compelling element of your presentation.

Rhonda, a copywriter for an ad agency, recalls her experience as an audience member for a presentation on creativity. Unfortunately, the first fifteen minutes were spent watching the speaker struggle with his computer, cords, and projector. Once he launched into his speech, she saw that his visuals were standard text slides. Rhonda was very disappointed. She had paid money to learn about creativity. What she got was an unimaginative presentation that was overly dependent on technology. The topic had been creativity, but the delivery was certainly not!

"My biggest failure became my biggest success."

I was scheduled to give grand rounds, which is quite an honor. I was very excited because I was going to be discussing my own original research, hypotheses, and thoughts, so it was pretty important to me. I was especially eager to help the group understand how my ideas could affect their patients and make them better clinicians. I arrived early to make sure the audiovisual (AV) equipment was set up correctly. I brought a diskette with my slides on it and a film of one of my patients to show, which I thought would be a touching end to my presentation. I had checked my diskette before coming and knew the slide presentation was on my A drive. But when I got to the room, I couldn't locate my slides anywhere on the disk. I even asked someone I knew in the audience for help; he couldn't find my talk either. At this point, people were starting to file into the auditorium, which included my boss and my boss's boss. What saved me was that I had thought to print out the presentation before I came. So at least I had the printed version of the slides in front of me to use as notes. When it was time to show the film, I pressed the button and the film started, but without any sound! I hadn't had the chance to check the film projector beforehand because I was so busy trying to make the slides work. I found out later that arrangements had not been made for the AV technician to stick around, so I had no one to help me. Fortunately, I had added a few subtitles to the film. So it wasn't as bad as it could have been, but it still didn't have the effect of making this kid come alive for the audience. I was able to pull on my reserves and keep my calm, and it turned out to be an interesting experience. In spite of all the apparent failures, the audience came to life. I don't know if they were showing me compassion or whether it was because I was able to focus so intently on this opportunity and my commitment to my ideas and to the children. I think sometimes when you show your vulnerabilities, the audience rallies around you and pulls for you to succeed. The audience, including my boss's boss, became very excited about my ideas. Later on, one of my colleagues said it was the most stimulating, interactive grand rounds she'd ever seen. I learned that I could speak from my heart and joke about what happened. I learned, too, that I don't need to rely on technology but that person-to-person sharing is probably better. The audience doesn't need perfection. When we share some-thing we're excited about, even in an imperfect form, the audience will listen and respond.

Karen, attending physician in psychiatry at a Midwestern children's hospital

Another tool in your toolbox is to develop content that appeals to the various learning styles your audience members will possess. Some people are auditory learners, meaning that they comprehend easiest by listening. Visual learners comprehend best through sight, and kinesthetic learners learn best via touch. Find ways to incorporate methods that will make an impact with each type of person.

Auditory learners appreciate word pictures. Examples, stories, metaphors, analogies, and quotations bring your words to life and create pictures for them in their minds. Share your past experiences ("When we did this for Company X. . . ."), colorful comparisons ("We need to move quickly. If we don't, we'll be just like road kill on the highway of success."), and testimonials ("We were ranked number three by *Business Blurb* magazine."). If your content includes abstract ideas, turn them into something more concrete and familiar to your listener (i.e., "It will cost 1.5 million dollars, the entire annual budget of this city's school system").

To appeal to the visual types, provide printed collateral materials (i.e., handouts, marketing pieces, articles, and colorful visual aids). Slides, video segments, flipchart pages, and props can fill the bill. Kinesthetic learners need to use their sense of touch to process information. Don, a vice president of a steel mill, brought a small piece of scrap metal to his presentations for community groups. He explained what it was (good for auditory learners), held it up for everyone to see (good for visual learners), and then passed it around for people to examine (good for kinesthetic learners). Robin, an image trainer, brings wardrobe items and fabric samples for the audience to touch and try on. Her presentations on business etiquette include handshaking exercises. Kinesthetic experiences can be sometimes challenging to think of but are well worth the effort. They can often bring the most impact to a presentation.

Juana's Move Juana's supervisors were pleased with her progress as a customer service representative. She was feeling more and more like one of the team and was becoming more assertive with her ideas. Because of her increased self-confidence, her boss asked her to begin doing informal presentations to the firm's Spanish-speaking customers on the various services the gardening center offered. Juana was nervous but thought this opportunity could improve her chances for promotion. So she put together a short speech on the garden center's offerings but was uneasy about the thought of so many people looking at her while she spoke. To help the audience focus elsewhere, she decided to gather examples of the different types of plants and flowers available at the center to pass around as she spoke. Her supervisor suggested she also fill small shopping bags with brochures, plant information, and seed packets as "take-aways" for the audience.

Who are the speakers you most admire? Why do you like them? What do they do that makes their speeches so interesting? Does it have to do with their words, their vocal delivery, their visual presentation, or a combination of all three? Make it your goal to develop all of the tools in your speaker's toolbox. Write content that is compelling. Develop your vocal variety. Find ways to make your body expressive. Produce visuals that are supportive and creative. If technology is a part of your presentations, know how it works *before* you go on stage. A complete tool kit will help you create presentations that are both interesting and exciting.

SUCCESS
CARD 26: *Build Your Case*

When you make the effort to build your case, you'll find that it gives you the capacity to persuade others to do, think, or feel whatever it is *you* want them to do, think, or feel. This is true whether you want to influence people to buy your product, clean up their rooms, change their opinions about the village referendum, or feel angry about the current crime statistics. To be effective at persuasion, your presentation needs to follow certain steps that involve both logic and emotion. Follow the steps in order, incorporate logical support and evidence, appeal to audience members' emotions, and you will likely succeed in persuading them to your side.

Before you begin your presentation, analyze the audience's attitudes about the subject. Do members already have an opinion? Do they agree with it, are they neutral, or are they opposed to it? If the audience already agrees with your position, your objective is to fortify the argument and motivate them to take action. If they're neutral or don't care, you need to convince them that it is important. Explain the relevance to their lives and present all possible solutions followed by the reason yours is the best choice. If the audience is opposed to your idea, your objective is to have members recognize the value of your position and, you hope, reconsider their views. Find the common ground between you, and watch that your words don't come across as an attack on their beliefs. Whatever the audience's attitudes, when you show that you recognize members' feelings and viewpoints, they will be open to listening to what you have to say.

Here are four steps to follow when building a persuasive presentation:

Step 1: *Grab the audience's attention.* Make members want to listen to you. "By the year 2007, gas-powered cars will be completely obsolete!"

Step 2: *State the problem clearly.* Use simple language and provide illustrations, statistics, and examples whenever possible. This will build a logical foundation for the solution you are about to present. "We have agreed as a family that we will all do our fair share of housework so that we can live in a clean and clutter-free home. However, as you can see by these photos, sweetie, your bedroom is 50 percent messier than last month."

Step 3: *Propose your solution.* To do this effectively, present your idea with passion and appeal to audience members' emotions. Ask them to visualize what would happen if they did (or didn't) do what you propose. Tell them how this idea will benefit them and use evidence as support. Think ahead to what their objections could be and address them. "This referendum will provide the money the town needs to build the schools our children deserve! If this referendum is defeated, classes will become more crowded, there will be fewer textbooks, and music, art, and gym classes will likely be eliminated completely. Do you want your children to have that kind of education? Look at the numbers in front of you. The money the district is asking for isn't much. It will be spread out over the next three years, and the school district has agreed to suspend all tuition and book fees for that same period of time."

Step 4: *Call for action.* This is where many persuasive speeches fail; the speaker hesitates to ask for the audience to take action. Make the request clear and specific. Unite both the logical and emotional elements of your speech and the audience will be motivated to do what you suggest. The more strongly you get members to feel about the topic, the more likely they will take action. "As you leave tonight, there are sign-up sheets in the back of the room for joining a neighborhood watch group. I urge all of you to get involved. Together, we can create a crime-free precinct."

"I changed my ways and learned to persuade."

A communications training class taught me how to market my ideas to lawyers. My own communication style was defined, and I learned how to communicate with people who have different styles from mine. In my sales presentations, I had always been someone who liked to jump right to the end, presenting the final outcome first. But lawyers, my primary clients, don't respond well to that technique. It triggers them to raise all kinds of objections, to be the devil's advocate, and look for reasons my idea won't work. I left that class thinking I needed to drastically change how I presented ideas to lawyers. I talked with a lawyer friend, and he helped me understand their psyche even more. He told me that lawyers like to look backward, to study precedents, and build off of history. He suggested I devise a way to build to my conclusion. I switched my selling style immediately. I now present bullet points, evidence as support, and make recommendations that lead to an inevitable conclusion: mine. Instead of walking into a frustrating argument over why my ideas won't work, I help them see why they would. This single change in strategy made it possible to implement my ideas. I experienced instant, dramatic success. I even went back to my earlier rejected ideas and presented them again in the new way. They have become some of my most successful projects.

Bernard, self-employed marketing director

Persuasion can be an important part of many presentations, formal or informal. Persuading people to do anything can be difficult because persuasion implies that change is necessary. People naturally resist change, but if you continue to show the benefits that will come to them as a result of your idea, it will be easier for them to make the move to your side.

SUCCESS
CARD 27 : *Keep Current*

When you're speaking, it's extremely important to be on the leading edge. Following trends will help you develop a topic that grabs immediate attention (i.e., what the aging Baby Boomers are doing, how people are adapting to the growing Hispanic workforce, how the downturn in the economy is affecting consumers and businesses, or the continual rebirth and renewal of the Internet). When you're in front of a group, you want to have the day's events available to you. The economy, people in the news, and the world scene change so rapidly that twenty-four hours can make a huge difference in how you could approach something. If you're speaking to younger audiences, be especially alert. Today's young people are quick to pick up on dated references; they're children of instant information. High school students create reports in computer-generated formats based on information they've taken the night before from the Internet. If you're in front of them, you need to be in tune.

William's Move   William never doubted his ability to be on top of the latest information in his field. After all, he was a recent graduate with honors from a top IT school. All the latest research was fresh in his head; he could discuss the current books in the field with all levels of employees at his new company. So when asked to make a presentation about what project teamwork was like to the new-hire orientation group, he prepared minimally and glanced at the news headlines when he logged on at work. There it was: a huge computer virus outbreak throughout his department. He realized then that he knew nothing about virus management that wasn't at least two years old, and he was going to be facing the brightest college graduates in a few minutes who would be asking him how the company was handling the outbreak. Quickly, he searched the latest manual, but he walked into the presentation wishing he'd kept up to date with his journals in the field.

131

The Internet is the easiest and quickest way to stay updated, and the daily newspaper is a close second. You can research a company's corporate news by clicking on a home page and surfing the site for daily events. At home, you can make a national news page the home page setting for your Internet connection and get information about the world every time you connect online. All the major Internet servers have news-filled home pages to meet that need easily. There are many highly respected newspapers in addition to your local paper. Try subscribing to one for six months and watch your perspective improve.

When speaking, you can bring clippings of newspapers and magazine articles with you to the front of the room. Highlighting and reading from the day's news shows you care enough to present the latest information. The same is true of current, hot books. Bring them with you, and read aloud some of the author's current statistics.

"If I hear old statistics again, I'll scream."

Nearly every time the company sends me to a presentation about communication skills, some speaker mentions the "58–35–7 percent" rule of body, voice, and words contributing to the meaning of a communication. I happen to have a communications background, and I pulled out my old college notes just to confirm how old this study was. Albert Mehrabian researched it in the 1940s, and it's a real red flag for me that the speaker isn't up to date. The only way I would accept that information as an audience member is if the speaker tagged the information as *classic* or *widely known*. Just discovering this has been a real lesson to myself to stay up to date with whatever I present.

Jerry, manager in a food services organization

Jerry and William know the value of presenting the most current information. Make news-reading and trend-watching parts of your daily life. Enlist others to help you. Tell them the kinds of information you're most interested in. They'll keep their eyes open and alert you to news about your topics when they see it.

Play the Game: It's Your Move

You've now played the Presentation Hand. You know the value of writing interesting content and how to make your presentations unique and persuasive. You also understand the importance of looking globally and staying current with your subject matter. So take a moment right now to choose one card to play. Write your card choice in your game plan at the end of the book. When you've completed the move, return to the game plan to fill in the results.

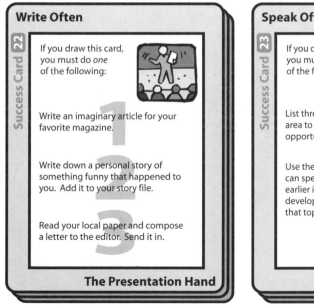

Write Often

Success Card 22

If you draw this card, you must do *one* of the following:

Write an imaginary article for your favorite magazine.

Write down a personal story of something funny that happened to you. Add it to your story file.

Read your local paper and compose a letter to the editor. Send it in.

The Presentation Hand

Speak Often

Success Card 23

If you draw this card, you must do *both* of the following:

List three to five organizations in your area to contact about speaking opportunities.

Use the list of three to five topics you can speak about that you created earlier in this chapter. Choose one and develop an outline for a speech on that topic.

The Presentation Hand

133

Be Unique—Look Globally

Success Card 24

If you draw this card, you must do *two* of the following:

Purchase a book of famous quotations.

Using your list of three to five possible speech topics, choose one and create a title that incorporates an acronym.

Subscribe to a business or news magazine. Buy a copy today and read it within the next five days.

The Presentation Hand

Know Your Tools

Success Card 25

If you draw this card, you must do *one* of the following:

Select a short story or section from a novel. Audiotape yourself as you read it aloud. Evaluate your inflection, rate of speech, enunciation, and volume level.

Select a short story or section from a novel. Videotape yourself as you read it aloud. Evaluate your facial expressions, gestures, and eye contact.

The Presentation Hand

Build Your Case

Success Card 26

If you draw this card, you must do *all* of the following within the next seven days:

List three things you'd like to be able to persuade others to do.

From that list, choose one and list every benefit that could come as a result.

Use that one topic and create an outline for a presentation incorporating the four steps of persuasion.

The Presentation Hand

Keep Current

Success Card 27

If you draw this card, you must do *one* of the following:

Using the list of three to five choose one and conduct an Internet search for the latest information.

Subscribe to a newspaper other than your local paper.

Create a filing system for collecting data on the three to five topics from your list.

The Presentation Hand

CHAPTER 7

THE LISTENING HAND

SUCCESS
CARD **28**: *Listen to Learn*

Listening is at the center of every move you make and, therefore, one of the most challenging hands to play. Listening will distinguish you as a key player, move you toward your goal, and establish your success. Nobody succeeds alone. You make decisions and choices based on listening to others. Dramatist Wilson Mizner once said, "A good listener is not only popular everywhere, but after awhile he gets to know something."[1] The good listener *is* popular and *does* learn a lot, yet when you ask people what causes communication problems in their lives, many will say, "Nobody listens." Social psychologists such as Ralph Nichols have studied listening valiantly since the 1950s, and it continues to be one of the most requested topics of today's professional development seminar audiences. No role in life or work can be successful without listening. No successful move can be made without listening.

If you've been in the game for a while, you've probably developed some habits that reveal your listening skill. Which habits are most like yours, those in column A or B?

135

A. I can listen to someone while reading my e-mail.

I know my job; I generally don't need too much advice.

I've got so many things to think about, I don't have time to listen.

I get through most days with good half-listening techniques.

B. I turn off my cell phone when I'm meeting with someone in person.

I ask probing questions to encourage people to talk.

I try to gather good ideas before making a decision.

I look directly at and concentrate on whoever is talking to me.

If you're like most people, you can relate to both sets of statements. When asked to rate themselves as listeners on a scale of 1 to 10 (10 = excellent), most people give themselves a 7. Would your rating be similar? Is a 7 good enough? How is it that you can achieve excellence—a 10, perhaps—in sports or cooking or computer technology but listening excellence somehow evades you? Writer Edgar Howe once said, "No man would listen to you talk if he didn't know it was his turn next."[2] Perhaps you're so busy talking that you forget that listening is 50 percent of the communication process, or maybe you think that listening should just come naturally, as a matter of course. Actually, you are equipped only to hear. You have to learn to listen. And you also have to listen to learn.

There are some myths about listening to let go of and some truths to build on. The myths tend to perpetuate bad habits. When you play the Listening Hand, you must believe and play the truths to win.

Myth 1: Good listeners are nice.   Truth 1: Good listeners are smart.

Myth 2: Listening is passive.   Truth 2: Listening is active.

Myth 3: Listeners lack power.   Truth 3: Listeners hold power.

Myth 4: Listening skill is innate.   Truth 4: Listening skill is learned.

The truths about listening are simple. You could have been brought up to think that listening is a nice, polite thing to do, and it is, but it's also a wise thing to do. Good listeners are smart because they are constantly taking in all kinds of information. When you listen well, you can't help but learn. Listening attaches meaning to the physical process of hearing; it allows you to make sense of everything you do. Listening is as active a process as driving a car on a snowy day. It takes the same amount of energy and concentration to listen well as it takes to watch how the car's windshield wipers clear the ice, to time the brake at the stop, and to test the iciness of the pavement. Listeners have power in relationships because they have understanding. They've gathered information and details that many might have missed. You're not born with an ability to listen. You have to learn and practice the skill. The truths are simple, but the skill of listening is complex.

How do you begin to play this hand successfully? The first step in learning to listen better is awareness. When you catch your thoughts drifting or your anger building a defense, you are aware. When you realize that a certain client's explanations always require your note taking, you're aware. When your child says to you, "Dad, you aren't listening to me!" you're aware. It's a larger first step than you might think. Too many people deny they have a problem. Be happy to be aware. Awareness will help move you to the second step, which is behavior change.

Anthony's Move   Anthony's lunch out with his co-workers taught him an important lesson in listening. At work, people were distracted by emails, faxes, interruptions, and the general hubbub. Away from the office, it seemed he could concentrate more on the interaction at hand. In a way, stepping out simplified the process. There wasn't as much information being exchanged, and it seemed to be more meaningful. He decided to see whether he could recreate the same concentration he had at the restaurant every time someone walked in his office. He vowed that every time someone walked in, he would look up and turn away from the computer. He even decided to have a small note pad nearby to take notes.

Anthony made the move from awareness to behavior change by altering a few simple daily habits. Imagine how it would feel if every time you walked into someone's office, he or she would turn directly to you or perhaps even pull out a note pad? In today's highly computer-based environment, it's easy to get lost in the computer screen. The first evidence of listening is eye contact. Make the choice to break your gaze with the screen and look up. With only a few cultural exceptions, looking in someone's eyes shows respect and caring. It's an easy behavior change to make if you're committed to concentrating.

"I learned to listen to their level."

The main thing I've learned after twenty years as a librarian is to listen for patrons' experience levels when they arrive. I really try hard not to be too exuberant until I watch their reaction to my first questions. I look for any confusion on their face. Only then can I figure out the amount of background information I need to give. When you're new, you tend to plunge into too many questions too quickly. I've also learned to listen to our foreign-born patrons. Just because people have accents doesn't mean they don't understand a library procedure. In fact, they often have more knowledge about our system than I would initially guess. Listening means not jumping to conclusions, in my book—no pun intended!

Ellen, circulation director for a large suburban library

Ellen learned to listen from years of experience answering library patrons' questions about the unknown. She simply couldn't function effectively in her job role without listening. For a librarian, the need to listen seems fairly obvious, but how about for you? In your life and work, can you afford not to listen? Think of all the ways that listening can make you more successful. If you're chairing a school event, why not call the past few chairpersons and listen to their experiences? If you're taking on project management, consider calling team members individually to get their input before you have your first group meeting. If you're applying for a new job, call someone who works for the company and listen to their experiences. If you're a working parent, feeling rushed at home, make a concerted effort to focus on only your family at dinner. Ask them about their day or how they feel about a current event. Focusing on them will build your spirit together.

"I learned about frogs."

Sometimes, as a mom, I felt like I spent the day nagging my kids rather than knowing them, especially my strong-willed son. But a family wedding taught me a big lesson. My son was ten at the time and we were on a late night family car trip to Cleveland for the wedding the next day. I was taking my turn at the wheel while my husband and small daughter slept. My son, typically full of energy, was wide awake in the back seat. I needed to stay awake too, and I didn't want to play the radio loudly, so I asked him to talk to me to help keep me alert. "Sure, Mom," he said, "Whadayawanna talk about?" I told him I'd talk about anything he wanted to talk about. "How about frogs?" he asked. I said that would be fine, and for the next hour or so we chatted about the difference between frogs and toads, and sports—basketball, soccer, and roller blading. He was interested in the financial income of Michael Jordan and Michael Jackson and how they got to be so rich. Now and then he would pause, but we'd continue to talk as I drove down the dark, deserted interstate highway. About an hour and a half later, when I finally stopped at a gas station, the bright lights woke everyone, and the magic of our discussion faded away. But I knew that I had taken the first step toward changing a bad listening habit with someone I love very much.

Sharon, busy professional and mother

What Sharon learned listening to her son in the uninterrupted environment of a car on a trip to Cleveland was a precious lesson in remembering what was important in her life. Taking the time to listen to someone important to you without distractions is a true gift—not to him or her, but to you. It allows you to fully receive who he or she is.

Perhaps you've heard of the classic communication theory of "the stranger on the train"—the phenomenon of the unwarranted amount of self-disclosure that occurs between two strangers who know they will soon part, never to see each other again. Why is it easier for strangers to share and listen than for those who are close? The answer is simple: Less risk is involved. Deep feelings don't have to be explained; they're just expressed. Mistakes and snafus are shared as normal, accepted parts of life. They don't have to be justified. There is less risk in sharing because there is less judgment on the listener's part.

You could find it difficult to self-disclose to anyone but your longtime friends and family. Try to keep an open mind. Try sharing easy things about your past or your opinions. When you're able to share more about yourself with a new acquaintance, make a mental note to remember how freeing it felt to share without being judged, reprimanded, or corrected. Try to allow that feeling to occur with those who mean a lot to you, both at home and at work. If you're a manager, you can open up more to your team. Did you know that most managers don't know simple things about their employees such as where they grew up or what their hobbies are, let alone how they really feel about the weekly meeting? Whatever your role in life, you can focus more on listening. What kind of listening environment have you created around you? With whom do you need to "take a trip to Cleveland" in some way?

SUCCESS
CARD 29: *Listen to Language*

If you've just made a move to a new project, job, or volunteer team, you'll find that experienced people are usually willing to talk. They're not always willing to talk about the positive things, however, and often you'll meet the most jaded, unhappy people on your first day. Listen openly, without making quick judgments. You'll be able to pick up cues to the type of culture surrounding you by listening to how things are described. People unknowingly give you cues to how they're used to operating by everything they do and say. If you listen, the cues aren't difficult to find.

"I knew I was on a real team."

I came from radio—a whole different world from the corporate world. I never had a "get up, take the train to work, carry a brief- case" job—ever. Not only was the content new but also the whole culture could not have been more different from a radio gig. In the real world, people stay at work from 8:30 to 5:30 or later. In a radio shift, you do about four hours with about an hour of prep time. Also, in my previous life on the radio, it was very independent and people were held accountable as individuals; at my current job, we really are a team. We don't just give lip service to that. For example, on the first day of training, one of the senior consultants came in to help us learn a new module. I was impressed when she said, " I know I'm supposed to do this at 12:15, but I have to make a phone call. Do you mind if I come back at 12: 25?" I was struck by how team-oriented the people were—right from the beginning.

Catherine, former radio celebrity, now a consultant for a business communication consulting firm

Catherine was happy to be entering such a positive, civil environment among consultants. The senior consultant who apologized sent a strong positive message that ten minutes meant a difference in her ability to serve her internal customers. Language tells you a lot about the other people in the game. You can listen for the order of what is covered in a conversation. Are details covered first? Do problems surface without solutions? Is the information a surprise? You can listen to the way language is used. Is it casual or very planned and articulate? How would you describe the overall tone of the information? It could be very logical and ordered or very creative and unstructured. Is there a serious or humorous tone?

Listening to language well also allows you to be able to ask questions well. If you can paraphrase or check in with someone about what you understand, you are demonstrating an ability to listen. You ought to be able to ask questions such as, What do you mean by that? or How does that work? or Why is that? Most people aren't very good explainers. You have to help them explain.

Linda's Move   Seated in Joe's office, Linda was excited about her first sales appointment for her new recruiting company. A former colleague, Joe had been agreeable to the meeting, even though he said he would have only half an hour. Linda planned the questions that she needed to ask to get an idea of the scope of his recruiting needs: the number of positions that opened on a yearly basis, the types of positions, and so on. She did some homework on Joe's company, went to its Web site, and copied a few pages about the key officers. She began with what she thought was the perfect overview, "Tell me about your current needs, Joe." His response quickly caused her to revamp her plan. "Well," Joe said, "I don't really think much about recruiting until somebody quits." Linda hadn't been expecting this response and tried to judge Joe's face for signs of anxiety, but he seemed calm and casual. "Oh, and, uh, is that often?" she blurted out. Joe laughed and said, "For some types, not soon enough!" They laughed, but Linda could see that she would have to re-structure her plan to get a better sense of how she could help. She decided to try probing more about exactly when Joe needed to recruit and in what areas, but he continued to lack the specific facts she needed. She left the call worried about how to word a proposal for Joe.

Linda was having difficulty getting Joe to explain his situation. Often, when you're new to the game, as Linda was in her new business, listening is a chal-lenge because you have so many other things you're worried about. Most peo-ple feel nervous about first meetings: first days with a new client, first-time social events, and first days on the job. In Linda's case with the evasive Joe, attempting to probe was a good choice. Even though her questions didn't lead her to essential information, they enabled her to better prepare for the next meeting. She can call colleagues and ask them for advice with similar compa-nies or experiences. She can return to Joe's company and research personnel records on her own. There are other ways to get the information she needs, and, in the process, she could discover why Joe knows so little about his em-ployment trends.

Many times, changes in work coincide with changes at home; for example, relocation, new schools, new bills to pay, and different transportation. If you're in a new work position where it seems you have lists and lists of questions, try to keep them geared professionally. For example, if you're concerned about getting off work in time to pick up your child at school, ask about the best bus route or the easiest parking lot to use, but don't include your personal worries. Keep your mind on your goal as you ask probing questions and listen for responses that move you toward it.

If you've made a move to a new group at work or in your personal life, you could hear a lot of jargon that is new to you. Professional, school, and community groups are all guilty of tossing around abbreviations and acronyms that experienced members understand. Publishers call a book that's not as good as others in its market "a brown suit." Speakers and actors talk about bookings, agents, bureaus, and exclusivity. Business managers discuss ROI (return on investment), the game plan, the cash flow, the market leader, getting buy-in, and crisis management. Human resource professionals discuss empowerment, being job ready, outsourcing, and outplacement services. When you're listening to the language around you, you'll be able to learn a lot about the attitude and awareness of your team members. Ask when you don't understand something; chances are that someone else doesn't get it either.

SUCCESS
CARD **30**. *Listen for Style*

Everyone is different. Hippocrates first talked about temperament styles in 400 B.C. His model classified four body humours that resulted in four different temperaments: choleric, sanguine, phlegmatic, and melancholic. As time went on, researchers including the Greek physician Galen, the German philosopher Kant, and the American psychologist William Marston continued to describe personality and emotions in four types or categories. Today, it is widely accepted that people have different ways to succeed in their environment. It's been proven over the centuries: If you listen for style, you will get along with people better.

Generally, you'll find it fairly easy to observe categories of people. There are those who are more direct versus indirect in how they approach you. Some people focus more on the work itself and others on the people who do the work. Some people are detail oriented; others like to think in big pictures. Some make decisions quickly; others need to think things through. Some people like to discuss thoughts; others prefer giving orders and instructions not to be discussed. If you observe and listen to others' behavior over time, you can adapt. Often someone's appearance will match his or her behavior. For example, an expensive suit and impeccable grooming will accompany elevated vocabulary and perfect grammar. But sometimes the two elements don't match up at all. Mixed messages in any combination should always cause a red flag— a caution signal—to go up for you. Keep your eyes and ears tuned in for the real truth about the other person's style; it will reveal itself to you if you're open to seeing it.

Style is evident in behavior. The keys to style awareness are to use your strengths, continually be open to opportunities for improvement, and adapt to others' styles. For example, if you're a detail-oriented type, be willing to work with people who have sloppy desks and no to-do lists. It can take counting to ten, some deep breathing, and trial and error, but you can do it. If you're outgoing and talkative, be careful not to overwhelm a quiet type. Try to ask questions and listen. Don't overwhelm your manager who is a big picture thinker with daily operations data. Listen and observe constantly. You'll discover things about people every day. For example, your personal assistant could enjoy data gathering but be uncomfortable with selling ideas. You can tell because you've listened to what he or she says about difficult client calls or new software tricks. Listen for what people say and do the most. You will discover their natural style as you listen, and you can encourage them to use their strengths.

"I listen for natural style every day."

I represent ninety-five people who are exclusive voice talent. I bring people on board at our agency because of an interesting quality in their voices, but I also listen to how they're interpreting the directions they're receiving when they read copy. My work is probably more about listening than anything else. I listen for whether they have an interesting voice, make the copy their own, and are comfortable with themselves. I listen to make sure they're not trying to be anybody else. Once we heard a young talent whose demo tape put him through hoops. That showed variety, but our advertising client needs to hear what that person really sounds like—not five interpretations. I listen for the ability that our talent has to explore their full and natural styles. Also, at our agency, we are very strong on talent relationships, so it's not just listening to the voice on tape but also to our conversations in the office. Even though actors come and go all day, I listen and learn from our fifteen-minute sound bite conversations. I'm listening for the agency, my advertising client, and me. I have a mailing list of six hundred ad agency clients, and they're always in the back of my mind; they hear so much that I have to simplify and interpret an audition for them so it's just enough for them to retain. And the easiest way to do that is to focus on natural style.

Joan, twenty-year veteran talent agent with more than ten years exclusively in voice-over

Although you could never have to listen to style with the intense concentration that Joan uses selecting voice-over actors, you can certainly listen for revealing sound bites: those meaningful cues to personality and naturalness that everyone in your life shares on a daily basis. The more evidence you find of someone's natural style, the easier it is to choose the right move with that person.

SUCCESS
CARD 31: *Listen with Your Eyes*

Any experienced cardplayer knows how much information is revealed by the slightest nonverbal nuance of the face. Any actor knows the amount of information revealed without words. Film actors, especially, are skilled in reading and reacting to body language. But there's a professional and personal place for listening to nonverbal communication as well.

"I listen to solve problems."

The biggest change in advertising over the last few years is a result of technology and email and how people are communicating. When you're talking face to face, you can react to what's being said. With email you're left with whatever set of words is on your screen.

The positive side is that if you're dealing with the transfer of information, it's all there. But it challenges listening.

Seeing how someone speaks is important. What's the body language? Is the person committed to what he or she is saying? Advertising is a relationship business; it's opinion; it's judgment; you just can't open a textbook and find the right answer as you often can in the medical profession, for example. In advertising, it's fluid; for example, you can get ten different opinions about an approach. A typical client complaint is that the agency contact doesn't listen. We try, but we need to infer a lot. We end up second-guessing. We think, They're asking for this, but what do they really want? It's a dance. My motivation comes from the ability to sell an idea. And listening skills are key to hearing what the client is saying, reading between the lines, and coming up with ideas that are solutions to the business problem.

Mary, executive and twenty-five-year veteran in advertising

Mary's experience as an advertising executive reflects the importance of face-to-face listening for clarity and creativity. Human communication would be so much easier if you could simply "mind meld" your thoughts directly into the other person's brain and not have to be bothered with listening to words and body language. The reality is, however, that body language actually reveals more than words. You can control what you say, but it's difficult to control your body; it sends out messages all on its own. What happens then? It's another case of congruence versus mixed messages. When the verbal and nonverbal don't match, we tend to believe the nonverbal.

When you listen with your eyes, tune into the other person's posture, gestures, eye contact, and facial expressions. Posture reveals attitude and level of interest in both the topic and you. What is the person's posture "saying"? Is he or she showing interest by facing you directly, or does he or she look suspicious with a sideways stance? Is the person slumped over, looking submissive or uncertain? Or is he or she filling the space with his or her body and exhibiting dominance and confidence?

You use gestures to help others understand. Have you ever tried to converse with someone who doesn't speak your language? What's the first thing you do? You use more gestures! Gestures are used to emphasize and clarify the spoken word. Palms up movements help propel the message toward the listener. Palms down gestures convey both emphasis and a mood of calm. Take note of gestures that reveal nervousnes—wringing hands, palm rubbing, and other movements directed toward the body. Rapport can be enhanced when gestures become somewhat synchronized. Conversational obstacles can often be overcome when the listener reflects the speaker's movements.

Eye contact is probably the most powerful form of nonverbal communication. In his book, *Eye to Eye: How People Interact,* Dr. Peter Marsh says, "How we look at other people, meet their gaze and look away can make all the difference between an effective encounter and one that leads to embarrassment or even rejection."[3] The ability to look directly at people and meet their eyes can help to make a positive impression. Honesty and the ability to look someone in the eye are also very closely related. If you're listening, you're expected to look at the speaker. As you look, consider his or her eye contact with you. Is he or she checking with you periodically to gauge your interest? Or is the person establishing authority over you by limiting the length of eye contact and frequency of glances? Eyes are very reliable mood indicators. It is difficult to fake genuine eye signals, so trust your intuition as you "read" another's eyes.

The reality about facial expressions is that, even when they're bad, they're good. An expression of any kind at least shows that people are involved. Be aware, though, that humans have become quite good at suppressing the display of some feelings and amplifying others. Researchers have come to agree that there are six basic emotions: happiness, sadness, anger, disgust, surprise, and fear. Interpretation of these emotions can be difficult because each one often appears in only one part of the face, either the lower face, eyes, or brows. The other two parts could be registering something completely different, as in a smug look, a combination of angry and happy expressions. Most people are skilled at manufacturing whatever expression society has deemed appropriate, so posed expressions are commonplace in many conversations. Eyebrows rise when surprised, "social smiles" are exchanged when agreeing, and jaws drop when astounded. It's often impossible to distinguish between conversational signals and true expressions of emotion. Consider facial expressions as a piece of a much larger communication puzzle.

Juana's Move   Partly because of her language barriers and partly because of her Latino culture, Juana had learned to watch the faces and eyes of her co-workers and customers with more intent than most. She was especially aware of other new employees because she remembered clearly how it felt to be new and overwhelmed. One day she noticed that Philip, an elderly part-time greenhouse worker, looked confused and a little sad after a busy afternoon when it seemed as if the whole city had been in buying annuals for spring planting. She walked up to him and asked if she could help him with anything. "Oh," he said, "You wouldn't know." She told him that she worked with the product catalog every day on the telephone and was learning a lot about annuals. After several more questions and smiles, Juana learned that he was embarrassed when he overheard a customer talking about "that old man who doesn't know anything." As a part-time minimum wage worker, he had been give only basic training. Juana told him about the product orientation training she had as a customer service rep and, with his permission, asked her supervisor to include him in the next session.

SUCCESS
CARD **32**: *Listen Up*

If you report to a manager, you know you have to listen to him or her. How well do you listen up? Do you listen without defensiveness? Are you accepting? Do you ask for more input? Asking for feedback is a mark of healthy self-esteem. If you have the courage to ask for help, you have the courage to take the next step. Superiors, especially, appreciate it when you seek their expertise, as long as you don't abuse their time. How you follow up to the feedback is just as important as asking for it, but asking is the first step.

Kathleen's Move   Naturally self-assured, Kathleen rarely asked for anyone's opinion. She was just one of those people who had good instincts the first time around. However, while volunteering to coach tennis, she met another player who taught her a different kind of lesson. Ryan was not only a great teacher but also a great learner. He would stay late to work with the "pro" on duty to continually hone his own skills. Sometimes Kathleen would play a match with Ryan, and as the months went by, she watched his serve improve to the point that she could barely return it. One evening, sweating and walking off the court, it hit Kathleen that even though you were good, you could always get better. You just had to ask for help and practice the advice you were given.

If you're good at your game, experienced, and successful, you still have opportunities to listen up. You can seek a mentor or circle of support among colleagues who are also good at their games. Sometimes called *forum, mastermind,* or *support groups,* these are selected groups of respected people who share common goals and standards.

"I asked everyone I admired."

I've learned that it's important to surround yourself with excellence. In the initial stages of your business, surround yourself with people who are already successful with what you want to do. Ask them politely, Would you mind if I take five minutes of your time? Or Is this a good time to talk? I would ask, What advice would you give to someone like me, knowing what you know now? Or, very specifically, What's the best way to get your article published? or What's the best association to join? What's the best way to get your foot in the door? I would suggest asking a minimum of five and a maximum of six people. That's enough to give you a sense of direction. I watched how people I admired looked, acted, and carried themselves. I made sure that I looked like the most successful.

I noticed that successful people take every single aspect of doing business seriously. They don't just talk about smiling on the phone; they smile on the phone. Lots of people have more credentials than I do, but I took it seriously when people told me to start marketing. I started marketing immediately. What was my biggest lesson learned listening? It was this: A lot of people get great ideas but don't take action. Write it down immediately and do it. Take action and stay focused. Discipline is important. You have to say, OK, I've learned this, now what am I going to do? Have the discipline to take action from what you learn.

Christine, business consultant, speaker, and author of *Wake Up and Smell the Competition*

149

Christine not only practices listening up on a regular basis to build her own business; she advises her clients to do the same. Who can you ask for advice? Whom in your life and work should you be listening to more intently on a daily basis? What are successful people doing that you're not? Don't be afraid to make the call. Most people love to talk about what they do.

SUCCESS
CARD 33: *Be Accepting*

True listening is listening without defensiveness or judgment. It is open and accepting. A good listener remains open not only to the ideas before him or her but also to the possibilities. If you're listening to the possibilities, your mind is open and creative. You're using your thinking time well because you're taking what's before you and moving it positively toward a goal you have.

"I listened like a shopkeeper."

In the 70s, when I was a single flight attendant based in New York City, I always liked the people who were the local shop owners. My community was my butcher, my pharmacist, my cleaners; they were my family. It's strange that you would think of community in New York City, but I always did. I dreamed then that if I ever got married and settled down, I'd be a shop owner. As the years went by, flying on the planes, I started talking to passengers about what they did for a living. At the time I didn't even know what the word *networking* meant, but I guess I was a natural at it. I talked to everyone so that since 1976, I had collected the names of about 170 suppliers whom I had met. Years later, my dream came true. When I finally did open my shop, South & West, my first suppliers were none other than the people I had met in my life and on the plane. People do all kinds of things! People design dog bowls, fashion silver Milagros, votives, ornaments, books—they are so creative. When you're in retail, your suppliers really are an extension of your family. I even refer to my store as "she." "She" has to take care of herself, and I take care of myself. We're family. I'm still flying four to five trips a month as a 25-year employee of the airline.

150

I'm stubborn. I would encourage people not to look back but to listen and dream. 'Your imagination is your only limitation'; that's what I believe.

Karen, mother, shop owner, and flight attendant

KEY PLAYER PROFILE: MARY ANN SMITH

"Listening is learning. It's the avenue for recognizing opportunities and it's also an early warning system. Constituents often come to us spontaneously and in a fury. First, we need to listen to understand the specific demand and then to find the larger underlying issues. For example, garage break-ins usually indicate broader problems; if we can work with the citizen and the police to gauge the time frame and the area of the break-ins, we can shut down the burglary operations.

"As a public official, it's important to see that complaints walking in the door are opportunities; if you were a salesperson, you would understand that it's an opportunity to provide good service and a better relationship. It's the same for our office. A complicating factor is the diversity of our community. It is a port of entry for refugees. When we listen, we have to look for subtler things. For example, a horrible financial crime was being perpetrated on the Asian community in the ward. We discovered that its members had fears dealing with the criminal justice system and going downtown to the large legal offices there, so the state attorney's office set up shop in our offices near their neighborhood in the ward.

"I would advise a new alderman in a community like ours to put into place a diverse staff. Get people who are passionate about issues such as public policy work or transportation or who represent different age groups and ethnicity. We have an Irish grandmother who can sit and listen to people's problems all day long; she doesn't have a college degree. We also have staff who are proficient in all the languages we need: Yugoslav, Spanish, Hebrew, and Yiddish. Diversity goes beyond economics and ethnic background. It's important to build it into all areas."

. . . Mary Ann Smith, 48th Ward Alderman for the City of Chicago, Illinois, since 1989, got involved in government through advocacy programs such as nursing home reform, fair elections, and Lake Michigan protection. She serves an economically and ethnically diverse community on the Chicago lakefront.

Like Mary Ann, the alderman, Christine, the business consultant, and Karen, the shop owner, you too can be accepting and open to the information that the people you interact with have to offer. If you don't ask, you'll never know. People you've listened to like to watch their ideas turn to action. Self-discipline is important so that you can move from acceptance to action. Listening takes energy.

Harry's Move   Harry listened to his voice mail and was happy to hear a message from the editor of the music association trade journal. Harry phoned him back with the hope that his articles had been accepted for publication. The editor explained that the issues were already set for the next twelve months and there was no room for Harry's pieces. Harry was very disappointed; he had thought this would be the start of a new direction for him. What the editor did offer was a spot as an unpaid proofreader, essentially a volunteer position for the association. Harry knew that it was an important job but not exactly what he was looking for. He told the editor he would think about it and get back to him. Harry spent the next day and a half giving it some thought. He also read through a few back issues of the journal and came to an unexpected realization. The job as proofreader would allow him to develop a deeper relationship with the editor and the opportunity to stay current with the newest trends and advancements in music. He decided to accept the proofreading job. It could only make his own writing better.

SUCCESS
CARD 34: *Acknowledge Mistakes*

If you've ever worked in a customer service role, you know that the first step in handling an angry customer is to say you're sorry. It's also a good listening step. It sets up equality between you and the speaker. It shows you're willing to listen to the next idea or step to solve the problem.

If you truly can't listen, say, I'm sorry, but I'm having trouble listening fully right now; I've got something else on my mind. Or Joe, this sounds really important and I'm having a hectic day. Can I call you back tomorrow? It's much better to acknowledge your mistakes and limits than to fake your way through a situation only to regret it later. Likewise, if you're truly sorry, say so. It will open you up to better listening, and the other person won't be so defensive.

William's Move   William was beginning to feel more comfortable as team leader. The project he had almost derailed earlier had moved forward smoothly, and the people on his team were back on his side once again. Then something happened that tested William's management skills. At the division meeting, his team was presenting a report that members had spent many weeks preparing. As he reviewed the information on page 5 with the group, William noticed that the figures had not been corrected to reflect their latest findings. Wanting to be accurate, William interrupted the presentation and pointed out the wrong numbers. He went on to say, "Jerry, we had those figures last night. Why didn't you get them into the final report?" Jerry's face suddenly flushed, he apologized, and quickly sat down. Another team member stepped in and finished the presentation. William's supervisor was in the room to see this unfold. He took William aside after the meeting and explained an important rule of management: Praise in public; discipline in private. He also pointed out that, as team leader, it was ultimately William's responsibility to see that the reports were accurate. William called his team member into his office and apologized for his behavior. He explained he was still learning how to manage and would work harder to be a good leader.

William acknowledged his mistake directly; you can send a note, offer an alternative, offer to learn more, send a gift, apologize in front of a group, or use any tactic that will let people know that you care. Very few days go by without opportunities to learn from listening. Whether you learn about someone else, yourself, your world, or your specific situation, you have opportunities to practice being a better listener every day. The next time someone asks you to rate yourself as a listener, wouldn't you like to say, I'm a 10?

Play the Game: It's Your Move

You've now played the Listening Hand. The best way to become a better listener is to practice listening a lot. So it's time to draw one of the cards following for your first move. With this hand, you might not feel very active, but remember that listening well is one of the most energetic activities in the game. Write your card choice in your game plan at the end of the book. When you've completed the move, return to the game plan to fill in the results.

Listen for Style

Success Card 30

If you draw this card, you must do *one* of the following:

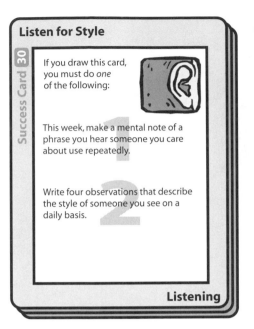

1 This week, make a mental note of a phrase you hear someone you care about use repeatedly.

2 Write four observations that describe the style of someone you see on a daily basis.

Listening

Listen with Your Eyes

Success Card 31

If you draw this card, you must do *one* of the following:

1 Make an effort to watch body language all day today.

2 Establish direct eye contact with everyone you meet today.

Listening

Listen Up

Success Card 32

If you draw this card, you must do *one* of the following this week:

1 Ask five people for advice on an issue with which you're struggling.

2 Ask someone you respect to lunch or coffee.

Listening

Be Accepting

Success Card 33

If you draw this card, you must do *both* this week:

1 Ask a colleague for advice on one thing you should change. Try it.

2 Select someone you'd like to accept more readily. Do it.

Listening

End Notes

1. Herbert Prochnow, *1,001 Ways to Improve Your Conversation and Speeches* (New York: Harper, 1952), p. 8.

2. Ibid.

3. Dr. Peter Marsh, *Eye to Eye: How People Interact* (Topsfield, MA: Salem House, 1988), p. 72.

CHAPTER 8

THE LEARNING HAND

SUCCESS
CARD 35: *Be Aware*

Once a year, on one day between December 14 and January 5, thousands of volunteer bird lovers participate in the Annual Audubon Christmas bird count. With binoculars and notepads, they count all the birds that they see. This helps them learn about the birds' patterns of behavior, survival, and growth trends. They are enthusiastically committed to the count because they learn so much about creatures they love—even in the chill of the winter season. If you're ready to play the learning hand, it's time to get your own notepad, guidebook, and binoculars because, like these naturalists, you'll be gathering information to help you succeed in areas to which you're committed. Play your learning hand with a keen and constant sense of awareness. A winning player never stops learning.

In her first workforce address in 2001, U.S. Labor Secretary Elaine Chao described a transformed, information-based economy. Calling for better education, training, and career self-management, she asserted that the days of the gold-watch employees—the workers who spend a career with a single company—were over. Although you could be perfectly happy with your current company, it is a fact that workforce turnover averages between 23 percent and 28 percent, depending on whether you have a government job or a retail position. If you're currently not employed and want to be, this statistic can be refreshing as you search; chances are that a job you like will open at some point. At any rate, you're in charge of your career more than ever before.

How will you know what you need to learn and when? Awareness is the first step. Stop, look, and listen to your situation and your life. What do you need to learn this week, this month, and this year? Observe the wise learners who are all around you. You will see people such as Debbie, a desktop publisher, who takes the latest classes in computer visuals every year to stay on top of technology for her clients. Maureen, a former manufacturing administrative employee, is studying for her real estate license. Ann, an unemployed actress, is a catering intern at the restaurant where she has worked as a waitress for five years. Steve, who once owned a thriving dinner theater, is successfully redeveloping the contracting skills he learned years ago from his father. Jill, a former owner of a small electrical contracting company, is successfully applying her electrical background as a top sales representative in the competitive telecommunications industry. Learning is ongoing, life enhancing, and career building.

Awareness can come in an illuminating moment after months or even years of observation and experience. Your timing for the right move will appear. Consider the excitement that Michelle feels in the following unedited letter to her mentor as she shares her new career choice:

To: bjones

From: mwilliams

Subject: So excited

Brenda, Good news! I have a new career in teaching! Other news—I'm moving out of state to start it. I have decided to apply for a teaching position for next year in a state that was awarded a grant from the government to train professionals transitioning into teaching. If accepted into the program, I would undergo intense training from March until August with a combination of theory and fieldwork. My first year of teaching would be considered an internship and I would be fully certified as a teacher after my second year. At the end of training and internship, I am guaranteed a three-year teaching contract. It will be a lot of work over the next few years with lots to learn, and I am so ready for it. I am getting so excited anticipating my new career. Thanks to you and the inspiration your words have offered me to find my true passion! Teaching! Absolutely! It took being in the moment of corporate training to realize what I really have a passion for is teaching! As they say, live and learn. I hope I never stop learning!

Best of luck, Michelle

When you look at all of the exclamation points, you see Michelle's genuine happiness knowing that she is finally on the right path. Michelle did her homework to build her awareness. In the months before the letter, she frequently met her mentor at small networking groups. She also developed a good sense of what a corporate training career was like by holding entry-level positions in two different companies and attending meetings sponsored by the local training association. By the time Michelle wrote the email, she knew what she wanted. You, too, can build awareness by attending events, observing people, taking new positions, and volunteering for special projects.

Anthony's Move   Having weathered one job loss, Anthony had developed a keen sense of observation about what was going on around him at work. Even though he was feeling comfortable in his role as an internal consultant, he kept an eye open when internal job postings occurred, just to see where the turnover was. His work writing the column for the annual report also forced him to actually read the annual report. That careful reading clued him in to the fact that his company was due for a merger with a long-time competitor. Mergers meant job changes. There would be a good chance that his job could be eliminated again. He was also aware that the IT staff he consulted with was in a precarious position. One of his roles, in fact, was counseling new IT team members, and there were always many of them as favored projects came and went. New product research and project management were volatile areas of the organization. Anthony promised himself to be ready for the next possible change.

Like Michelle and Anthony, you gain awareness over time. Practically, you can join groups, observe job postings, read reports, and listen to the water cooler chatter or the neighborhood buzz. You could hear a little voice in your head telling you what your next move should be. You also want to listen to your heart.

"I help people end and begin."

For all of us, the end of the year is always challenging and full of activities, especially if you are a small business owner. I usually felt exhausted and did not look forward to beginning the next year. Many years ago I decided to change that and I created a year-end workshop called "Endings and Beginnings" as a way to help people put closure to the past year and enter the new year with enthusiasm. The workshop, which I still do, is very special and occurs only once a year. It has three purposes. The first is to list and celebrate all of the accomplishments and miracles of the past year, for example, the happy surprises and great people who have come into your life. The second purpose is to let go of failures. When you really confront disappointments and failures, you can not only come to closure but also see what you need to do next. Is there a healing ritual, for example, that would help you? The third focus of the workshop is on unfinished business: the nagging stuff that saps energy, such as tax work, papers, and even messy basements. After this, you're ready to look ahead and design goals for the next year that are heart based—not "should" based. Heart awareness is the first step.

Robin, career consultant and author of *No More Blue Mondays: Four Keys to Finding Fulfillment at Work*

According to Robin, heart awareness gets beyond the ordinary, daily to-do list. It provides a broader focal point. It puts things in perspective. Your heart awareness can point you back to your family, your home, or a cause in which you believe. Take time to assess where you've been and where you're headed as you learn both head and heart awareness.

SUCCESS
CARD **36**: *Ask for Help*

Asking for help is actually a sign of healthy self-esteem. If you seek help in the form of feedback, you become not only more aware but also more confident because you get answers and advice. People find you easier to work with because they learn that they can give you help in the form of constructive criticism without fear. Tell yourself that asking for help is a sign of strength, not weakness. People who help each other naturally feel more camaraderie. At work, you could find that comraderie pays off in company loyalty. A study by the Wharton School of the University of Pennsylvania showed that firms with high levels of closely connected employees are more inclined to retrain their employees rather than hire new ones. Why? With good teamwork, employees know what to ask each other and are aware of each other's strengths and challenges. Advertising agencies, medical offices, and construction companies are typical types of companies that rely heavily on this type of information sharing. It's clear that open, communicative relationships are valuable; they make it easier for your organization to keep you.

A women's publishing association conference featured a panel of female publishing executives. In the question and answer session afterward, the panel addressed many standard questions about how to get started in a publishing career. Then one young student asked, "Looking back, is there anything you would have done differently?" An officer of one of America's largest publishing houses answered first: "I would have asked more questions. I think at work people are afraid to ask questions, when, really, most of us are quite willing to answer. I would have asked, Why do you do it this way? Or Have you considered this? That's what I would have done differently."

Linda's Move   After her disastrous appointment with Joe, Linda knew she needed some help. She'd never really been taught how to sell; she hadn't needed that skill as a company employee. Now, on her own, however, she needed to improve her selling skills—fast! She decided to start an informal networking group of people in her same situation. She posted signs at the library and sent out email feelers to some consulting groups in her area, looking for people who would like to share ideas regarding selling. Three people showed up at the first coffee shop get-together. Linda talked about her past unsuccessful selling experiences and shared how doing homework was not enough for a sales call;

she knew she needed to ask better questions. And with that, the group took off, exchanging sales techniques and humorous stories from the trenches. Linda learned a lot that morning. Asking questions of her peers would enable her to ask her clients better questions.

You could be a person who finds it difficult to ask for help. Think about what you fear about it. Is it appearing inferior or lacking in knowledge? If so, ask for something small first, for example, where something is located. Build gradually to more important questions. Perhaps you're a shy person who fears approaching people in the first place. Again, start by asking for the help of someone you know best. Every organization has people who naturally take others under their wing; choose one of those people first. Then be honest with yourself. Are you really asking people for help, or are you just going through the motions? Do you really listen when they give it? Are you willing to help them in return? Are you just making mindless small talk in the lunchroom every day? How can you become an integral part of the group? Don't you want to be the person whom the company retrains rather than outplaces? Every day, work to increase your chances of becoming an integral part of the team. It will pay off.

"I make mistakes on a daily basis."

My philosophy is this: it's you. It doesn't matter what your employer has done to you or whom you want to blame. Most people are doing what they want to do, so if you want to change, it's up to you to do it. I used to write meetings for a large mortgage company so I knew that the mortgage business was a good one—very busy. In fact, I went into the business because my own mortgage broker would not return my calls about refinancing. About that same time, I went to a neighborhood Dad's Club breakfast, and one guy was talking about how he saved money refinancing and what a great mortgage broker he had. I asked for the broker's number. Well, I ended up using the firm, and at the closing appointment, I happened to mention my interest in the field. As it turned out, the firm was also interested in training me. I had a lot of questions and still do. I think it's key when you're in a new job to just say, "Tell me that one more time." The first time you ask, it's embarrassing because you feel like you're exposing your ignorance. But then you quickly become known as a person who wants to get it right. It's all about the customer. When you can get the best information from the experts, you can do the best job for your customer. In sales, you're selling solutions, and I can find solutions when I ask the experts for help.

Rob, mortgage consultant with a brokerage that funds more than half a billion dollars a year, and who was salesman of the month after two months on the job

A common area in which people need help is technology. Even if your life involves limited technology, it's very important to be knowledgeable when you need to be. It's not even funny to say you're computer illiterate any more. No one is asking you to be a wizard, but your associates at least expect you to ask educated questions. It's the difference between asking frantically, How do you turn this darned thing on? and saying calmly, I'm not familiar with the power switch location on this model.

Catherine, a former radio personality turned business consultant, had used email at the radio station but had never needed to use a laptop. When she discovered that, as a consultant, she would have to use one, she was a little nervous. Every time she touched it, it appeared to her as if something too fast would happen and she would scream. It was hilarious to everyone who watched as well as to Catherine. Whenever something happened on the screen, she was surprised. She asked Bill, the computer guy, as she called him, for help. With a good sense of humor, Bill readjusted the computer so the touch pad wasn't quite so sensitive. She then realized that the technology problem she faced wasn't totally due to her lack of experience. Catherine now asserts that people come to her for help; in addition, she has learned how to use spreadsheets and technological tools that she never had to use before.

Rob and Catherine asked for help directly. If you're employed, it makes sense to ask the boss for 15 minutes of time to find out what you need to learn next. In addition to asking questions of your manager, friends, and co-workers, you can join a support group or take a class to develop your skills and abilities. The coaching field is growing fast; you can find a coach to help you in every major city in the United States. Search under coaching or coaching and training alliances on the Web. With a little experimentation, you will find the right fit for you.

SUCCESS
CARD 37: *Develop Yourself & Take Responsibility*

Develop Yourself

French author and diarist Anais Nin wrote in *Winter of Artifice,* "Life is a process of becoming, a combination of states we have to go through. Where people fail is that they wish to elect a state and remain in it. This is a kind of death."[1] If you feel stagnant in your life, you are probably ready to make a move. That move can involve a considerable amount of self-development.

"I advise that you're never too old."

We're an open-admissions community college. I see lots of folks who represent the first generation to go to college at any age— twenty-six, thirty-six, forty-six, or fifty-six. They learn from life and want to go back to get an education. I deal a lot with people who didn't follow the formula. Education means choice when you have no other options. I see people who've run out of options. For example, I have adult women whose husbands have left them and their supplemental job now needs to be full time, or people who have to learn a skill to stay employed with new technology. What's growing is the reeducation—the retraining of adults. Senior citizens are coming in because they want to learn computer skills, and we have a custom-paced program for them. We have a woman in her seventies who came in because she wanted to email her grandson. She was very nervous at first, but she got so enthused that now with the advanced classes, she's putting on PowerPoint programs with clips, music, and special effects. She's a computer lab assistant now, helping others in the program.

**Billie, admissions adviser
at a Midwestern community
college**

164

If you're an older or experienced worker making a job change, you could find that your wisdom and experience are less important than the recent computer courses you've taken at a local college. Many interviewers will check your resume to see if you've gone back to school and if you're keeping up your knowledge with new skills. You could also want to apply for a bridge job: a part-time, short-term position that helps you move between one career and another or retirement. The Employee Benefit Research Institute estimates that between one-third and one-half of older full-time workers will hold a bridge job before finally quitting work. Older workers are seeing retirement as a process, not an event.

Whatever your age, if you want to be employed, you will find that self-development through formal education pays off. Lifetime earnings are far higher for college graduates. The Economic Policy Foundation in Washington, D.C., cites that a degree from a vocational or technical school can mean almost $1.5 million in earnings during a work lifetime compared to about $852,000.00 for a high school diploma. A bachelor's degree is worth more than $1.9 million over a lifetime. The average college graduate makes twice as much as a high school graduate. The impact of technical change and globalization has increased jobs in careers that require more education. If your employer doesn't provide assistance, investigate loans, grants, and scholarships. If you end up paying for education on your own, research www.irs.gov for information about federal tax credits such as the lifetime learning tax credit. Don't give up easily if you want formal education to be your next move.

Self-development is often challenging. It could become necessary when you weren't really planning to be re-educated. For example, after the September 11, 2001, attacks on the United States, many people were forced into developing new skills outside traditional classrooms. One in four workers in New York's Chinatown lost a job in the three months following the attacks. Chinese workers in the devastated New York garment district were signing on for beauty school while other people waited in the wings for the garment workers' spots if they decided to quit. The meeting and travel industries were greatly affected as were thousands of other workers in the New York area. All of those people had to make new moves. Many had to develop new skills.

Technology's volatility could also have affected you. You could be one of many who are stunned by rounds of layoffs in the aftermath of the dot-com crash and the weak economy. As you plan your next move, make a note that companies prefer people who are well rounded, able to work in teams, and communicate effectively. Although a few years ago you could have been hired based on your great technical skills, today you'll need to have evidence of your ability to communicate and adapt. You could feel as if you're stepping out of your comfort zone. Imagine how the Chinese garment workers felt while learning the art of the manicure!

William's Move   On the intranet early one morning, William noticed the Bulletin Board flashing a "Sign-up Today" for the upcoming training department's in-house course, Communication: The Key to Effective Teams. He didn't need a coach to tell him he needed help communicating with his team. He sent a quick email to his manager asking for a day off to go to the session. He received an affirmative reply and cleared his calendar. The day of the training session arrived; William came with a list of problems and concerns, required by all for entry. Right away he saw three other team leaders he knew, and he felt less alone with his less-than-perfect leadership skills. The facilitator guided them all through a careful overview of how effective teams work; the day was discussion filled, and the analysis of different work behavior styles got especially heated. William learned that he needed to be more patient when people make mistakes. He left the class with an agenda for a special team meeting with his team to discuss communication standards. He knew he had to ask, not tell. He planned to hand out a feedback form to his team to help him understand how he was doing as a leader.

Take Responsibility

A mother tells a favorite story about her son. Once, when he was eight, he got a letter in the mail, addressed to him personally in child's printing. Mysteriously, there was no return address. When he came home from school that day, he eagerly opened it because he didn't receive much mail. He read it out loud in his best second-grade style:

Dear Robbie, This is a chain letter. Please do not break the chain. Send a post card to the first child on the list and a copy of this letter to five other friends and in 30 days you will receive hundreds of post cards from all across the nation. You will be a part of a World's Record for the longest children's chain letter in existence. It will be entered in the *Guinness Book of World Records*. You have 48 hours to send copies of this letter. Please don't break the chain.

As she listened, the mom sighed, envisioning days of letter writing ahead of her, but at the same time her son shouted, "WOW! Can I do it, Mom? Huh? Huh?"

"Well, sure you can," she answered. "But chain letters take a lot of time and work, Robbie. This will have to be *your* project—not mine!"

"That's O.K.," her son responded. "I'll do it on my computer."

He was learning keyboarding in second grade, and he ran to the family computer. Much later, he came back with five copies of the letter. Seeing his hard work, his mother suggested that he call a few friends to see who might like to receive a chain letter. First, he called his best friend, Jared, next door. She overheard him ask, "Hey do you want to be in a chain letter? Yeah, well you send it to five friends and you get all these postcards. . . . OK." Click.

With disappointment he said, "Mom, Jared doesn't want to do it."

She suggested that he call his cousin Leon in Pittsburgh.

"Hey, do you want to send a chain letter? Yeah, well, you send it to five friends and get postcards. . . . OK." Click.

"Mom, Leon doesn't want to do it. Do you think the kids on the block might?"

She started to say yes when he yelled, "Yeah!" and he was out the door with five letters in hand.

Very shortly, he returned with all but one letter delivered.

The mother was truly amazed. "Robbie, great job!" she said.

Nonchalantly, her son answered, "Yeah, Mom, everybody wanted to do it."

She wondered what his technique was, but at that moment his friend Jason came over to play. Brightly, Robbie turned to Jason with the remaining letter in hand.

"Hey, Jason," he asked, "Want to be a part of a world's record?"

Then the mother knew. Her eight-year-old salesman had changed his strategy. No longer was he even mentioning the chain letter. He knew his customer, all right. What child doesn't want to be a part of a world's record? He took responsibility for his success, and he repositioned the idea so he would achieve it.

Like Robbie, you too could have projects that don't go well at first. You could want to give up, but keep in mind that instead of giving up, you can just reposition. Sometimes you need to look at things from a different perspective. Robbie began to see his buyer's point of view more clearly with each failure. Repositioning an idea will often lead to success.

"I didn't listen to the naysayers."

When I was sixteen, I started a company where I did promotions for nightclubs and bars using email lists and flyers. When I was eighteen I had an idea to wrap trucks with advertising, like it was wrapping paper—all around the truck—like a present. I worked to get funding, and I had partners who were older. What I learned from that venture is that the business world is very cutthroat and that it's important to surround yourself with people with the same dreams and visions that you have. I also learned the basics of business, accounting, management of people, and customer relations. It gave me great people skills—the overall ability to relate and adapt to any and all situations when you're put in with a variety of people.

I realized that restroom advertising was a more viable business. It was already somewhat accepted in bars and restaurants, and I started thinking, Where can we do it with high traffic areas—areas with a lot of people? We started with ballparks. Now it's in all kinds of large stadiums. I have an office manager, two attorneys, a few salespeople, a technology person for the Web site, and a financial person. Since landing the White Sox Comiskey Park last spring, we are signing two to three stadiums per month now.

I've learned to follow my own dreams and I would tell others not to be deterred by naysayers—because there will be a lot of them.

Woodrow, age twenty-four, founder and president of AdCommunity, a company that places advertising in restrooms at major sports stadiums

Robbie and Woodrow are both young entrepreneurs. They both took risks and followed their instincts to reach success. You don't have to start a company to learn how to work with people and figure out problems. A group of dentists in a large urban area has met every Friday for fifty-four years to schmooze, shop talk, and share opinions about difficult cases. They are single practitioners who enjoy the gatherings because they don't get out of the office much. The weekly get-togethers have been accredited as a form of ongoing education by their state's academy of general dentistry. Many current members are the children of original forum members.

If you want to change how you spend your time or your work, you can look closely at areas that have been hobbies or part-time jobs in the past. Maybe you used to ski, knit, bartend, or sing. Why were you attracted to these areas? How could you make the next move to include them more fully in your life? Chances are that something about that hobby or pastime fulfilled you; perhaps it heightened your self-esteem because it came easily and you did it well. Perhaps now is the time to develop it further.

"I believed in magic."

I've always loved scouting. I'm an Eagle Scout. I've held other jobs, but for the last thirteen years I was one of only about 4,000 professional Boy Scouts in the United States. I was good at what I was doing. Promotions came. Pay raises came. I moved to four different areas of the country to lead districts. I was serving in a liberal district when the Boy Scouts were challenged on their standards for membership, which the national organization said did not allow for gay leadership. It became difficult for me to create new units and to market activities in my area after that, so I was appraised as a marginal performer and asked to resign. After thirteen years and many Chief Scout Executive Winners Circle and *Boy's Life* magazine awards, I was fifty years old and unemployed. I had loved being a professional Boy Scout; I had won many of the awards because I simply challenged myself to be better each year.

For some time, I found that the hardest thing I had to do was get out of bed in the morning. I filed for unemployment while my wife continued working in a skilled job in a bakery. We celebrated every time we got the bills paid. We couldn't eat out any more; I grew a beard because I stopped shaving; I became lazy because I had no purpose. Even though I had gotten an MBA degree while in scouting and have a degree in accounting, the job hunt was difficult. Finally my parents told me about someone they knew who was a signing agent as a mobile notary. I took the training and if I had one signing every ten days, I was thrilled. I kept looking and thinking about what else to do. I had been a professional magician, and so I went back into training. With the help of a friend who allowed me to make the tuition in several payments, I attended the Magic 2 Motivate program to learn how to become a motivational speaker with a magic base. I remember the long discussion with my wife as to whether we could afford my flight to Orlando at the time. The class was inspirational, and now I promote my magic everywhere—to Kiwanis, Rotary, and Cub Scouts. Not long ago, I thought I had I lost my identity; now I still have my beard; it's part of the new me. I think I have finally found where I belong. It's not the end of the world.

Steven, magician and motivational speaker

Steven's experience illustrates what can happen when you take responsibility for your happiness. He was in an unhappy pattern; finally, he took advice, asked for a friend's help to fund his training, and is now following his passion for magic and motivation.

You can learn alot through daily life and volunteering. Karen, a stay-at-home mother of three boys, cochairs the school fund-raising auction. She develops her skills in managing people and territories, in presenting, and in making sales calls. Alex, a busy dad and graphics artist with an ad agency, designs the logo for the program book. He develops his listening skills as he works with Karen to get it right. Guy, a restaurant owner, writes the copy for the school newsletter. He develops his ability to write, edit, and meet deadlines. Michele, an interior designer, heads the site details and develops her negotiating skills with the suppliers and venue managers. Even a school auction can be a valuable training ground for responsible learning.

SUCCESS
CARD 38: *Read*

Few people read anything of worth once they graduate from high school. Reading can be the conduit, however, for countless ideas that propel you forward. Today, you can read online, via email, or on paper. Formats change as technology allows. E-books are growing slowly in popularity, roughly by 10 to 15 percent per year. Perhaps you're attracted to reading in this format. If you travel or like the technology, you could have found a great way to learn in your spare time. Especially popular with students and people who love handheld devices, dedicated reading devices allow you to download books over the telephone line. One company's best selling e-book is the international version of the Bible. Some publishers now provide complimentary e-book editions with their print titles.

In contrast to the high-tech format of the e-book is the growing popularity of the traditional, home-based, low-tech format of the book club. Ranging from free-for-alls that are open to anyone and any book to set groups with set books, a dues base, and a paid moderator, book clubs are growing rapidly. National news shows have focused on the phenomenon, and bookstores around the country cite statistics showing a 200 percent increase in the number of clubs. Often they give discounts to registered book club members. Members range from retired people to busy executives. Why such interest in reading? People say they want to use their minds again.

Originally designed to promote literacy, book clubs date back to seventeenth-century England and France. Benjamin Franklin organized a book group to encourage reading among his young apprentices in colonial Philadelphia. Many of these societies evolved into community activist groups that helped fund libraries, oust child labor, and promote women's suffrage. Great Books clubs, promoted by University of Chicago academics after World War II, are still alive in many schools, businesses, and libraries. One executive is reading Homer on the commute to and from his job as a Pfizer Inc. executive.

Juana's Move   Her experiences helping the older gardener and her friends with school applications made Juana realize how much she liked developing others. At the weekly staff meeting, the personnel manager announced that the supervisor in her area would be retiring in six months and that the position would be offered to internal employees first. She signed up for a community college English pronunciation class and a beginning business course. For the English class, she had to read two children's books a week out loud to practice pronunciation, so she collaborated with her ten-year-old daughter, and they chose books together at the library. Soon Juana found herself in the enviable role of reading with her daughter nightly before bedtime again, as she had been in when her daughter was three. One day at the library, they saw a notice for a mother-daughter book club, and Juana allowed her daughter to talk her into attending. Now they would be reading and discussing books in English with other people.

Parent-child discussion groups, such as the one Juana and her daughter found, are the most popular at many libraries. Reading formats are changing every day, but reading is still recommended as one of the easiest, least expensive ways to learn. A middle-age business owner talks about how his father, who is eighty-four now, was always an avid reader. Although his father was only a high school graduate, his son felt he was one of the most intelligent people around. His father would always come home from his factory job, do a few chores, and then read the paper. Later at night he read the *Readers Digest* and *National Geographic*. Another person remembers a great Aunt Sylvia who read political biographies and *The New York Times* and stayed sharp until age ninety-nine when she died.

"I read so that I can start a new career."

I've been a dancer for as long as I can remember. It's all I've ever done. I studied dance in college and went on after graduation to work all over the country in various companies. But I've always known that I wouldn't dance forever. I've been interested for many years in developing a sideline that could turn into my next career. I'm a voracious reader. Reading is what has kept me sane and grounded. Other dancers tease me all the time about how much reading I do. I read everywhere, on the tour bus, backstage before performances, during rehearsal breaks, everywhere. I'd like to get into computer graphics, so I read every book on the subject I can get my hands on. I don't want to get another degree, and I don't think I'll need to. I think everything I need to know about computers and graphics, as well as how to start my own business, is out there in books."

**Eduardo, semiretired
professional dancer**

Reading can be inspiring, stimulating, and incredibly relaxing. French lawyer and political philosopher Charles de Montesquieu once wrote that he had never known any distress that an hour's reading did not relieve. Read on!

SUCCESS
CARD 39: *Learn Generations*

Another important piece in the learning puzzle today is the opportunity to talk with and learn from the other generations in your life. For decades, Baby Boomers have dominated the demographic landscape. The Boomers, who grew up post-World War II in the late 1940s, 50s, and early 60s, set many standards due to their large numbers. Each generation has different attitudes about work and life. The wise learner considers these differences, which can be as simple as differing tastes in food, drink, or music or as complex as how they like to be rewarded for a job well done or how they approach project management.

Harry's Move   Harry's former student, Sean, was now in the midst of his first year as a high school music teacher. Sean kept his promise and invited Harry to be a guest conductor at the school's winter concert. He asked Harry to conduct the National Anthem, which would serve as the concert's finale. Sean also invited him to come to school and sit in on the various music classes the day before and day of the concert. Harry was flattered and looked forward to getting in front of a chorus once again. It was a three-hour drive, and Harry arrived in time for the concert choir rehearsal after lunch. Sean introduced Harry to the chorus and let him begin working immediately on the song. Harry had brought along an old arrangement of the anthem that he had used years ago with his own choruses but could quickly see that the kids didn't care for it. Sean, a little embarrassed, stepped in to intervene and convince the choir that this arrangement would be just fine for the concert. Harry felt hurt that the kids didn't like it; he also suddenly felt very old, but he decided to try something. He asked the kids to talk with him about what they didn't like. It took several minutes of beating around the bush, but one student finally said that maybe it would be better if it sounded like the National Anthems that had been performed on TV recently. They wanted it to have more of a pop "boy-band" type of sound. Harry thought, Why not? So, with Sean's help, they all worked together and created an arrangement on the spot that everyone seemed to like. When they were finished, Harry couldn't help but think, Well, I guess you *can* teach an old dog new tricks! As he drove back home after the concert, Harry decided he would approach a few music publishers with this new, updated arrangement.

Today's newest young adults, the Millennials–Generation Y, born between 1977 and 1994, are largely the offspring of the Baby Boomers and are set to take over as trendsetters and influencers. Generation Y is technologically precocious; they can't remember not having handheld phones and computers at home. They are highly adaptable and tend not to need the "high touch" that older generations do. They can take in lots of information and multitask easily. If you're in Generation Y, you can learn from older generations—even Generation Xers—about perseverance and etiquette. Generation Xers, who grew up in the 1980s, have been maligned for overfocusing on material goods and on six-figure salaries, but change, the dot-com crash, and the economy have sobered them. If you're a Generation X member, you can share your thoughts and feelings with the very different generations between which you're sandwiched.

"I trusted the advice from a Generation Xer."

I'm twenty-four years old, so I guess that makes me part of Generation Y. My dad died just a few years ago, and I inherited a large sum of money from his life insurance. I also had quite a bit of debt at the time and needed advice about how to handle all of this. I talked with lots of people, my mom, my roommate's parents, even a financial manager, but couldn't make a decision. As all this was going on, I was spending a lot of time with my roommate's older sister who was living with us for a while. Judy was five years older, a Generation Xer, and I had always thought she was great with money. She knew a lot about investing and had been able to save tons of money. Judy gave me the advice and direction I needed. We researched the Internet together and she went with me when we talked with different banks. She encouraged me to negotiate with my debtors and invest in diversified mutual funds. I'm glad she was around. I was much more comfortable talking with someone closer to my own age. I respected her and she spoke my language.

Kim, intern in the telecommunications industry

SUCCESS
CARD **40**: *Learn Cultures*

If you're playing the Learning Hand today, you're playing it in the midst of all sorts of cultural diversity. Labor Secretary Chao cites a growing shortage of qualified workers and encourages us to move faster to introduce new populations and nontraditional employees into the workforce. What does that mean for you? If you are foreign born, you could need to quickly learn the culture into which you're assimilating. If you're working with people of more diverse cultures, you also need to learn about them to make your own life easier. Even if you're at home, you'll find that your school, church, and community are affected by growing numbers of people from around the world: Koreans, Poles, Vietnamese, Indians, Pakistanis, Chinese, Cubans, Mexicans—the list goes on. You're probably finding that other cultures offer a colorful mosaic to events and plans.

If you're lucky, your organization will help you learn about other cultures. As one example, America's Hispanic population jumped by 58 percent between 1990 and 2000. Hispanics will compose 22 percent of the U.S. workforce by 2010. To respond, a construction company in Des Moines, Iowa, is giving bonuses to employees who learn to speak basic Spanish on the job—but learning the language is only the beginning. It's also important to know that for Hispanics, family values are very important. Children are most important in their lives; extended family such as aunts, uncles, and grandparents also get great care. Hispanics need flexible hours to manage their personal lives. If you work with them or employ them, you need to understand their perspective.

The growing Hispanic culture is only one of many cultural groups about which to learn. Middle Eastern cultural influence is also spreading throughout the world. These groups have practices that are based on centuries of religious beliefs and traditions that transfer to work and all aspects of life. Middle Easterners express themselves differently and hold unique values in comparison to those with Western culture backgrounds. They are a wonderfully complex and historic group who are already influencing the Western workplace. European cultures are also constantly changing with the political and economic climate. Follow what's in the news in Europe to stay in tune with today's global climate.

Kathleen's Move   Nicely positioned for a globally based career, Kathleen knew that language fluency would help her progress. She had spent a year in Tokyo, six months in Portugal, and three months in Denmark. Sometimes she could hardly believe it; when she became a sales rep, she really had no idea that she would find international business such a driving force in her life. International airports and hotels had become her second homes, and she was becoming a fast student of cultures. Once, waiting in the airport in Denmark, a fellow American told her about a Web-based language course in Danish. The relationship with the World Health Organization in Denmark was key for her company, yet few in the company could speak the language. Since Kathleen knew that Danes were very humorous, and humor was a big part of the culture, she went to www.danelink.com to connect with a Danish language course. She looked forward to laughing at the next meeting when the Danish purchase manager cracked a joke.

In addition to learning about ethnic cultural diversity, you will also find it valuable to learn the organization's culture. This culture is often unspoken, as Don discovered in his experience with an airline and Tina learned with a government agency.

"I've completed my Ph.D. in emergent change."

In the last year and a half, I went from a very healthy health care organization of 1,200 people to a huge airline that was knee deep in union problems and other industrywide issues. I think the biggest adjustment for me was the change of cultures. It wasn't the content of the job. It was how people communicate—the degree of honesty and frankness in the communication—how it transferred up and down the hierarchy. It takes a while to figure out where your influence and power are. The cosmic division between union and management and how that showed up everyday surprised me. I needed to tread carefully with open eyes and open ears. In my former job if I saw a change was needed, I could put together a team to implement it; in the larger organization, my ability to affect change is so spread out that I get frustrated. For example,

when I came onboard, there was very little orientation to our division, so one of the first suggestions I made was to provide an orientation. It took so long to get this point across, yet alone to implement it, that I began to learn how to navigate a little differently. It got to the point where instead of seeking permission for something, I just did it. My motto has become, "Go ahead and do it and ask for forgiveness later." My advice to anyone who wants to learn the culture is to start early, even when you're in the interview process. Ask questions such as, What happens when you suggest ideas here? How are people oriented? How are the values manifested in day-to-day operations? What is an example of when integrity was especially important?

Don, project manager, leadership, airline industry

"I am learning to listen to learn."

I wasn't looking for a new job; through my volunteerism I received a phone call and it was another state agency that sounded perfect for me, so I took the job. The transition for the first three months was hard—not so much the work but coming from a single-person office to having co-workers, supervisors, and team members. I was set in doing things the way my old agency did them. For example, at the new agency, the meetings were too long and too disorganized, so I think a lot of the time I was mentally thinking of changing processes to make them shorter. I had questions every step of the way about how they did things. I had a problem with listening; I wanted to jump right in. It's a skill I continue to work on. Although I have trust now because of governmental changes and a new upper-level management team, I still work on understanding why the culture has been the way it has. It helps to have the new team. They're coming in the way I did—wondering why things were the way they were.

Tina, training program manager for a government agency

Both Tina and Don learned to listen to a new organizational culture and to ask questions to figure it out. As is true for all learning, they began with awareness, asked for help, took responsibility, researched and read, and continue to make moves for improvement. They admit they made mistakes. Learning any culture takes time and patient understanding. Learning in general isn't perfect. It's just another way to set yourself up for success.

KEY PLAYER PROFILE: JOSEPH L. BADARACCO, JR.

"With the fall of the celebrity CEO, the timing for a book on quiet leadership has been good; people are looking again at what it means to be a leader. Overall, the reaction to the concept has been positive, although some people wonder if quiet leadership is too cautious. In the book, I talk about being a realist and that having the time to think is OK. Even though I write about being realistic, in practice, it's hard to free up your mind to see a wide range of scenarios. We want the world to be pretty orderly and stable, and it's disconcerting to see the other happening. Yet, in most business organizations today, there's more of a risk in doing things too hastily. You want to avoid situations where you have to quickly get the answers; instead, try to understand what's really going on in the situation both technically and politically. Talk to a number of different people; have a lot of small conversations. You're trying to figure out what's going on from several different points. Know what's expected. All of this gets you ready to say, 'Well, I'm going to try X and Y.' And no one is surprised. In general it's important to be as candid with people as you can. They need to understand what you're doing and why. When times are tough, people will sense if they're not being dealt with honestly. At Harvard Business School I think the basic approach is the quiet leadership approach. We have to work in persuasion and influence if we're going to build a case among the tenured faculty here. So, yes, I guess I am a quiet leader."

. . . *Joseph L. Badaracco, Jr., is the John Shad Professor of Business Ethics at Harvard Business School and the author of* Leading Quietly: An Unorthodox Guide to Doing the Right Thing *(Harvard Business School Press, 2002) which is a* New York Times *Best Seller. A Rhodes scholar, he has written three other books on managers' ethical responsibilities.*

Play the Game: It's Your Move

The Learning Hand has been dealt. You've had a chance to think about all the ways you learn. Which self-developmental idea will propel you forward? To find out, play them all and compare results. Remember to write your choice in your game plan at the end of the book. When you've completed the move, return to the game plan to fill it in.

Be Aware

Success Card 35

If you draw this card, you must do *one* of the following:

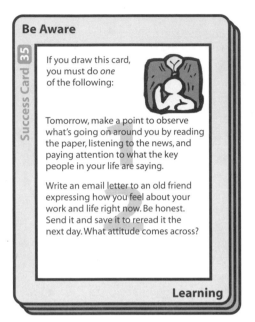

Tomorrow, make a point to observe what's going on around you by reading the paper, listening to the news, and paying attention to what the key people in your life are saying.

Write an email letter to an old friend expressing how you feel about your work and life right now. Be honest. Send it and save it to reread it the next day. What attitude comes across?

Learning

Ask for Help

Success Card 36

If you draw this card, you must do *one* of the following:

Ask someone for help about anything you're working on this week.

Interview two professional coaches to discover how they help others.

Learning

Develop Yourself & Take Responsibility

Success Card 37

If you draw this card, you must do *both* of the following:

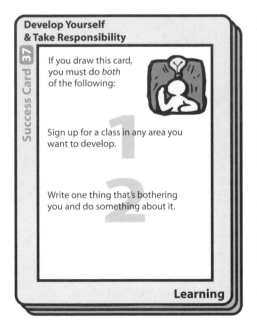

Sign up for a class in any area you want to develop.

Write one thing that's bothering you and do something about it.

Learning

Read

Success Card 38

If you draw this card, you must do *one* of the following:

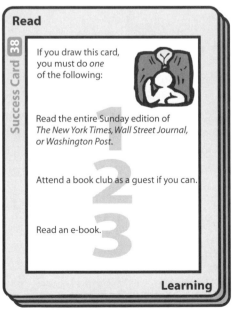

Read the entire Sunday edition of *The New York Times, Wall Street Journal, or Washington Post*.

Attend a book club as a guest if you can.

Read an e-book.

Learning

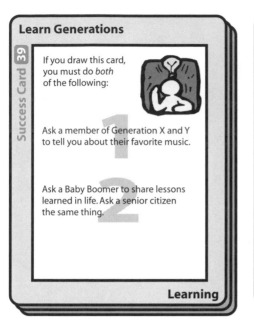

Learn Generations

Success Card 39

If you draw this card, you must do *both* of the following:

1 Ask a member of Generation X and Y to tell you about their favorite music.

2 Ask a Baby Boomer to share lessons learned in life. Ask a senior citizen the same thing.

Learning

Learn Cultures

Success Card 40

If you draw this card, you must do *both* of the following:

1 Pick one cultural group whom you live or work with and research it on the Web or at the library.

2 Invite a member of another culture to lunch but ask him or her to select a favorite restaurant of his or her culture.

Learning

End Note

1. Anais Nin, *Winter of Artifice: Three Novelettes by Anais Nin* (Columbus: Ohio University Press, out of print).

CHAPTER 9

THE BALANCE HAND

SUCCESS
CARD **41**: *Address Anxieties*

The search for balance in your life could be one of the reasons you're reading this book. Something seems out of whack. You're not happy with where you are or what you're doing, and you're struggling to find meaning and fulfillment in your life or career. Your work could be stressful because of a recent layoff, reorganization, or increase in competition. You've been asked to take on more work to cover the departure of others. You're putting in longer hours than normal to keep *your* job secure. And if you're not part of the traditional workforce, you're probably juggling children's schedules, a household, and community involvement. The gutters need cleaning, healthy meals are a rarity, and you lie awake at night thinking of all the things that still need to be done. You're craving balance, serenity, and direction.

It *is* difficult to achieve complete balance in life. It never fails: As soon as one part of your life starts to go well, another part becomes a challenge. Balance remains an objective we all desire, and you don't want your next move to throw what little balance you have into a tailspin. Anxiety can result from external forces. Is your life being consumed by overscheduling, too much clutter, toxic relationships, or overwhelming family responsibilities? Anxiety could stem from something internal. Perhaps your physical health is not good because of poor eating habits or inactivity. Anxiety itself has been linked to ailments from heart disease to immune system disorders. You could be engaged in unhealthy self-talk, your head filled with

183

thoughts of failure or self-doubt. Anxiety could also result from doing too many things that don't mesh with what you value. You could be spending too much time on activities that aren't important to you but not enough on goals about which you're passionate.

It's time to reflect again on the principles and goals you chose in Chapter 2, The Preparation Hand. These decisions should set the course for the moves you need to make. Compare the life your principles and goals describe to the life you currently lead. By making the move to create a life based on what you value, you will be moving closer to creating a life filled with balance. The internal and external challenges will either disappear completely or become more manageable because of new and improved work and life strategies. Don't let the idea of making a move itself create anxiety for you, either. Most people are fearful of change, but the moves you are about to make can take you to a better place. Balance is just ahead.

You can try a number of strategies to deal with the anxieties in your life. Some are related to your work life and others to your life at home. Many of the ideas are surprisingly easy and work well to reduce anxiety, no matter where you are in your life journey.

Most people begin their days already behind. Having stayed up a little too late the night before, they hit the snooze button twice before getting out of bed, then race through a shower, skip breakfast, and drive ten miles over the speed limit to their first appointment of the day—and they wonder why they feel overwrought and anxious! It's important to allow yourself to get adequate rest. The National Sleep Foundation reports that 31 percent of U.S. adults sleep less than seven hours each weeknight. Do you know how many hours of sleep your body needs? The next time you take a vacation, keep track of the number of hours you sleep without waking to an alarm. It sometimes takes several days for your body to readjust to a no-alarm-clock natural waking time, but eventually you'll be able to determine how much sleep your body requires. Then try to get that amount of sleep each night. That often means going to bed earlier than you are used to, which, of course, isn't always possible. You can operate at a sleep deficit for a while but not for long. Eventually, your mind and body will rebel, and you'll need to replenish the "sleep bank" again with several longer nights of sleep. Take a moment right now to think about your evening habits. Can you change any activities or lifestyle choices that would allow you to get more rest?

184

Another way to relieve anxiety is to allow yourself to start each day quietly. Thirty to sixty minutes of private quiet time right after you wake up can provide clarity and focus, two qualities missing from most days. Bernie, a restaurant manager, runs on his treadmill. He does so in complete silence, with no TV on and no newspaper in front of him. The quiet felt uncomfortable at first, but now he looks forward to being lost in his thoughts. He considers this time to be his most productive hour of the day. Allison, an aerobics instructor, likes to write in her journal. She used to write in the evenings before going to sleep but now prefers journalizing in the morning after she's had a chance to "sleep on things." LaWanda, an engineer, uses her morning quiet time to read. She enjoys reading popular fiction during vacations but uses her regular mornings to read and reread the great books of literature. She finds they help her gain a perspective on her fast-paced, information-overloaded life. She finds comfort in seeing how history repeats itself, and the books illustrate lessons that she can often apply to her life today.

People with high anxiety levels are people who usually expect perfection and rarely delegate to others. Do you have those tendencies? Perfection can be a time waster. Although precision and excellence *are* important to most things you undertake, focusing on details that only you will notice eats up time that could be used more productively and causes undue stress. Most parents of young children will tell you that perfection flew out the window as soon as the kids were born. Personal grooming must be delayed until late in the day; housework happens only when guests are expected. Changing your mindset from it must be perfect to this is good enough considering everything else I have on my plate at the moment is the battle cry of anxiety-free people everywhere.

Another question to ask yourself is whether someone else in your life could handle this better (and maybe even do a better job) than you. Just because you *can* do something doesn't mean you always *should*. Multitasking can be overrated! Delegate, delegate, delegate—to team members, family members, roommates, assistants. Delegating to others will decrease your overload and take advantage of others' skill sets. It can also teach others the values of personal responsibility and teamwork. List the various tasks you face at work and in your personal life. Which could be broken into smaller pieces and delegated to one or more others? Take each big job and divide it into specific tasks. Then create a chart of each person's responsibilities, set appropriate deadlines for each task, and schedule times for periodic updates. Jack, a retired TV engineer and union representative, believes his parents instilled in him the attitude that "if you want it done right, do it yourself." He used to take on too many responsibilities at work and with the union because he believed he was the only one who could get the right results. Along the way, he developed high blood pressure and an ulcer and saw the demise of two marriages. As he neared the end of his professional career, he started to realize that the price of always being in control and in charge had too big a price tag. He began to groom his replacements and tried hard to give up his controlling tendencies. In doing so, he found he could help others learn better and faster how to do his job. It was a lesson he wished he'd learned sooner.

Are you having enough fun? Laughter is a great anxiety reducer. You've undoubtedly noticed how one good laugh can instantly change your mood or diffuse an argument. Many doctors believe that laughter reduces pain and suspect that it can have the power to promote healing. One study of college students showed that those with good senses of humor had fewer colds and upper respiratory infections. Laughter could indeed be the best medicine. Do what you can to laugh more each day. It may be a cartoon-a-day calendar that gives you a chuckle. Perhaps it's reading a humorous newspaper column each morning or spending more time with friends who make you laugh. Watching TV and film comedies, stand-up comedy routines, and reading humorous books can also lighten a heavy load.

Having fun doesn't mean you always need to be doubled over with laughter. Engaging in a hobby or sport is a fine way to release tension and get your mind off your worries. If you think you don't have time, find a way to schedule it. It might mean you have to sacrifice something else in your calendar, but all work and no play can make you not only dull but also full of anxiety. Kari, a lawyer, enjoys those unexpected periods of "found" time that crop up occasionally. Open, unscheduled pockets of time used to be spent fretting over some issue at work. Now Kari takes that time to step outside for some fresh air, close her eyes for a few minutes of rest at her desk, or wander through the boutiques located in her building's lobby. By taking advantage of those unexpected open periods, she allows herself some personal time and an opportunity to clear her head and enjoy herself.

Doing something for someone else can release anxiety for both parties at the same time. Volunteering your time and talent helps others in need and provides a way to get your mind off whatever is plaguing you at the moment. Coaching a kid's sports team, preparing meals for the homeless, or providing companionship to residents of an elderly care facility are all ways to serve your community and put your own life and troubles in perspective. Jackson, an accountant, enjoys spending each Thursday night at a local church helping underprivileged kids with their homework. It clears his mind of his troubles, and he leaves each evening with a fresh perspective on his own life.

Anthony's Move   After a year in his new position, Anthony was able to take his first extended vacation. He planned to spend part of it in Florida visiting amusement parks with his grandson. His grandson was very excited with the idea of spending private time with his grandfather, and they enjoyed planning the details of the trip together. The day before Anthony was to leave town, his boss called him into his office to talk about Anthony's vacation. Expecting a casual conversation about the current status of his projects and his travel plans, Anthony was surprised when his boss explained that he expected Anthony to take some of his work with him and participate in two conference calls while away. "Things sure have changed," Anthony thought. "It was never like this at my old job." He'd heard that many companies were shrinking workers' leave time and asking them to continue to work while away, but he didn't realize it could happen to him. Anthony spent the drive home worrying about how he was going to balance time with his grandson with work responsibilities.

It has become more and more difficult for us to get away from it all. Thanks to cell phones, pagers, email, instant messaging, and laptops, it has become possible, and often expected, to work a "24/7" workweek. Some people like the ability to be connected instantly to others. Many chief executive officers and vice presidents use email to stay in constant communication with employees, shareholders, and customers. Their open door policy has evolved into an open mailbox policy. Managers often use a combination of email, instant messaging, cell phones, and voice mail to stay in contact with far-flung team members. Ramon, a managing director, uses instant messaging to get immediate status updates and customer information from the home office. Many families enjoy the instant connection that email and cell phones provide. Parents are able to stay in closer contact with children; long-distance relationships stay healthy and strong.

187

If you're in a position to choose how available you are to others, consider the two schools of thought regarding incoming calls and email. Some people prefer to process them as they come in and take immediate action, whether that is to answer them, pass them along for someone else to handle, or trash them. Others prefer to schedule one or two times each day to deal with voice mail and email. Messages are logged as they come in and then handled at a more convenient time later in the day. Caller ID is becoming a favorite tool of families and home-based business owners. Incoming calls can be identified and screened for the ultimate in control. Experiment with both strategies and find which one works for you.

If you're currently in the workforce, is there a way to spend part of your normal workday working from home? That can be a good way to reduce anxiety and allow you to see your family, get dressed in the daylight, and commute after the rush hour. Dante, an applications specialist, was ready to resign after an especially busy product rollout. She had two small children and wanted to see more of them while they were young. Her employer came up with an innovative idea; he let her design a work schedule that worked for her needs. She suggested a schedule in which she worked eight months on and four months off. She's been working that schedule now for more than ten years. With many companies stretched thin by layoffs, employers are often willing to do anything to keep their good employees happy. If your employer isn't as flexible as Dante's, it might be possible either to reduce your work hours or to work part of the time from home.

Perhaps a larger move is in the cards for you. Many people, especially parents of young children, are making major career decisions to bring more balance into their lives. Some are leaving their conventional jobs to start their own companies; others are selling their businesses and rejoining the traditional workforce.

"I sold my business and got a 'real' job."

I had my own business for many years. I owned and managed a health food store in the suburbs. It was a good life and I enjoyed being my own boss. Of course, it could be overwhelming at times with hiring and firing, covering floor time for sick employees, and so on. It could be a lot of long hours, but I was proud of the store and what I was able to create. Then, the kids came along, and, then, the divorce. I needed more balance in my life and flexibility with my schedule. My kids needed to know that I would be there for them. An opportunity came up to work for one of my health food product lines as a sales manager. I explained in my interview with the company that I needed flexibility. I felt that was more important at this point in my life even than salary. The company hired me and let me work two or three days from home on my computer. I spend the other days calling on customers. I took a pay cut but have so much more time to be with my kids. And for the first time in my life, I can be part of a book club, garden in my back yard, and see friends, too. It's funny, I never thought I could stand having a 'real' job, but it's the best thing I could have done.

Dana, sales manager, health food products

Do you need to make a major move to reduce your stress level? Get into the workforce? Get out of the workforce? Ask for a raise? Take a pay cut? It all goes back to knowing your goals and what you value. Take time to think about what a perfect life would look like to you, and then begin taking the steps to create it.

SUCCESS
CARD 42: *Simplify Daily*

Simplify—sounds like a great idea, doesn't it? Is it easier said than done? Not at all. You can try a number of ideas that will streamline your routines and simplify your daily life. The first thing you have to do is clear the clutter. Clutter can take on a life of its own and mess up yours in the process, causing psychological stress, mistakes, lost income, lower productivity, and embarrassment.

Think about all of the places that hold the clutter in your life:

- Desktop
- Drawers
- Closets
- Basement, attic, and garage
- Car trunk
- File drawers

Then think of all of your clutter:

- Loose photos
- Mail
- Email
- Magazines and newspapers
- Tax receipts
- Children's toys

Once you deal with the clutter, you'll be able to create new routines that will ensure that the clutter won't reappear. Don't try to clear all of the clutter in a single try; it's too overwhelming. Do it in chunks, tackling only one of the clutter areas at a time. Begin by taking everything out or off of the space. Take this opportunity to clean that area thoroughly while it's cleared. As you put things back, sort as you go, grouping similar items: computer discs, bills to be paid, sweaters, tools, action figures, and so forth. Place the things you need most frequently in the most convenient spots. Be ruthless as you sort, throwing away everything that is a duplicate or no longer relevant to your life. If you can't throw it away, consider selling it, donating it, or storing it out of sight.

Like the wire hangers in your closet, paper has a way of multiplying when your back is turned. Consider storing more of your paper and photo clutter electronically. In fact, take digital photos of sentimental items and keep the photos instead of the things, such as kid's artwork or an old prom dress. Locate your prime real estate: the places you need open to do your work, such as your desktop, the kitchen counter, or workbench. Put everything you need to get at throughout the week within arm's reach; move everything else away. Respect your prime real estate and keep it clear. If this all seems too overwhelming, consider hiring a professional organizer. You can locate those in your area by contacting the National Association of Professional Organizers. A day spent with a professional can jump-start the organizing process and teach you the skills you need to maintain the order.

As you work to clear your clutter, experiment with some new, simplified routines. If you are computer proficient, set up a program to pay your bills online. Depending on where you live, you could also do your grocery shopping online and have it delivered to your door. More and more busy people are shopping online for gifts from books to flowers to food. You can even send greeting cards via email. Here's a classic reminder: Handle any paper material only once. Sort all mail and papers immediately into one of five categories: to be read, to be done, to be thrown, to be filed, to be paid. Keep your reading pile handy and grab a few items when you know you'll have some down time such as while traveling, waiting for an appointment, and before going to bed. Items requiring action, such as correspondence, forms, and questionnaires, should be kept in a to-be-done area and scheduled into your calendar. Keep a wastebasket handy and toss everything you don't need or want into it. File papers immediately or schedule filing time into your calendar as a daily or weekly task. Create a to-be-paid file and schedule bill paying into your calendar.

Juana's Move Like many other working mothers, Juana's life was hectic. It was especially difficult in the mornings, when Juana, her husband, and their three children all rushed around to get ready and out the door. Getting dressed, making lunches, and gathering homework were making everyone in the family tense and snippy with each other. Juana found that when she arrived at work, it took her a while to relax and get the smile back in her voice, an important quality for any customer service representative. On a break, she decided to spend some time searching on the Internet for ideas that could help with time management. After just a few minutes of searching, she found a newsletter that offered some good ideas. She thought that they were so easy she should have thought of them herself. The newsletter suggested she spend ten to fifteen minutes at the end of each workday clearing and organizing her workspace for the next day's business. She found other tips that would be helpful at home. Before bed that night, she made a to-do list for the next day. The newsletter recommended she go even one step further and prioritize that list by highlighting the tasks, calls, and errands that absolutely *had* to be accomplished the next day. Juana also enlisted the help of her children and asked them to pack their school bags, make their own lunches, and set out their clothes for the next day before going to bed. Juana looked forward to an easier morning.

SUCCESS
CARD **43**: *Breathe In and Out and Manage Thoughts*

Breathe In and Out

We take breathing for granted. It's something our bodies do naturally, in and out, thousands of times each day. The problem is that many people breathe incorrectly. When asked to take a deep breath, most people will suck in their stomachs (if they're not already holding them in) and raise their shoulders. This kind of shallow, upper chest breathing, can actually lead to hyperventilation. You don't need to be gasping for air to be hyperventilating; you're simply breathing more than the body needs. This can prevent adequate oxygen from reaching your brain and the other cells of your body and can result in physical symptoms resembling panic attacks. Check the quality of your breathing, especially during emotional times. Shallow inhalations and strong exhalations often accompany anger. Fear is partnered with shallow, fast, and irregular breaths. Impatience is associated with short, jerky breaths. Guilt produces a restricted breath. Pay closer attention to how you breathe throughout the next few days and watch for any variations, positive or negative.

Abdominal breathing, also called *diaphragmatic breathing*, should be the goal of anyone who wants to improve the quality of his or her life; it promotes relaxation, detoxifies the inner organs, and promotes blood flow. The diaphragm is shaped like an upside-down bowl and acts as a partition between the heart and lungs above and all of the other internal organs below. Deep breathing takes advantage of the fact that the lungs are larger at the bottom. When you inhale, the diaphragm is forced downward by the expanding lungs and the stomach protrudes. As you exhale, the lungs empty, the diaphragm relaxes back to its domelike shape, and the stomach contracts. The more the diaphragm can move, the more the lungs can expand, bring in more oxygen, and release more carbon dioxide. You automatically breathe from the abdomen when you lie on your back and usually when you're seated, although this is not necessarily *deep* breathing. A conscious effort must be made to breathe deeply. The Sherpa guides of the Himalayas are experts at breathing, largely because their very lives depend on it. Each time they breathe, they focus on exhaling completely and expelling every bit of air. This technique creates a richer intake of oxygen for them, which increases their energy and endurance.

The following are some diaphragmatic breathing exercises to try:

1. Pant like a dog, keeping your shoulders still. Notice how your stomach bounces in and out.

2. Lie on your back and place a book on your stomach. Watch it rise and fall as you breathe.

3. Sitting in a chair, lean all the way over so that your chest is on your lap. Let your arms hang down to the side. Breathe in and out several times deeply and slowly, noting where the expansion occurs.

4. Stand or sit with your hands on your waist and breathe in through the nose. Sigh out through your open mouth and throat. Let your stomach cave in as you blow out every ounce of air. Wait until you feel you must breathe, and then inhale slowly, feeling the lungs filling deep down. Don't let your upper chest move.

5. Breathe in, and then exhale quickly as though you were punched in the stomach. Inhale, taking five short, quick gasps through your open mouth to fill your lungs completely. Feel your stomach grow larger and larger with each inhalation. Then exhale, blowing out over the course of five short exhalations. Repeat.

6. Stand facing a partner. Lean toward your partner with his fist pushing into your stomach. Say "ho, ho, ho." With each "ho," your expanding stomach should push you away from the fist.

Now that you know how to breathe from the diaphragm, make an effort to monitor your breathing more carefully throughout the day. Ban shallow breathing from your life.

William's Move   William was beginning to miss college days when all he did was go to classes, schmooze with the professors, and get good grades. He could do no wrong. Now, every day as he drove to work, he couldn't stop thinking about everything he had to do and how his team would react this time to his ideas. One morning, waiting at a stoplight, William realized that, while thinking these thoughts, his jaw was tense and his neck was tight. The waistband on his pants was also feeling a little snug. He realized that he was concentrating so hard on doing a good job at work that he hadn't taken the time to participate in the physical activities he used to enjoy. He remembered hearing some coworkers talk about the new health club across the street from the office. William decided to check it out after work. A treadmill now and then might be good for both his mind and his waistline.

The news is filled with stories touting the benefits of regular exercise. Recent studies have shown that benefits can be realized with only fifteen minutes of exercise a day. Besides helping to control weight and develop lean muscles, exercise minimizes the risk of dying from coronary heart disease and of developing high blood pressure, colon cancer, and diabetes. It can reduce blood pressure and help to maintain healthy bones, muscles, and joints. It can also reduce symptoms of anxiety and depression and promote feelings of well-being. Another benefit to exercise is the deep breathing that results, pumping oxygen into the lungs and promoting blood flow throughout the body. Is exercise part of your daily routine? If not, you could consider joining a gym or taking up a sport. Even walking and gardening can increase the heart rate and encourage deep breathing. Yoga, a form of spiritual discipline, has become a popular form of relaxation and exercise. It teaches breathing techniques and develops strong, flexible bodies. One popular form of yoga, hatha yoga, is a physical exercise regime that utilizes different poses for the purpose of strengthening and cleansing the body. Some yoga poses can even be done while sitting in a chair; they are great to do at the office or if your mobility is limited.

"I learned to breathe."

I joined a yoga class soon after my mother suffered a massive stroke. I was incredibly stressed out and wanted tips on how to calm myself without using medication. I went to my first class the same day Mom was released from the rehab facility. I remember that I wavered that day, trying to decide whether or not to go to the class. But it was the best thing I ever could have done. I was trying to balance a full-time job, family, and home, and when my mom had the stroke, I felt like my life was a total shambles. We had no clue about what to do about Mom and had more questions than answers. Would she need a nursing home, in-home care, or what? Yoga saved me and provided a way for me to think and take care of myself. I learned breathing techniques that immediately helped me handle my overload. It cleared my mind and helped me relax at bedtime so I could get some sleep. And now, at my job, I'm finding I use the breathing techniques to calm myself when things get stressful. I remove myself from the rush and concentrate on my breathing, and I can get through the day so much easier.

Micki, ladies floor manager of a retail clothing store

Manage Thoughts

Do you have an inner voice that says nice things to you, or does it talk trash? Everyone has a voice inside his or her head that feeds thoughts into the brain. The challenge is that the voice often fills heads with negative ideas rather than positive ones. As you prepare to make a move in your life, it's important that you learn how to control the self-talk and feed yourself only positive, encouraging thoughts.

Positive thinking may not come naturally to you and can be especially challenging if you're trying to find balance and make a work or life change at the same time. You could be feeling confused or fearful. Perhaps you're questioning your abilities or plans for the future. You need some serious "think time." Remember when you stepped back and took stock in Chapter 2? You analyzed what you value and what you now want. But what is it you do well? What are your strengths and talents? Before you go any further, list your strengths. This step takes you beyond your joy sensor. Instead of listing the things you enjoy, write from the perspective of what you already do well, such as these possibilities:

- Playing golf
- Writing killer proposals
- Playing jazz piano
- Communicating with my spouse
- Building consensus in meetings
- Cooking
- Finding creative solutions to problems
- Caring about the earth and its resources

Stuart, a classic character on "Saturday Night Live," was a self-help junkie, and the skits featured him as host of a TV show on which he attempted to help others through his own brand of psychotherapy. Each skit ended with Stuart looking into a full-length mirror and affirming that he was good enough, smart enough, and that people liked him. The skits were a send-up of the self-help industry and had audiences laughing at the seemingly futile self-talk Stuart was feeding himself. Stuart never seemed to have a true and clear picture of his actual strengths and abilities. You, however, have that picture and need to feed your head with healthy and sincere self-talk. Turn your list of strengths into your own mantra. Post them on your bathroom mirror and read them each morning and night. Keep reminding yourself of things at which you are good. Positive thoughts produce positive attitudes.

"I found having a sense of perspective is important."

I attended a training class on the subject of building strong customer relations. The trainer began by talking about perspective. He said we needed to understand how we view ourselves and our place in the world and how customers might view us. He told us that understanding these perspectives would make us better at our jobs. He drew a dot on the board and said that represented us. Then he drew a half-circle above it, like an upside-down bowl, to represent the world around us. He then added several fat arrows above the curve pointing down at the top of it. They represented all of the pressures in life, such as money, family, career, love, and health. At different points in our lives, one of these areas becomes more important or demanding than the others and pushes in on the circle. He explained that at those times, we have to move out from under that circle and travel way out above the arrows to get a better perspective, to see the big picture. From that vantage point, we can look back and see that our whole lives are made up of many facets. One facet could require some additional time or effort, but it should never take over our entire lives. We never want to let the difficult parts of life swallow up everything else.

Kerry, law firm receptionist

You've probably heard the phrase "garbage in, garbage out." Garbage can consist of self-defeating thoughts and also can involve engaging in activities of low or negative value. Enrich your mind with quality endeavors. Read some of the great works of literature. See thought-provoking films. Have uplifting conversations with interesting people. Volunteer for a worthwhile cause. Too much pop culture can be dulling to the brain. When you envelop yourself with intelligence and quality activities, you will bring more brilliance into your own life and thoughts. Norman Vincent Peale believed in the benefit of "mind-emptying" twice a day. This frequent mental catharsis allows you to drain your head of all the insecurities and fears you are harboring. The opportunity then exists to refill that mind, and he cautioned that you must do so quickly, with creative and healthy thoughts. Then, when the worries and negative thoughts try to come back, they find an "occupied" sign on your mind's door.

Linda's Move   Linda's workdays were long and sometimes difficult. She was making some inroads with her contacts, but she thought her business would be further along than it was at this point. She knew that being self-employed would be challenging but hadn't realized just how long her workdays would be. She was usually up before daylight working at her desk and often went back to her office each evening after dinner. There didn't seem to be enough hours in the day to handle all of the details of being a business owner. Linda wasn't sleeping too well; she had trouble going to sleep and staying asleep. Her husband had even given her a small notebook and light-up pen to keep at her bedside so she could make notes and lists as she thought of things in the middle of the night. One afternoon, she called her husband at work and broke down talking about the pressure she was feeling. She shared how concerned she was that she wasn't bringing in more money and how tired she was of having to work so hard to get new accounts. Her husband came up with an idea for Linda to try. He told her that, as a master list maker and scheduler, she should *schedule* time to worry. He thought that if she could file those self-defeating thoughts away until a specific time, she could free her mind to be more productive. It sounded a little silly, but Linda decided to give it a try. She scheduled 3:00 to 3:15 each afternoon as her time to fret. The first day she tried this idea, it didn't work at all. She found her mind racing throughout the day about things that were going wrong, and when 3:00 rolled around, she thought it would be better for her just to keep working. On the second day, she became more aware of her "thought attacks" and quickly jotted down what was on her mind each time. When 3:00 rolled around, she looked at her list of frets and spent fifteen minutes thinking hard about the positive things she could do to fix them.

Linda is learning the value of managing her thoughts. She is learning how to think more productively and deal with negative thoughts. You also need to find ways to isolate yourself so that you can process what's going on in your life and to think strategically and creatively about yourself. Schedule private time each week away from things that beep at you and beckon you to answer. If you don't, you'll spend most of your time engaged in task work rather than knowledge work.

SUCCESS
CARD 44: *Say No*

Saying no can be an easy way to achieve more balance in life. Balance requires controlling your anxiety, your clutter, your breathing, and your self-talk. You must also control your choices. Do you let yourself get overscheduled with more activities than time allows? Are you involved in toxic relationships with people who drain your energy? Have you developed some bad habits? Do you let others interrupt you or take advantage of your time? Women are frequently guilty of trying to be people pleasers. Saying yes is just easier than facing the conflict or rejection that often results from saying no to something. Avoiding saying no can also be tied to culture. Japanese rarely use a direct no; in that culture, indirectness is seen as a sign of maturity and power.

No is a favorite word of young children. They say it easily and often. If they don't like the food, clothes, friends, or toys, they have no problem letting you know. This is part of the growing-up process; by saying no, they're exploring their boundaries and expressing their free will. Something happens as you age, however: You are bombarded by cultural messages that encourage you to conform and seek the approval of others. You want to be seen as a nice person, so you placate others rather than run the risk of offending them. You could allow yourself to get maneuvered into situations you're not comfortable with. You may accept unjust criticism without challenge. Quite often we can't even say no to ourselves; we allow ourselves to procrastinate, to give up, to give in, to shirk responsibility. The inability to say no when you need to can lead to a number of unhappy conclusions; you could be moving yourself further and further from your values and goals and heading toward feelings of isolation and resentment.

Harry's Move   Harry was approached by others in his building's wing to take a position on the tenant board of directors, the group that creates and enforces the guidelines for the retirement community. He knew he had some of the skills needed for that position. He was a good communicator and had the desire to keep the community well maintained and desirable to prospective tenants. In his heart, though, he knew he didn't really *want* to do it. He'd heard the meetings were long and the directors were more talk than action. Harry didn't want to appear unappreciative or unsociable to his new neighbors; they must have thought a lot of him to nominate him. Would saying No, thank you cause his neighbors to think less of him? Harry spent a restless night worrying about the offer.

You can try some strategies to feel more comfortable saying no. First, you need to analyze your speech for nonassertive, tentative speech patterns. Have you ever heard yourself say, kind of . . . , maybe . . . , well . . . , don't you think . . . ?, or I guess . . . ? If so, you're robbing yourself of the opportunity to speak with authority. Make an effort to speak more directly. Avoid turning sentences into questions, remove hedges from your language, and give instructions rather than suggestions.

- Say, The security system breaks down frequently, instead of The security system breaks down all the time, doesn't it?
- Say, This is the best choice, rather than I kind of like this one better.
- Say, I will need this done by Thursday at 5:00, instead of Do you think maybe you could have this done by Thursday at 5:00?

These changes won't turn you into a demanding or mean-spirited person. It's the difference between being assertive and aggressive. Trying to prove you're better than someone else is *aggression*. Assertive people value themselves and can speak directly about what they believe.

The next technique is a good one to try when you want to avoid conflict. Try framing your no response between two more positive phrases. It can help others accept your refusal with a minimum of hurt or angry feelings. First, make a statement that acknowledges the other person's request; this will tell him or her that you listened and understand. Second, state your refusal and your reasons that you can't do it. Third, tell the person what you *can* do.

Example

I understand that you want me to finish the project by Friday at 5:00. But I have two other projects that are also due that day and don't have any more time to devote to it. I *can* have the outline and preliminary graphics to you by then.

Having a clear idea of your goals and what you value can help you set boundaries for yourself. Take some time at the beginning of each year to create a personal set of policies, your own guidelines for how much you will take on, volunteer, or donate. Then, when you're approached to do something, you can lay down the law and say no. I'd like to help you out, but I have only enough time in my schedule to take on one pro bono project each quarter. Kids, you're each going to be able to play only one sport this year. It certainly sounds like a good cause, but I've already made all of the donations I can this year.

"I shouldn't have volunteered."

Have you ever in retrospect said to yourself, What was I thinking? That's what I thought a few weeks after I said yes to chairing a major fund-raiser for my community. It seemed like a good idea. The funds raised would build a park on the corner for all of the neighborhood children, including those in adjoining neighborhoods who lived in apartments without lots of lawn space to run. Now, I'm a working mom and little did I know that this should be a job for a stay-at-home person—any person without another job. I began with a positive attitude, but I could see right away that my ideas were considered radical when I suggested that we set up an email newsletter among the committee rather than just phoning each other all day long. That was the first heated discussion I lost to the old guard. Actually, until I accepted the job, I really didn't realize there was an "old guard." But now that I've experienced volunteerism overload, I can guess that nearly every volunteer activity has a tradition attached. And you have to decide if you're man or woman enough to challenge tradition. Well, this project has taught me a lot about leadership, and that's been worth it. But, y'-know, I should have just said, No, when they asked me. I'm a cre-

200

ative thinker and I like to try new things. This project was a constant reminder of why things in this world take so long to change.

Jenny, graphic artist and neighborhood volunteer

Jenny learned the hard way about taking on more than she should. Strong personal principles and an "eye on the prize" will help keep you balanced and free to make the next best move for you, whatever it is.

SUCCESS CARD 45: *Family Plan*

When we feel off-balance, often all we need to do is reconnect with our family. Not all families are the same. Yours could have only a few members or hundreds. Perhaps you count only immediate family members; others can include pseudofamily: a neighbor always called Grandpa, a babysitter who was more like an aunt, a best friend's parents always considered to be a second set, and so on. Ask yourself: Who composes your family? How often do you connect with them? What is the quality of your relationships? A truly dysfunctional relationship demands professional help. Most families are able to weather the storms together and stay healthy and strong throughout the years. Taking the time to reconnect and stay in touch can help you feel grounded and secure, two qualities that are especially important to someone looking to make a move at work or in life. What can you do to keep the lines of communication open with family members? What can you do to make your relationships even stronger?

"I learned about myself through my Dad's writings."

My dad was an amazing man. He came to America from Lithuania after losing his family in the Nazi death camps. He arrived in a strange country and didn't speak the language. He spent his life going from job to job, although his dream was always to be a teacher. He wasn't able to achieve that, but he really pushed me to go into teaching. During my college years, I took a class on genealogy, and it was the greatest class I ever took. I learned so much about my family's history and began to understand why my father was the way he was. I had insight now into the relationships he had with other relatives and why some were happy and some were strained. My dad finally earned his college degree at age 75 and, when he died at 79, he was just two credits short of earning his master's degree in history. My mom recently came across a box of his college papers and, yesterday, my family went through them together. Most of the papers were for a psychology class he took for which he had to write about topics such as his family and his parenting style. That was an eye-opening experience; to be able to hear in my father's own words how he viewed himself and his family. He wrote about my twin and me and I could see how differently he viewed the two of us. The things he said were very true. It probably had the most impact on my college-age son. John became very excited when he read through the papers—and he read every single one. He realized how much he and his grandfather were alike, beyond the fact that they both majored in history. He kept saying, "Grandpa and I think just alike!" It all came through in Dad's writing. John felt a real connection with him. He also said, "I'm not alone." It was a very emotional evening for all of us and I'm so thankful we have these writings from Dad. What a treasure.

Rosalie, arts marketing company president

Documenting your family's genealogy and stories is important to the generations who follow. As Rosalie and her son discovered, writings from her father offered insights into how they came to be the way they are today. Larry, a management consultant, asked his elderly father to document his experiences fighting in World War II. His father did so and also went on to write about his days working in his dad's small town grocery store in the 1930s. Larry cherishes both papers. He learned things about his father that were never discussed when his father was alive. Larry was also left with fascinating accounts of world history and Americana from someone who actually had experienced them.

Diaries, journals, and videos provide information and wisdom we can never get from photo albums. Written and filmed accounts can help later generations feel grounded and give them a focus and direction for the future. Why is it that so many adopted children and orphans search for parents and relatives? For most of them, undoubtedly, it stems from a need to feel connected and that they are part of a larger grand design. They search for answers, of course, but also want to feel as though they belong to a certain place and a time. Ask your older relatives to document their life stories and lessons learned. Be sure that you do the same. Family histories can bring balance to future generations.

Reunions are a fun way to reconnect with your existing relatives and are popular annual events for many families. Chris's family has gotten together in a little town in Michigan the third Sunday of August for more than 100 years. The numbers have dwindled in recent years, and the family name is now less common, but the reunions are still highly anticipated events. Some families plan less frequent get-togethers but make them more extravagant. Billie's family meets every two years and makes it a group vacation. One reunion was spent on a cruise; another took place at a dude ranch. Many resources are now available to help families plan reunions, including Web sites, software, and travel services.

Kathleen's Move   Because she was such a high achiever and busy traveler, it was easy for Kathleen to forget to connect with her parents, who she knew loved to hear from her. She knew because they always stayed on the phone a long time and asked lots of questions about her life and travels. They thought she was such a success; little did they know how lonely travel could be. On one such call, her mother asked if she could plan to be there for a family reunion the next summer. Slightly irritated, Kathleen chirped that she didn't know her travel schedule yet. However, as things turned out, she was able to go. In a bad mood at first, trying to relate to all the cousins and their broods of kids, she slowly began to relax as old stories of childhood erupted. When someone remembered her constant lemonade stands and the high prices she charged, she had a long hidden insight into her sales career choice. Of course! She had always liked the sale! Someone else reminded her of Scout cookie sales, and then her younger brother told her what a pushover she was for anything Barbie oriented. All the memories and good humor brought her back to her roots. When she left the reunion, she caught a flight to New York and then to Denmark. But she had changed her outlook. She was, for the first time in months, really relaxed.

If you're a parent, it's important to do everything you can to create balance in your own family life. It's difficult to do with so many demands on parents' time, energy, and finances. One government study states that roughly 37 percent of the total U.S. workforce is composed of parents with children under the age of eighteen. The typical middle income married couple with children works nearly six weeks more than their counterparts did ten years ago. Another study found that between 1969 and 1999, working couples lost an average of twenty-two hours a week of family and personal time. You're feeing more stressed and tired just from reading this, aren't you? And if you're a single parent, you're probably feeling even more so. All you need is to put a little more plan into your family plan.

Family balance is rarely achieved without some reflection, evaluation, and strategizing. Does your family take time to get together to talk? Parents' response to the challenge of spending quality time with their family is often to do an activity together. It is certainly valuable to read a book together or to go bowling or to a movie, but it is vital that families also get together to talk. Many families swear by family meetings; regular get-togethers at which siblings and parents catch up with each other, resolve conflicts, and discuss future plans. Consider calling your family together for a meeting and give it a try. Talk about the upcoming week or month and any problems that need to be smoothed out. Then talk about the meeting itself. How often would your family prefer to meet—weekly, daily, over a meal, at bedtime? Create a schedule and stick to it. If your family isn't used to talking together, it could take a while for it to feel comfortable. Stick with it.

Some families undertake an evaluation process similar to those done in corporations. These can be geared more toward children "grading" their parents: giving feedback regarding communication, availability, patience, support, favoritism, and so on. Don, a health care executive, and his wife found this evaluation process to be a wake-up call. Their kids told him he needed to play more games with them and take less work on vacation. They told their mother that she needed to be fairer when mediating arguments between them. This type of evaluation can be sobering for parents to hear but is a good way to improve family interaction and performance. Try this at one of your family meetings.

Also use your meeting time to bounce around ideas for bringing more balance into family life. Fun time can be scheduled into everyone's calendar, with specific dates and times for doing things together such as traveling, taking lessons as a family, or just watching videos together on the couch. It could mean that outside involvements need to be scaled back. Perhaps a reward system could be set up for doing chores or expressing kindness to each other. Brainstorm a little, and you'll be able to devise strategies that everyone can agree on.

SUCCESS
CARD 46: *Affirm Yourself*

Balance in life is not all about change, as in changing the ways you manage thoughts, say no, or deal with anxiety. Balance also encompasses other qualities you could already possess, which should be explored and celebrated. These particular traits and values can be the very things that bring you a sense of peace and joy. Affirm yourself by saying yes to:

- *Challenge:* Experiment with new ideas and experiences.
- *Personal growth:* Never, never stop learning.
- *Calculated risks:* Find the excitement in adventure .
- *Intuition:* Realize that "gut" feelings rarely lead you astray.
- *Quiet:* Rejuvenate your spirit with solitude.
- *Friends:* Cherish the people who know you best.
- *Hope:* Believe that dreams can become reality.

KEY PLAYER PROFILE: THOMAS M. BREMER

"I love my work. At a young age, I was fortunate enough to find a profession in which artistic skills can be expressed while helping improve another person's quality of life. People told me when I went into business for myself that I would be working long hours and under incredible stress and pressure. But my family and I have found it to be quite the opposite. Sure, we all have to work and produce, but there can be a lot of freedom if I surround myself with good people who are on their way up with their own goals and objectives. People like that step up to the various challenges, which frees me up to pursue other business goals. I never got a business degree and perhaps, because of that, I do business in a unique way. We don't punch a time clock here and I don't believe in employment contracts. So far, all of my key employees are long-term employees. We have an agreement that we will act like adults and take personal and professional responsibility for what we do. That's great for me because I don't have to micro-manage everyone. I also don't let myself get upset about things at the office. I try to make our office a pleasant one to work in—and both employees and clients respond to that.

"It can be a little scary to start your own business, but you can't allow yourself to be fearful. Fear is the great inhibitor. I took two big steps back before opening my current business. I sold my shares of my first medical practice and went back to school to fulfill requirements for residency and board certification. I did this so that I could eventually be sole owner of my own facility. I ended up doing my residency working for a competitor at a third of what I was making before, but that's what I needed to do to reach my goals. It was a win–win for both of us. Eventually, I was able to buy that practice outright. For twenty years, I thought I wanted to live in Northern Michigan and have been working toward that goal. But when the chance to buy my competitor's practice came up close to home, my gut instinct was to go for it. I listened to my intuition and I'm happy I did so. This has been a very good fit for me. The business has grown every year and I now have two facilities.

"I remember reading something in a book written by a CEO: 'I want to spend the first half of my life making money and the second half of my life giving it away.' That hit home with me. I thought that was what I'd like to be able to do with my life and my business. I realized I could set up my company so that the young people I employed could eventually take it over, and I could reach my goal of giving back to the community. And this year, it has all started to happen for me.

"I was invited by the organization Healing Hands for Haiti to travel to Haiti for a week to work in a medical clinic in Port-au-Prince. This was another case of listening to my intuition; I knew this would be a great experience. Not only could I fit people with good prosthetics, I would have the opportunity to teach others there how to do what I do. People in Haiti have lost limbs due mostly to infection. Much of the country is affected by broken sewer systems and inadequate medical care, so one small cut can easily turn into a raging infection, which can necessitate an amputation. I didn't know going in that I would have armed guards outside my door every night or razor wire around the fences, but I certainly saw the need to help the people there. Some came from the city; others traveled for hours in the back of pickup trucks and then would sit for several more hours waiting to be seen at the clinic. This experience totally changed my perspective. It gave me a worldview that I never got from TV. I couldn't come home the same person. I'm now their prosthetic coordinator and am training their students. Some of them are even traveling to the States and will live with my family while they learn the trade. What an opportunity this will be for my family and staff —a real-life lesson in cultural diversity.

"This experience has given me a new sense of direction and balance. I can't change the world, but I can change one thing at a time. I have the ability doing what I do to build bridges and give to others in need."

. . . *Thomas M. Bremer, president and owner of Bremer Prosthetic Design, Inc., is an American Board Certified Prosthetist, a member of the American Academy of Orthotists and Prosthetists, and director of an accredited residency program through the National Commission on Orthotics and Prosthetics Education. He lectures extensively on emerging technologies and health care trends and is an avid sculptor.*

Play the Game: It's Your Move

You've now been dealt the Balance Hand. You've learned strategies that can help you deal with life's challenges and embrace the future. Which cards will move you toward a more balanced life? Choose one now, and then write your choice in your game plan at the end of the book. When you've completed that move, return to the game plan to fill in the results.

Address Anxieties

Success Card 41

If you draw this card, you must do *two* of the following:

Go to bed tonight one hour earlier than usual.

Set aside thirty minutes tomorrow morning for reading, writing, or exercising.

On paper, design your perfect work schedule: total number of hours spent working each week, month, or year and work location (home, office or road).

The Balance Hand

Simplify Daily

Success Card 42

If you draw this card, you must do *one* of the following within the next seven days:

List the clutter areas at work or at home and the amount of time you estimate each area will require to get organized. Schedule time to deal with clutter area 1.

Select one "prime real estate" area and reorganize it.

For the next seven days, take every new piece of paper you receive and immediately place into to be filed, to be read, to be done, to be paid, or throw it away.

The Balance Hand

Breathe In and Out— Manage Thoughts

Success Card 43

If you draw this card, you must do *two* of the following:

From the list of breathing exercises, choose either #4 or #5 and practice three times every day for one week.

List your favorite forms of exercise and the ways you can incorporate more of them into your life.

Begin reading a classic piece of literature you've always wanted to read.

The Balance Hand

Say No

Success Card 44

If you draw this card, you must do *two* of the following:

Keep a tally of each time you speak tentatively this week.

Try surrounding a no response with two positive phrases.

Create a set of personal policies guidelines for how much you'll volunteer, donate or take on for the next twelve months.

The Balance Hand

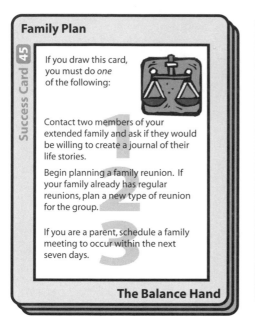

Family Plan

Success Card 45

If you draw this card, you must do *one* of the following:

Contact two members of your extended family and ask if they would be willing to create a journal of their life stories.

Begin planning a family reunion. If your family already has regular reunions, plan a new type of reunion for the group.

If you are a parent, schedule a family meeting to occur within the next seven days.

The Balance Hand

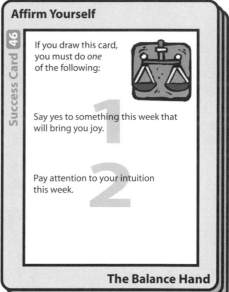

Affirm Yourself

Success Card 46

If you draw this card, you must do *one* of the following:

Say yes to something this week that will bring you joy.

Pay attention to your intuition this week.

The Balance Hand

CHAPTER 10

THE FLEXIBILITY HAND

SUCCESS
CARD **47**: *Accept Change*

"Rain, rain, go away. Come again another day. Little Johnny wants to play," the nursery rhyme invites. How do you prepare for the cloudy weather? Just when you least expect it, it arrives and changes how you want to play. After a fabulous start and great progress in the game, you roll the dice one more time, and you're asked to return home. Or you draw a card and you have to give away your best prizes, the ones that took you the longest to get. However, you know that if you still want to play, you have to be a good sport. This is the skill of the Flexibility Hand. Just when you think you know the rules, they change. People who play this hand well are able to accept change, let go, change habits, break old rules, and move forward to the future.

And the rains came. . . .

The wedding plans were set. Everything was in its place. The hotel was reserved, the flowers had been ordered, the last guests had RSVP'd, and the cake frosting finally selected. Then the rented tuxes arrived—surprisingly, in lime green.

They were the best next-door neighbors you could want. The women co-hosted birthday parties. The men grilled out. The boys played into dusk with sticks and bugs. Then Jay's corporate headquarters moved, and new neighbors moved in with a red-haired baby girl who couldn't play with sticks and bugs at all.

211

The team was thriving, largely because of Joe. Everyone loved him. He was a manager unlike any boss they'd had before. He was a truly genuine, caring kind of guy. Unexpected corporate battles were making national news, however; mid-level managers were getting outplaced right and left—and then the company outplaced Joe.

The kids were grown and settled in cozy apartments with nice start-up careers. She was in her early sixties and her hobby as a porcelain artist had grown into a nice little home-based business that allowed her and her semiretired husband to travel to interesting trade events. A yearly physical checkup seemed routine—and then there was the cancer diagnosis.

"The best laid schemes o'mice an' men, gang aft agley," wrote Robert Burns in 1786 in his poem "To a Mouse." Burns' inspiration occurred when he accidentally upturned a mouse's nest while plowing a field. The challenge of disruption and the force of change have fed the creative minds of great writers for centuries. When the reality of change hits you personally, it can be either inspiring or devastating.

Some of the changes you face are universal human conditions: birth, life, death, partnership, relocation, children growing up, progress. Other changes you face are tied to the times you live in: technology, the market, war or peace, the economy, or transportation. For example, job loss has been a devastating change for many people in recent history. In fact, in the first two years of the twenty-first century, more than two million jobs in the United States were lost. When you lose your job, you often lose your bearings because your job is the anchor that grounds your identity. Even being transferred to a different location can be a big adjustment.

"I accepted the commute."

Change is not a negative but a way to learn more. I'm a city person, but because of a change in jobs and a physical move of the office from the city to the suburbs, I've had to adapt to a totally different work environment. I was used to working in the city where people met for lunch or drinks after work; in the suburbs, people bring their lunch and their cars to work every day. It's a different social culture. Although I prefer the city, I really enjoy my flexible schedule; I have some noncommuting days when I work at my home office, and on the days when I do commute I've learned to enjoy the drive through the forest preserve where I often see deer and hawks. And I've learned about suburban issues like having to attract business to a bedroom community or expanding the tax base. Overall, I guess I am concentrating more on the content of the work rather than the environment, and my colleagues make up for the change in location. I have five people reporting to me—two managing editors and three assistants. Recently, I was out of the office for a month on disability and I had to be able to plan in advance, delegate, and rely on their good will. We have fun; for example, I have a reputation that when people work for me, they have babies and they go out on maternity leave—so when I said I would have to have surgery and I would be out a month, they found this great 'get well' card showing a woman with a baby that read, "Whatever you have, thank goodness it isn't this." My colleagues make the difference. You're not going to get too far without being flexible. The world will always be full of change and if you can't flex with the change, you'll be unhappy and unproductive.

Deb, director of publications for an international association

Deb did a great job of appreciating small moments throughout a sizable change in the daily structure of her life. When the company asks you to commute farther or work with new people, let the small things bring you happiness. The small things will begin to add up.

Linda's Move   At year-end of Linda's first year in business, she looked at her gross revenues and wondered if it was worth it all. She was now paying herself less than she made in her first job after college. She no longer wore the designer suits, and she leased a car. She sighed and answered the home phone line to hear her preteen tell her that the girls' basketball team really needed another driver at 4:00 P.M. on Tuesday for the game. She glanced at her calendar and noted that not only could she help, but she could also watch the

4:30 P.M. game—two activities that would have been impossible when she was a full-time corporate employee. As she added the basketball note to Tuesday, the phone rang again; it was Scott Winfield, her client, Joe's assistant. Scott said Joe was planning next year's budget and wanted to get a proposal from her for continuing the fine work she was doing with the recruitment. Her first repeat business! Feeling more upbeat, Linda booted up her computer, found the proposals file, and went to work. This proposal would come together more quickly because she had a base of information on Joe's needs. She might even have time to get a chicken in the oven before 5:30. A home-based business surely had its ups and downs, but she hadn't felt so productive and meaningful in years.

Both Deb and Linda learned to find happiness in specific aspects of change. For Deb, it was her colleagues and even her commute through the woods. For Linda, it was a chance to be both a mom and a professional who earned a repeat customer. Earlier you read about your joy sensor. Remember it now and be mindful of what brings you joy during change. Change in life is inevitable. You might as well accept it and find happiness where you can.

SUCCESS CARD 48: *Let Go*

Living an active life means living through setbacks and failures. Try asking anyone you know, What's the last thing you did that was perfect? See what kind of response you get. Most people will not be able to come up with much. Getting through imperfect, difficult days, weeks, and months is a challenge for anyone, and people who get through most successfully are able to engage in some form of letting go. Some people exercise; some write poetry or call old friends. Others talk to themselves.

> **"I have this mantra."**
>
> You know how you say little things to yourself all the time to spur yourself on—like Hurry up, don't be late or Lose those pounds, lose those pounds? It's as if you have a mantra or a self-talk script of some sort. Well, in times of stress, my self-talk has always been, Put

it in perspective, Lou, just put it in perspective. I know this sounds a bit academic, but that's what helps me adjust my attitude. I think I read it in an article somewhere a long time ago, and it just stuck. It's taken me a while to really use this well. I mean it's one thing to say something positive and it's another thing to really put it into action. Like when traffic is bad—that's when I usually practice my mantra. The more severe the situation, the harder it gets to make the mantra work; for example, if I'm really angry with somebody or when I lose a major account at work. But if I can just repeat it and believe it, I can always adjust my attitude.

Lou, industrial sales rep for a large manufacturing corporation

With a little effort, you can put bad traffic in perspective. With a little more effort, you can put an argument with a colleague or the loss of a major account in its place. To be flexible is to let go. Like Lou, you could adopt a mental mantra, a simple mental incantation to adjust your attitude. Some people say, "This too shall pass." Others use, "Don't worry. Be happy." Maybe your mantra is just "Chill," or "Take it easy." Nobody else will do this for you. The mental commitment is yours. Buddha once wrote, "We are what we think. All that we are arises with our thoughts. With our thoughts, we make the world." Your thoughts are yours to master.

"I let go to let come."

What you really have to do is be still; you have to do nothing. I was a clergyman and found that what I had once loved to do, I didn't love to do any more. I rented an oceanside cabin just because I didn't know what else to do and, in reflecting back, I realized that many things came to me then. Now I know that the answers are there waiting for you if you just let go—really, really do nothing. The point is that it's only when you let go that things will reveal themselves. For me, it wasn't as if all of a sudden I had this great insight. Things sorted themselves out. I remember what's important to me and what my basic values and principles are. One of the things I realized was that I liked the values that I had in my life; I just didn't like the structure in which I was working. I left the ministry and came to California to be retrained as a family therapist. I came up with the concept of *Stopping*—which is doing nothing in order to wake up and remember who you are. If you want to practice Stopping, use *Still points*—brief moments of doing nothing in between the events of your day. First, cease what you're doing. Second, take a couple of deep breaths. Third, turn your energy and your focus inward. That's it! Many of my patients say that practicing Stopping has changed their lives. They tell me, "If I don't practice Stopping, I lose my way." I think you have to learn to let go to let come. Stopping is *Doing Nothing* as much as possible. It is only during this time of quiet stillness that you truly rest, that your own wisdom becomes accessible and creativity finds fertile ground.

**David, family therapist
and author of *Stopping:
How to Be Still When You Have
to Keep Going***

You could be holding on to bad relationships. You could be holding a grudge needlessly that's affecting your morale. Is there someone or something that you just don't want to be tied down to any longer? Speaker and psychologist Beverly Smallwood, Ph.D., often ties an audience member to her with a rope around each of their waists when she speaks about change. The visual of two people tied with rope really demonstrates how you can carry around dead weight—all those past issues never addressed and those past relationships never healed. What should you do when change that you don't like, don't want, and don't need surrounds you? Let it go. When you get a parking ticket, the best thing to do is to pay and mail it. Let it go.

Anthony's Move The inevitable happened. At least he was prepared this time. When the manager called him into the office, he recognized the look. It was the look of an uncomfortable human being: the mouth grim, the eyes avoiding direct contact. Anthony sat down, looked at the uncomfortable man across from him, and heard him say that he would be asked to "re-interview" for his internal consulting position. "Major changes above" were creating new jobs, and this specific internal consultant position was being reengineered. The meeting was brief, and Anthony re-interviewed the following week. He did not get the new job. It was a blow to his ego, but now it was over. One thing he had learned about job loss was that the sooner you let it go, the better. That night he began. He let go of his love of consulting and sales. He let go of the teams of people he was just getting to know better. As he let go, he felt lighter with each past memory that was released. By the time he went to bed, he was still sad, but his damaged ego had begun to heal.

SUCCESS
CARD 49: *Communicate*

Women in pioneer America got together for quilting bees. Farm life was often hard, and quilting helped connect them. They gathered around a large wooden frame and all worked on a single quilt. They often quilted outdoors when daylight was plentiful during the long summer days. You can imagine that they laughed about their children or worried about their families' crops as they quilted, sitting on a variety of mismatched farm chairs. This was their network—their bridge to each other. A quilting bee was their telephone—their communication connection.

Today, especially in times of change, it's important to communicate with other people as much as you can. Arrange your own form of a quilting bee, even if it's just coffee or drinks at the local pub. Like the traditional bees, it could also be a hobby-based gathering. Scrapbooking is one popular way for women to get together to talk and create, often with their children. Men and women can also connect during a sport, such as golf or a softball league. Take time to reunite with people you haven't seen in a while, such as high school friends. When you compare your feelings with others in your own age range, you'll typically find some common ground that will help you feel more at ease. Retreats are popular for many reasons; the main one is that they inspire relaxed communication. You can plan your own retreat by asking friends to contribute to room rental and food at a local low-cost hotel.

Kathleen's Move   When her company announced a merger with another large pharmaceutical firm, Kathleen was thrilled; she loved change and all that it brought: new adventures, untried waters, and new travels. Not everyone felt the same way. The other sales reps were talking after work, wondering what product they would be selling next week or even if they would keep their jobs. Kathleen could tell that people were under stress. In the old days, she would have laughed it off, glad that she felt differently, but now that she was more in tune with others, she had a wild thought. Why not recreate the family reunion she had so enjoyed with her own family? Why not treat her co-workers to a similar experience and call it a company reunion? It was important to have it soon. It could be a picnic. She could even arrange tennis matches at the local park district courts. It would give people a chance to get together, have fun, and vent a bit, too. She decided to approach her manager about the idea tomorrow.

If your organization is in the midst of a change, merger, or acquisition, it's important to talk about it. Ask your team leader or your manager to help you understand what is happening. Volunteer to organize a meeting. If you manage others, you should tell your team members that you appreciate them. Try to provide incentives and opportunities to keep people motivated and interested and don't forget to provide forums for people to talk. People don't like to guess about why things are happening. Negativity can fester if it's not given a way to vent.

"I prepared others for the impending change."

A number of years ago, I was hired as an account executive at an ad agency specifically to join a new team that was being formed. And two months later, the team leader suddenly resigned to join another company and left all of us out in the cold. It was obvious that this had probably been in the works for awhile, but he never gave us any indication. I always remembered how that felt and vowed I would never do that to someone else. Jump forward a few years and I'm working at another agency. I knew within six months that it was a dead-end job. I had a disagreement with management and felt I wanted to go elsewhere. But I had hired someone to work with me, someone I respected. She came to the agency expressly because of me. I hated the idea of leaving someone who was depending on me. So I filled her in on my plans, off the record. I told her that I was interviewing and wanted to give her a heads-up. I didn't want her to be surprised by anything, as I had been before. She resigned the day after I did. I think it's important to prepare people for change.

When you're honest with people, especially about difficult news, they respect you for it and believe you'll always do the best thing for them.

Melanie, senior partner, advertising agency

If you're new on the scene, it's important to take the initiative to establish important communication links. Do it as soon as possible. In the first chapter, you met Gary, who moved his family to the South to build a career in financial services. Even before his family joined him, Gary knew that gaining the trust of the other employees in the organization would be important. He got to know them, learned their culture, and communicated a lot. One day, one of the key players said to a major client, "You've known me for 30 years; now let me tell you you've got to see Gary; he's got some good ideas." Gary learned that he had to communicate to the internal team first.

Like Gary, Melanie, and Kathleen, you will find that a move to communicate is a move to connect. People today are too busy, for the most part, and communication is often poor because of assumptions. People assume that they are understood. They don't take the time to check. Don't be afraid to ask questions and, if you're in a communication disconnect, take the initiative to say something to correct it. One moment to clarify will waylay hours of guess work and frustration.

SUCCESS
CARD 50: *Change Habits*

When you want to change a habit, how long do you think it will take? Chances are that it will take much longer than you want. Most skills and behaviors take months and years to change. If you've ever hit a backhand in tennis or changed a diaper, you know how experienced you get with practice. If you've ever managed people or chaired a project, you know how much better you are the second time around. So the first key to changing habits is the honest awareness that it will take time. Research actually suggests that it takes from three to six months to change an old habit.

The next key is to have realistic expectations. Dieters are told that if they fall off for one meal, it's important not to just give up and eat chocolate chip cookies all day. They should get back on track the next day or even the next meal. No matter what change you're undergoing, allow yourself some imperfection. You will probably fail in some aspects, especially at first. In fact, studies of people who are successful at long-term change suggest that they just don't let themselves fall into the "all-or-nothing" trap. They monitor their behavior. They create incentives for themselves to stick to their goals. They also see difficulties as little detours rather than major washouts.

Another key to changing habits successfully is to redouble your effort. Try harder. People who succeed do what others don't do. Don't judge yourself too quickly. Self-evaluation is good, but give yourself a chance. You need to ask yourself, Was that attempt sincere or was it just a half-hearted one? Am I really committed to this? Maybe I need another plan. Maybe I need help. The good news is that most people who fail the first time try again. Only 15 percent give up totally.

"I looked at me and I dealt with me."

You know how it is when people speak truth to you and you know it's the truth but you avoid it? At the age of seventeen, I was going into the Marine Corps because I was a tough, bad kid and I thought it would be good for me. But my parents were influential in health care and government; my father was a doctor. So rather than let me enlist, they got me into an apprentice construction engineer program. They thought that the money I could make as an engineer would straighten me out. Engineering became my life for twenty-six years. I became a director and big boss, had lunches, dinners, cocktail parties, kickbacks, trips, and huge contracts. And there was lots of drinking and drugs. Everybody liked the connections I had and the money that I had. I was a drug addict for 33 years.

What finally changed me was fourteen years of recovery programs—all of the talk and all of the treatment places paid off. People in those programs would tell me to go into sales and get out of engineering. So I did and things were going well. Then I had a traumatic accident in which I broke my arms, legs, and hands; first they told me I might lose my leg, then that I would not walk again; I was in a walker for two-and-a-half years with pins and rods through my leg.

These were bad times and nobody would take me in. I panhandled on the streets as a tour guide. I'd watch people who looked like tourists pull out maps and I'd approach them; I remembered the telephone numbers to the clubs and the restaurants that I used to go to and I used my old connections to get those tourists into clubs. Sometimes they'd ask me if I was homeless and they'd help me. I'd lost 40 pounds and had a beard but I was tan because I'd fall asleep on the beach. In the morning in those days, I'd look at myself in a gas station mirror and say to myself, You look good, man. You look tan. I would get high. I was lying in a park by America's most famous treatment center. A guy gave me a sandwich and a pop and said, "Call this number." It was the number of the treatment center. I didn't throw it away; I called and he remembered me. I went on a waiting list and he told me to remain drug and alcohol free and if I did they'd test me and I'd get in to the program. And they let me in. Afterwards, I went to a halfway house for men and became manager of the house. When I left, I got a job as a manager at a candy factory but got in a car accident and went back to the halfway house with a walker again and casts everywhere. Finally the owner of the house asked me to leave because I was a liability. I had no money, no medical insurance.

Nobody was chomping at the bit to take me. I had cried wolf too many times. I humbled myself and called my mother and finally moved to Florida and lived with her. I improved physically and got a job at a hotel as a chief engineer. They took a chance on me even with the cast and the cane. I made money but then I relapsed again; I went into treatment and there I met a doctor and she helped me. She asked me to write a page about who I was—who was Michael? I couldn't do it. If you've got to look at you, you've got to deal with you. And I finally did. I always wanted to work with horses; I'd loved them all my life. Nobody in my family had anything to do with horses. Now I manage a ranch. It's a dirty job. I love it.

Change is when your mind, your soul, and your heart all think as one. That's complete change.

Michael, horse ranch manager and horse owner and lover

Michael's incredible story ended in love . . . and horses. He never gave up on himself. He knew that he was better than the face he saw in the mirror. Everyone stumbles, and if you accept your stumble as just a setback in a natural process of getting ahead, you will never give up on yourself. What can you do to move on? One thing is to get specific. Specifics really help. It's the difference between saying, I wish I had a bigger income, to I'm going to get online tonight and research what I need to do to advance my skills. It's the difference between complaining, I wish I could talk; to my teen, to committing, I'm going to take a teen parenting class. Researchers once thought that people should address only one change of habit at a time; today there's strong evidence to suggest that it's possible to tackle multiple habits, provided that they're related. So you could take a teen parenting class as well as work on cooking simple meals at home. They both relate to improving your habits with your family, and together they support your core values.

Juana's Move Juana decided to work on her confidence as an English speaker. It had been such a habit over the years to tell herself that she was bad at it; she wasn't sure that she could ever believe she was good. But her pronunciation classes were paying off. One morning, when a new group of garden maintenance workers arrived, she spoke to them in English first, without even thinking. She was jolted by the surprised look on the workers' faces. She realized that they expected her to give them instructions in Spanish. This incident led Juana to believe that she was truly on the road to confidence as a bilingual speaker. Just for fun, she spoke only English the entire day, even though she didn't have to. Interviews for the service supervisor position were being held this week, and to buoy her confidence, Juana came up with her

222

own self-talk: I am good. I speak well. I am good. I speak well. She signed her name on the interview sign-up sheet. She knew that now she had a strong chance for the position.

Aristotle is noted for saying, "We are what we repeatedly do. Excellence, then, is not an act, but a habit." Why not make it yours?

SUCCESS
CARD 51: *Break Rules*

Children have a special perspective about breaking the rules as this story illustrates. A mother and her six-year-old daughter were in the kitchen. She was doing dishes while the child was eating a peanut butter sandwich at the kitchen table.

"Mom," she said, "you know how when you have an *emergency* and you do something you're not supposed to do?"

"Yes . . . ," the mom answered cautiously, knowing her daughter's past antics and wondering what she had conspired this time.

Her daughter continued brightly, "Like just now I had peanut butter stuck on the roof of my mouth and I had to gulp my milk."

The mother, trying hard not to laugh, solemnly said, "Honey, that's OK; you did what you had to do."

Perhaps you, too, have felt that you're stuck with peanut butter on the roof of your mouth. You gulp your milk, but you have an awkward sensation that something is just not right. It's just not supposed to be that way. It could be that you're in a crisis situation, or it could be a sense of misalignment: What you value most just isn't in the right position in your life. The top five global values, according to a 2002 Roper Reports Worldwide survey, are first, protecting the family, then honesty, health and fitness, self-esteem, and knowledge. In 1990, 70 percent of U.S. consumers considered being an executive the number one status symbol. Ten years later, only 68 percent agreed, replacing that status with having a second home. If you're like most, you're looking for ways to get out of the rat race. You want to protect what you value most, and you don't mind breaking the old rules that your parents followed if it means more happiness for you.

William's Move   As he commuted back and forth to work each day, William realized he had a nagging thought that kept popping into his head. That inner voice was telling him, "I'm not sure how happy I am at this job." William tried to ignore it for a while. After all, he had a great job with a very promising future. He had lived up to all the expectations of his traditional Asian parents, graduating from a top school with excellent grades and getting an impressive start in a good career. But corporate life was not quite what he had expected. Office politics played too much of a part in this company, and he was not interested in playing. When Friday came, William invited two of his closest friends from the office to go out for "attitude adjustment hour." As always, the conversation first centered on work. And, much to his surprise, William heard himself voice his dissatisfaction to his friends. They commiserated with him for a while and revealed that they felt the same level of frustration. One of them said, "You know what? We should just start our own business." They laughed at first but then started to bounce around a few ideas. William made a comment about the number of homeless people in the city and wouldn't it be great if they had access to the Internet and email. Their new business idea began to unfold: They would create a nonprofit organization that focused on bringing free Web access and email capability to the homeless population. As he drove home, William got very excited thinking about this possible career move. He knew he would have to wait for the perfect time to break the news to his parents. He wouldn't say anything to them until everything was worked out in detail.

It's not easy to break the rules. It's just not the way people are raised. In a game, rules make everything work. They keep people on track. If you break a rule, supposedly, you are punished and you have to go back home. Sometimes, however, risk taking means breaking old patterns of behavior and defining new expectations. Maybe you need to build a new game.

"I learned to take new directions."

There are two ways that my life has led me to trust new direction—one professionally and one personally.

Our business has a fairly regimented career path set up in operations. I began my career as an assistant manager of a restaurant;

I was promoted twice and the next traditional step would have been to be a district manager. But I took a side trip as a trainer for about two and a half years and then went back into operations feeling more confident because of my experience training others. I made several moves in and out of training and management. Because of my operational services background, for a while I was a manager of assessment services at the corporate offices where I gained experience working with consultants and executives. It was a broadening experience. We were growing quickly and so if you were doing a good job, you got approached. But I'm glad I said yes so often. In our industry, people often aren't willing to relocate to take a new management position. But, I tell them that every city has a suburb that pretty much looks like the one they live in now, especially if you're a middle manager. I find that many people are fearful because they've never been anywhere else. What I try to do is encourage them to go out and explore: Take trips within a day's drive from home. See what else is out there. When people say "I can't leave. My whole family lives here," I say, "Well, there are airplanes!" Another trap for people is that they get comfortable. They think that if they go to another office, perhaps they won't like their co-workers. I would encourage people to take ownership and responsibility for building their careers. I've moved five or six times, and everywhere I go, I expand my life experience. Stepping out of the traditional path can lead to better opportunities.

The other new direction came after I lost my teenage son in an auto accident. I was fortunate to have people around me at work who were comfortable with me and were able to talk with me about it. But many wouldn't. There were people who wouldn't call. I learned that I needed to talk about the person I lost. I wanted to; people shouldn't be afraid to reach out. After that experience, I put a different perspective on what was important. The things that I used to sweat about I don't worry about now; what I found was that, surprisingly, it has lowered my stress level. Also, I'm not as risk averse. I am more willing to speak up and to be frank. I am finding that people are looking for someone to tell them the truth. They don't find that everywhere.

> I guess what I've learned in life is not to look at change as good or bad but rather to ask myself whether I'm doing the right thing for me.
>
> **Chris, regional training director for a large quick-service company**

How you deal with change in your life is up to you. You can make your own rules. Take your own path. Learn over time what you value most and live your values. Beth Copeland Varga writes a heart-tugging ode to the passage of time in her essay, "Mothers' Wishes come True Too Soon." She is inspired to write as she watches a neighbor's little girl playing in the backyard next door: "A sunburst of tousled blond curls, short chubby legs, a round rosy face," as her tired-looking young mother follows her around the yard. Beth is transported back in time to when her own fifteen-year-old daughter was a toddler: "The sticky lollipop feel of her hand as we crossed the street together, the weight of her head on my shoulder as I read to her at bedtime." Later, she pauses at her teen's doorway: "A typical teenager's room: an empty 7-Up can on the desk, stuffed animals, rumpled sheets, balled-up socks on the floor, CDs scattered like dominoes across her carpet, a wet towel in the corner. . . ." She shares, "We're passing through the fire of adolescence, the years of slammed doors and driver's ed, of hormones, MTV and curfews. The children who once clung to me and vied for my attention now talk on the phone behind closed doors and roll their eyes skyward when I offer suggestions about clothing or hairstyles. . . ." As more memories come, she realizes how important it is to cherish the moments with your children. She closes the essay: "The wishes of sleep deprived mothers come true. Little girls grow up and move away. And their mothers stay home, missing them. Wishing for one more dandelion bouquet."

If your heart and mind tell you that you need to take some time heading in a new direction, as William and Chris did, or appreciating your small children, as Beth did, do it. Take a time out. Take a detour on the game board. Wait one turn. Skip two spaces instead of one. Break the old rules of the game.

SUCCESS
CARD **52**: *Move Forward*

The last play in the Flexibility Hand is to move forward. Nothing happens without action. Great ideas and attitudes are only the beginning. You need to put them into play. Watch, listen, and learn what's going on around you so you can make a winning move.

"I was laid off but I moved on."

I had been in the telecommunications industry since 1980, working for a company that had seen several transformations as the telephone industry grew, broke apart, and rebuilt itself. In the mid-90s, my company was Wall Street's darling, but by the end of '99, the company started to spiral downward. In December of that year, right before Christmas, I was let go. Officially, I was "relieved of immediate duties" and was given sixty days to find another job within the company. I never had any plans to switch careers, and if I did leave, I was sure it would be of my own volition. But now that decision was made for me. I spent those sixty days calling everyone I knew within the company, but there just weren't enough jobs to go around. On my last day of work, I packed up my office and left. It was devastating. I never had the need to market myself before; my job transitions had all

been pretty seamless as the companies I worked for recreated themselves. But now it was different. Many of the people who were outplaced set about reinventing themselves, but I wasn't ready to leave telecommunications yet. I took advantage of the outplacement services offered me and took workshops on interviewing and resume writing. I worked my network but had no luck. The telecommunications job pool was just too saturated on the East Coast.

I traveled to Seattle to visit my son at school. I stayed with an old friend who was a real estate broker. As I learned more about his work, I started thinking—was this something I could do? When I returned home, I talked with lots of real estate companies and related businesses, did Internet research, and then took a short training course. I was feeling good about myself again and started to feel encouraged in my job search. As I continued to look for work, I started to also consider the retail industry. I thought it could be fun; it would certainly be different than anything I had ever done before. I interviewed for a home products store opening up close to me, and wouldn't you know, I got two job offers in one day—one with a real estate company and one with the store! I decided to work in retail. Even though the other job would mean more money in the long run, I could make money faster in retail. So now I'm a department manager at the store.

My wife and I have always wanted to move back west, and we've decided to do that now. She's in pharmaceutical sales and we both see this move as an opportunity for a fresh start for both of us. We know we'll be able to find work when we get out there. In fact, I think I'm probably more marketable now than I ever have been before. My confidence has certainly improved, probably because of all the interviewing, retraining, and communication skills practice I get everyday with my store customers. If I hadn't been laid off, I'd still be working at the telecommunications company. There were times at my old job when I questioned my happiness. If I had ever really asked myself if I was happy, I wouldn't have liked my answer. I think I'm better off now having gone through what I've gone through. I'm not bitter about the past or scared about the future. I've found satisfaction doing something different with my life.

Tim, department manager of a home products store

Sometimes the best moves forward are made after careful looks backward. Tim not only discovered a new career, but also he and his wife took the opportunity to relocate to an area they loved. They were excited by the fresh start. Moves offer a chance for greater happiness and adventure, often when you least expect it.

KEY PLAYER PROFILE: GAIL WARD

"I used to drive by the empty lot and the sign said 'Future Site of Region 2 High School.' I would think to myself, Wow, that will be the most amazing school . . . what a perfect urban environment. I really had no intention of leaving the elementary school where I was principal; I just had a new contract and I was very happy. However, I was aware that my name had begun to be tossed around as a possible principal for another high school in the city. Still, I wasn't interested in moving. Months went by, and later, during a meeting with the superintendent I said, 'The school that's going to be interesting is the one that you're building.' We talked about the Region 2 High School, which was now named Walter Payton College Prep. A month later, I received the call to interview for the very school that I had watched being built. I realized that this was my dream school. People dream of opening schools and my dream came true. What an adventure!

"I am absolutely a flexible person. A principal's day is a day of decisions—you're continually moving from one decision to another—from the very minor to the very major ones. So much change can happen in one day when you're consistently responding to students, parents, teachers, and constituents. The variety challenges you and forces you to prioritize constantly. It's not that different from what parents do every day—managing changes in their kids' schedules, car pools, and social arrangements—except that it's compounded by the number of children, parents, teachers, and administrators with whom you must deal.

"When you're forced to do multi-tasking, you're going to make mistakes. I don't look back; I keep moving forward. I happen to think that mistakes are good. From the errors I make, I develop a toolbox of things that have worked well and a list of things that have not. The good news is my toolbox is very large! In my job, when something happens that I don't expect, I try to move forward to an end goal, and I understand that I will learn along the way.

"Change entails risk. When you travel in the unknown, there are opportunities to craft something new that would make a difference for students in the future. Utilizing a $30 million building entails risks; the potential rewards available to the students demand that a principal take meaningful risks.

"The school has now been open nearly three years. This year we had over 6,000 applications for less than 200 openings. It's one of the highest performing schools in the city and we still do not have a senior class. Why is the school so popular? Our priorities are first to have a happy student, second to nurture a hard working student, and third, to promote an involved student. The student's happiness and well-being come first."

. . . Gail Ward, principal of Walter Payton College Prep, has been an educator for thirty years in one of the largest U.S. urban school districts and a principal for nearly ten of those years. Gail heads up the team at this thoughtful, academically distinctive college prep school that nurtures leaders.

Being able to learn from mistakes and move forward is a lesson repeated in many of the hands in the game. People who have the biggest toolboxes have the most wisdom when it comes to fixing things. Toolboxes equip you to meet the demands of life and work today. They also help you prepare for the future.

"I've always loved the future."

I first became interested in the future when I was in high school. Even then I realized that if I could stack the deck in my favor by knowing what was coming, I could make better decisions. In college, I joined the World Future Society; I subscribed to the *Futurist* magazine and found it fascinating. I was like a sponge and I wanted to learn about as many things as possible. Knowledge is power. The more knowledge you have, the better decisions you can make. At the age of 28, I published a national magazine, *The Complete Buyers' Guide to Stereo Hi Fi Equipment;* I was the youngest magazine publisher in the country at the time. I learned that my clients were most likely to buy advertising with me if I had information that was meaningful to them. I became one of the most successful women in the consumer electronics field by gathering information and sharing it. I would connect the dots—I would put together seemingly unrelated things and come to quite accurate conclusions.

Now I see that people are having difficulty coping with the speed of change. Change and the increasing speed of that change are throwing people off balance; and just when they get their balance back, something comes by so fast that it throws them off balance again. There are so many wild cards today that throw people off balance—manmade wildcards such as the oil market, corporate events, terrorism and natural disasters like hurricanes, severe winter storms, and volcanic eruptions. I always give my audiences and readers of our *Herman Trend Alert* electronic newsletter the following advice: Learn all you can about your field and all of the fields that are related to yours. Learn so much that you become valuable just because you know what you know about your field. That kind of networking and intelligence gathering makes you hard to replace.

Joyce, strategic futurist who helps individuals and organizations position for future success and profitability

All solutions lie in the future. You can study the past and experience the present, but you're always looking forward to get better. Who would have ever thought that google—"to google someone"—would become a verb that would be trademarked? Who would have guessed that authors would write and editors would edit books on a computer screen without ever seeing each other? Who would know that our average life span would keep rising every year? You never know when or where your next opportunity could lie.

Harry's Move   As he walked to the dining hall one evening, Harry had a realization: He was truly happy here at the retirement community. He had made some good friends and was enjoying seeing more of his grandchildren. His retirement, followed with his wife's passing, had prompted him to reevaluate his life, and he was pleased with the new avenues he was exploring. His association with Sean, his former student, was turning into a business venture as well. After the experience of working with Sean's choruses, the two men began discussing ways to continue partnering in the future. Harry had the experience; Sean had the youthful perspective. Harry agreed to continue working with Sean's choruses and to mentor Sean on his teaching and conducting skills. Sean volunteered to help Harry create new versions of his older choral arrangements and help him design a Web site. The idea of writing articles to-

231

gether as a team, ones that could be offered to publications or on the Web site, energized them both. They decided they would next explore the idea of writing a series of textbooks and selling them over the Internet.

Play the Game: It's Your Move

To be flexible in life is to be free from bindings and hard-and-fast rules. Rules exist to guide you, not to stifle you. Plans change. Lime green tuxes can actually look nice with yellow boutonnières. New neighbors bring new stories and fun to the block. New managers who are even more motivating than the old join the company. Unexpected diagnoses put life's real treasures into perspective. Your Flexibility Hand, played well, will allow you to play all of these situations and move forward. Now it's your turn to play.

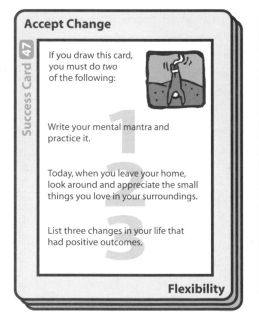

Accept Change

Success Card **47**

If you draw this card, you must do *two* of the following:

1 Write your mental mantra and practice it.

2 Today, when you leave your home, look around and appreciate the small things you love in your surroundings.

3 List three changes in your life that had positive outcomes.

Flexibility

Let Go

Success Card **48**

If you draw this card, you must do *one* of the following within the next seven days:

1 Phone someone and apologize or clear up a misunderstanding.

2 In your bath or shower, let go of your worries.

3 Look through an old scrapbook to let go of any sadness you feel.

Flexibility

Communicate

Success Card 49

If you draw this card, you must do *two* of the following:

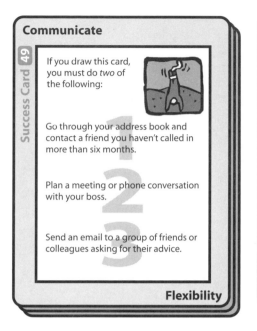

1 Go through your address book and contact a friend you haven't called in more than six months.

2 Plan a meeting or phone conversation with your boss.

3 Send an email to a group of friends or colleagues asking for their advice.

Flexibility

Change Habits

Success Card 50

If you draw this card, you must do *one* of the following:

1 List three of your habits that you love and engage in them more often.

2 Select a habit you've tried to change in the past but failed, and try again, starting today.

Flexibility

Break Rules

Success Card 51

If you draw this card, you must do *one* of the following:

1 Take a time out even though your to-do list is full.

2 Do one thing you've never done before.

3 Do something that makes you feel a little bit naughty.

Flexibility

Move Forward

Success Card 52

If you draw this card, you must do *all* of the following:

1 Go online and read about the future.

2 Take action on an idea you've been tossing around for months.

3 Get advice from someone to propel yourself forward.

Flexibility

233

CONCLUSION:

END GAME? NEVER!

Play to Win

You are approaching the end of this book, but it's just the beginning for you. You've already played several cards for each chapter, and you've taken the first steps toward your next—and best—move. What have you accomplished already? Perhaps you've written your short- and long-term goals, identified an event to attend this week, and written a letter to the editor. Perhaps you've organized your clothing, become more observant of others' body language, and created a set of personal policies to safeguard your precious time and energy.

The beauty of this game is that you are in control. Each card has several different action steps from which to choose, and you can select the steps that are right for you at this moment in time. The important thing is to keep choosing. The more you play, the easier your move will be to make. You can't help but win!

Wise Moves

Every time you choose a card, your wisdom grows. Wisdom comes from experience, and the cards invite you to expand your insight, practice new skills, and increase your knowledge. Age doesn't matter in this game. Wisdom is within everyone's reach. Choose a card, select an action step, and move toward your goal with increased wisdom.

Courageous Moves

The mere thought of making a move can be scary. You already have plenty of challenges in your life; why add another one? Making a move is important because you're tired of being stuck or lost or burned out. Don't let fear of the unknown overtake you. It takes courage to take a risk. Keep playing the game and choosing cards. They'll ask you to try new things, think in a new way,

235

and, occasionally, take a step outside your comfort zone. It's okay to be a little scared. Courage is all about being afraid and doing it anyway.

Strategic Moves

Think back to the last time you played a board game. Did you focus only on your game piece? No, you kept an eye on the entire board and all the other game pieces, too. The same is true in this game. Look past yourself and see the big board beyond you. As you prepare to make your move, consider the other players and study their moves. Plan your strategy, but realize you'll need to be flexible along the way. You could even find you'll be able to jump ahead a few spaces.

Well-Timed Moves

Is there ever a perfect time to do anything? Probably not. Many people get trapped thinking they have to wait for just the right moment to ask for a raise, quit their jobs, buy a house, or have a child. And that moment never presents itself. If you stay informed and keep an eye on trends and current events, however, you'll become good at predicting the best moves to make. Sometimes, a move requires a "leap of faith." You have to believe that you've prepared yourself for this moment—and just jump! The cards in this game will help keep your engine tuned and your skills sharp so that you can make your next move when the time is right for *you*.

Play On!

This is a game that can be played over and over again. Each time you play a card, you're going to learn something new about yourself or the world around you. The action steps will keep you energized and actively involved in making smart moves. Each time you need to make a move or want to be prepared to make the right move, play the cards.

Make it your goal to play every card within one year's time. Keep shuffling the deck and mix up the hands, and then choose several cards each week. Select your action steps and make the time to complete them. These steps and the results you achieve will lay the foundation for success. It's Your Move: Play On!

The Game Plan

What follows is a complete list of all cards included at the end of each chapter. Place a check in the box next to each action step as you undertake it. Then record the results you achieved in the space following each step.

Card 1: Step Back and Take Stock

If you draw this card, you must do *one* of the following:

☐ Schedule two hours of uninterrupted time into your calendar this week for some think time. Required: Get out of your office or home.

My results: _____

☐ Spend one evening connecting with immediate and extended family members. Talk with them about the qualities that define your family.

My results: _____

Card 2: Dream Again and Define Values

If you draw this card, you must do *both* of the following:

☐ Spend an evening looking through scrapbooks and photo albums from your youth.

My results: _____

☐ Ask three good friends to identify what, in their opinion, you seem to value. Compare their responses, add your own, and select the top three.

My results: _____

Card 3: Write Your Goals and Plan in Pieces

If you draw this card, you must do *one* of the following:

☐ Write three long-term goals and three short-term goals for yourself.

My results: _____

☐ List three action items you could accomplish for one of your goals. Do one of them tomorrow.

My results: _____

Card 4: Know Their Goals and Define Yourself

If you draw this card, you must do *one* of the following:

☐ Become familiar with your organization's mission statement this week. Discuss it with two other people at work.

My results: _____

☐ Spend time tonight selecting your wardrobe for tomorrow. Make choices based on qualities that tie you to the organization's values.

My results: _____

Card 5: Make Family Room

If you draw this card, you must do *one* of the following:

☐ Reschedule your after-hours commitments this week so that you have at least one full evening free. Spend that time alone, with friends, or with family.

My results: _____

☐ Write three new goals for yourself that are not career related.

My results: _____

Card 6: Shine Through

If you draw this card, you must do *one* of the following:

☐ List everything you have to be thankful for today.

My results: _____

☐ List all of the angels in your life.

My results: _____

Card 7: Embrace Change and Allow Failure

If you draw this card, you must:

☐ Write three changes in your life that have resulted in positive directions for you.

My results: _____

☐ Write one thing you would do if you were guaranteed success. Tape it on your bathroom mirror.

My results: _____

Card 8: Find the Window

If you draw this card, you must do *one* of the following:

☐ Make your own list of ten things you can and can't control.

My results: _____

☐ Pretend someone asks you, Today, what are you working hard at that is worth doing? Answer out loud.

My results: _____

Card 9: Say Yes—Give More

If you draw this card, you must do *one* of the following:

☐ Sign up to help serve dinner to the homeless in your area.

My results: _____

☐ Sign up to tutor a child in your school or community.

My results: _____

☐ Find a volunteer agency in your community that needs help. Do something.

My results: _____

Card 10: Take Risks—Be a Cheerleader

If you draw this card, you must do *one* of these:

☐ Contact someone who is tackling a difficult project and express your support.

My results: _____

☐ Write a new motto for your family or business that represents the risk taker and cheerleader in you.

My results: _____

Card 11: Forget Perfection

If you draw this card, you must do *both* of the following within the month:

☐ Begin a cooking, handiwork, or hobby project that you are fairly sure won't be completed perfectly. When you're finished, tell a friend.

My results: _____

☐ Write the words, "The person who never makes a *mistake* probably isn't doing anything" on a piece of paper and tape it where you will see it every day.

My results: _____

Card 12: Show Up and Be Visible

If you draw this card, you must do *one* of the following:

☐ Go do one thing you've been putting off.

My results: _____

☐ Look in the newspaper today to select an event to attend this week.

My results: _____

Card 13: Arrive Early and Have Energy

If you draw this card, you must do *both* of the following:

☐ Locate the next meeting on your calendar and plan a way to arrive fifteen minutes early.

My results: _____

☐ Plan your opening greeting so that it conveys energy and a positive attitude.

My results: _____

Card 14: Start Talking and Talk to Everyone

If you draw this card, you must do *both* of the following:

☐ In the next twenty-four hours, make three contacts outside your comfort zone.

My results: _____

☐ At the next meeting or event you attend, introduce yourself to two new people.

My results: _____

Card 15: Sign Up and Reach Out

You must do *one* of the following in the next seven days:

☐ Ask to attend another department's meeting to research an article you're writing.

My results: _____

☐ Volunteer for a cause you believe in at work or in your personal life.

My results: _____

Card 16: Reignite Supports—Refer Work— Advertise—Make Dinner

You must do *two* of these three activities:

☐ Send a handwritten note to your oldest client or friend. Don't ask for anything.

My results: _____

☐ Call a long-time client or friend and recommend another long-time client or friend.

My results: _____

☐ Invite a client or co-worker to dinner.

My results: _____

Card 17: Follow Up

If you draw this card, you must perform *both* of the following deeds:

☐ Send a thank you note to someone who was kind or thoughtful this week.

My results: _____

☐ Send a newspaper or journal article to a cherished client.

My results: _____

Card 18: Know Your Buyer—Understand Perceptions

If you draw this card, you must do *both* of the following:

☐ Starting today and for the next six days, list every different "role" you play each day.

My results: _____

☐ Ask three good friends to describe their impressions of you when you first met.

My results: _____

Card 19: Know How—Choose Appropriately—Enhance Yourself

If you draw this card, you must do *three* of the following:

☐ Book a professional color analysis consultation.

My results: _____

☐ Review your organization's dress code. If there is none, begin composing one for yourself.

My results: _____

☐ Divide all of your clothing into each of the four levels of dress. Note the piles that need more and less.

My results: _____

Card 20: Entertain With Flair—Give Gifts

If you draw this card, you must do *two* of the following:

☐ Look ahead to the next holiday on the calendar. Spend an evening planning an imaginary party based around that holiday.

My results: _____

☐ List the most treasured gifts you have ever received.

My results: _____

☐ Order a set of personalized stationery.

My results: _____

Card 21: Celebrate You

If you draw this card, you must do *one* of the following:

☐ Create a name for your particular sense of style.

My results: _____

☐ Make an appointment for your favorite services at a local day spa.

My results: _____

Card 22: Write Often

If you draw this card, you must do *one* of the following:

☐ Write an imaginary article for your favorite magazine.

My results: _____

☐ Write a personal story of something funny that happened to you. Add it to your story file.

My results: _____

☐ Read your local paper and compose a letter to the editor. Send it in.

My results: _____

Card 23: Speak Often

If you draw this card, you must do *both* of the following:

☐ List organizations in your area to contact about speaking opportunities.

My results: _____

☐ Use the list of three to five topics you can speak about that you created earlier in this chapter. Choose one and develop an outline for a speech on that topic.

My results: _____

Card 24: Be Unique—Look Globally

If you draw this card, you must do *two* of the following:

☐ Purchase a book of famous quotations.

My results: _____

☐ Using your list of three to five possible speech topics, choose one and create a title that incorporates an acronym.

My results: _____

☐ Subscribe to a business or news magazine. Buy a copy today and read it cover to cover within the next five days.

My results: _____

Card 25: Know Your Tools

If you draw this card, you must do *one* of the following:

☐ Select a short story or section from a novel. Audiotape yourself as you read it aloud. Evaluate your inflection, rate of speech, enunciation, and volume level.

My results: _____

☐ Select a short story or section from a novel. Videotape yourself as you read it aloud. Evaluate your facial expressions, gestures, and eye contact.

My results: _____

Card 26: Build Your Case

If you draw this card, you must do *all* of the following within the next seven days:

☐ List three ideas you'd like to be able to persuade others to do.

My results: _____

☐ From that list, choose one and list every possible benefit that could come as a result.

My results: _____

☐ Use that one topic and create an outline for a presentation that incorporates the four steps of persuasion.

My results: _____

Card 27: Keep Current

If you draw this card, you must do *one* of the following:

☐ Using the list of three to five topics, choose one and conduct an Internet search for the latest information.

My results: _____

☐ Subscribe to a newspaper other than your local paper.

My results: _____

☐ Create a filing system for collecting data on the three to five topics from your list.

My results: _____

Card 28: Listen to Learn

If you draw this card, you must do *one* of the following:

☐ Choose two listening behaviors you're going to change on a daily basis.

My results: _____

☐ Take "a trip to Cleveland" with someone you care about this week.

My results: _____

Card 29: Listen to Language

If you draw this card, you must select *two* of the following:

☐ Ask probing questions today when someone you care about talks.

My results: _____

☐ List on paper any jargon you use in your work or life.

My results: _____

☐ Ask for an explanation of any jargon you hear this week.

My results: _____

Card 30: Listen for Style

If you draw this card, you must do *one* of the following:

☐ This week, make a mental note of a phrase you hear someone you care about use repeatedly.

My results: _____

☐ Write four observations that describe the style of someone you see on a daily basis.

My results: _____

Card 31: Listen with Your Eyes

If you draw this card, you must do *one* of the following:

☐ Make an effort to watch body language all day today.

My results: _____

☐ Establish direct eye contact with everyone you meet today.

My results: _____

Card 32: Listen Up

If you draw this card, you must do *one* of the following this week:

☐ Ask five people for advice on an issue with which you're struggling.

My results: _____

☐ Ask someone you respect to lunch or coffee.

My results: _____

Success Card 33: Be Accepting

If you draw this card, you must do *both* this week:

☐ Ask a colleague for advice on one thing you should change. Try it.

My results: _____

☐ Select someone you'd like to accept more readily. Do it.

My results: _____

Success Card 34: Acknowledge Mistakes

If you draw this card, you must do all *these* the next time you make a mistake:

☐ Say you're sorry.

My results: _____

☐ Say out loud, " _____ was a mistake, and I'm sorry I did it." Then, say out loud what you'll do to move on.

My results: _____

247

Card 35: Be Aware

If you draw this card, you must do *one* of the following:

☐ Tomorrow, make a point to observe what's going on around you by reading the paper, listening to the radio news, and to what the key people in your life are saying.

My results: _____

☐ Write an email letter to an old friend expressing how you feel about your work and life right now. Be honest. Send it and save it to reread it the next day. What attitude comes across?

My results: _____

Card 36: Ask for Help

If you draw this card, you must do *one* of the following:

☐ Ask someone for help about anything you're working on this week.

My results: _____

☐ Interview two professional coaches to discover how they help others.

My results: _____

Card 37: Develop Yourself and Take Responsibility

If you draw this card, you must do *both* of the following:

☐ Sign up for a class in any area you want to develop.

My results: _____

☐ Write one thing that's bothering you and do something about it.

My results: _____

Card 38: Read

If you draw this card, you must do *one* of the following:

☐ Read the entire Sunday edition of *The New York Times, The Wall Street Journal,* or *The Washington Post.*

My results: _____

☐ Attend a book club as a guest if you can.

My results: _____

☐ Read an e-book.

My results: _____

Card 39: Learn Generations

If you draw this card, you must do *both* of the following:

☐ Ask a member of Generations X and Y to tell you about their favorite music.

My results: _____

☐ Ask a Baby Boomer to share lessons learned in life. Ask a senior citizen the same thing.

My results: _____

Card 40: Learn Cultures

If you draw this card, you must do *both* of the following:

☐ Pick one cultural group whom you live or work with and research it on the Web or at the library.

My results: _____

☐ Invite a member of another culture to lunch but ask him or her to select a favorite restaurant of his or her culture.

My results: _____

Card 41: Address Anxieties

If you draw this card, you must do *two* of the following:

☐ Go to bed tonight one hour earlier than usual.

My results: _____

☐ Set aside thirty minutes tomorrow morning for reading, writing, or exercising.

My results: _____

☐ On paper, design your perfect work schedule: total number of hours spent working and work location.

My results: _____

Card 42: Simplify Daily

If you draw this card, you must do *one* of the following within the next seven days:

☐ List the clutter areas at work or at home and the amount of time you estimate each area will require to get organized. Schedule time to deal with clutter area #1.

My results: _____

☐ Select one "prime real estate" area and reorganize it.

My results: _____

☐ For the next seven days, take every new piece of paper you receive and immediately place into to be filed, to be read, to be done, to be paid groups, or throw it away.

My results: _____

Card 43: Breathe In and Out—Manage Thoughts

If you draw this card, you must do *two* of the following:

☐ From the list of breathing exercises, choose either #4 or #5 and practice three times every day for one week.

My results: _____

☐ List your favorite forms of exercise and the ways you can incorporate more of them into your life.

My results: _____

☐ Begin reading a classic piece of literature you've always wanted to read.

My results: _____

Card 44: Say No

If you draw this card, you must do *two* of the following:

☐ Keep a tally of each time you speak tentatively this week.

My results: _____

☐ Try surrounding a no response with two positive phrases.

My results: _____

☐ Create a set of personal policies for how much you'll volunteer, donate, or take on for the next twelve months.

My results: _____

Card 45: Family Plan

If you draw this card, you must do *one* of the following:

☐ Contact two members of your extended family and ask if they would be willing to create a journal of their life stories.

My results: _____

☐ Begin planning a family reunion. If your family already has regular reunions, plan a new type of reunion for the group.

My results: _____

☐ If you are a parent, schedule a family meeting to occur within the next seven days.

My results: _____

Card 46: Affirm Yourself

If you draw this card, you must do *one* of the following:

☐ Say yes to something this week that will bring you joy.

My results: _____

☐ Pay attention to your intuition this week.

My results: _____

Card 47: Accept Change

If you draw this card, you must do *two* of the following:

☐ Write your mental mantra and practice it.

My results: _____

☐ Today, the first time you leave your home, look around, and appreciate the small things you love in your surroundings.

My results: _____

☐ List three changes in your life that had positive outcomes.

My results: _____

Card 48: Let Go

If you draw this card, you must do *one* of the following within the next seven days:

☐ Phone someone and apologize or clear up a misunderstanding.

My results: _____

☐ In your bath or shower, let go of your worries.

My results: _____

☐ Look through an old scrapbook to let go of any sadness you feel.

My results: _____

Card 49: Communicate

If you draw this card, you must do *two* of the following:

☐ Go through your address book and contact a friend you haven't called in more than six months.

My results: _____

☐ Plan a meeting or phone conversation with your boss.

My results: _____

☐ Send an email to a group of friends or colleagues asking for their advice.

My results: _____

Card 50: Change Habits

If you draw this card, you must do *one* of the following:

☐ List three of your habits that you love and engage in them more often.

My results: _____

☐ Select a habit you've tried to change in the past but failed, and try again, starting today.

My results: _____

Card 51: Break Rules

If you draw this card, you must do *one* of the following:

☐ Take a time out even though your to-do list is full.

My results: _____

☐ Do one thing you've never done before.

My results: _____

☐ Do something that makes you feel a little bit naughty.

My results: _____

Card 52: Move Forward

If you draw this card, you must do *all* of the following:

☐   Go online and read about the future.

My results: _____

☐   Take action on an idea you've been tossing around for months.

My results: _____

☐   Get advice from someone to propel yourself forward.

My results: _____

IT'S YOUR MOVE

PROGRAMS

We want to help you make the moves that are right for you. Our highly interactive results-oriented "It's Your Move" keynotes, workshops, and coaching series will show you—and your organization's attendees—how to put the "It's Your Move" strategies to use immediately.

For more information on the "It's Your Move" programs, please contact:

Connie Moore, Sales & Marketing Rep
Maxey Creative, Inc.
Speaking and Listening Programs to Inspire Stellar Communication
5407 N. Lakewood
Chicago, IL 60640

Phone: 773/561-6252
Fax: 773/275-5417
Email: cmoore@cyndimaxey.com
Or visit www.cyndimaxey.com

Jill Bremer, AICI, CIP
Bremer Communications
Image and Communication Skills for Business
826 N. Ridgeland Avenue
Oak Park, IL 60302

Phone: 708-848-5945
Fax: 708-8484-6011
Email: jill@bremercommunications.com
Or visit www.bremercommunications.com

Also available from Maxey Creative Inc.:

SEMINARS (Half Day to Two Day workshops)
<u>Presentation Skills</u>
Speakerskills®
PEAK Meeting Facilitation Skills
Training from the Heart

Interpersonal Skills

How to Fine Tune Your Communication Skills: Seven Keys to Success

How to Give and Receive Feedback

Constructive Conflict: How to Work Together Better

Management Skills

Coaching and Mentoring for Excellence

Creating a Motivating Climate

Delegating to Your Team

CONFERENCE PROGRAMS (45–90 minutes)

RSVP: How to Respond to your Customers©

Putting it in Perspective: How to Manage the Stress and Change of Life and Work

Selling Your Ideas: How to Manage your P's and Q's

Are You Training from the Heart?

Ten Ways to Motivate (or De-Motivate) your Staff

What You've Got in Your Pocket: Recruiting and Motivating Volunteers

One on One Coaching

Private coaching in Presentation and Interpersonal Communication Skills

Also Available From Bremer Communications:

SEMINARS (Half-Day to Two Day workshops)

Image Insight®

Group workshops in First Impressions, Wardrobe Strategies, Business & Social Etiquette, Dining Etiquette, Workplace Civility, and Communication Skills.

SpeakAbilities®

Group workshops and private coaching in Presentation Skills, Preparing for the Media, Trade Show Demo Coaching, and Booth Training. Speechwriting services also available.

Executive Image Coaching

Private coaching in Wardrobe, Etiquette, and Communication Skills.

256

CONFERENCE PROGRAMS (45–90 minutes)

Polishing Your Professional Image: Using the A, B, C's

Building Relationships Through Business Etiquette

Civility in the Workplace: How to Build a Spirit of Respect

First Impressions Fast: Setting Yourself Up for Success

Index

8 reasons why you should read the Financial Times for 4 weeks RISK-FREE!

To help you stay current with significant
developments in the world economy ...
and to assist you to make informed business
decisions — the Financial Times brings you:

1 Fast, meaningful overviews of international affairs ... plus daily briefings on major world news.

2 Perceptive coverage of economic, business, financial and political developments with special focus on emerging markets.

3 More international business news than any other publication.

4 Sophisticated financial analysis and commentary on world market activity plus stock quotes from over 30 countries.

5 Reports on international companies and a section on global investing.

6 Specialized pages on management, marketing, advertising and technological innovations from all parts of the world.

7 Highly valued single-topic special reports (over 200 annually) on countries, industries, investment opportunities, technology and more.

8 The Saturday Weekend FT section — a globetrotter's guide to leisure-time activities around the world: the arts, fine dining, travel, sports and more.

FT FINANCIAL TIMES
World business newspaper